11th AIRBORNE

To:

Wing Commander

Joseph Hill

R.F.C.

"Ardua Ad Astra"

Tom

8-15-80

UP AND AT 'EM

OTHER BOOKS WRITTEN OR EDITED BY
STANLEY M. ULANOFF

ILLUSTRATED GUIDE TO U.S. MISSILES AND ROCKETS

FIGHTER PILOT

MATS—THE STORY OF THE MILITARY AIR TRANSPORT SERVICE

BOMBS AWAY!

THE FIRST WAR IN THE AIR, 1914–1918 *Illustrated*

MAN IN A GREEN BERET

AIR COMBAT CLASSICS

WINGED WARFARE *by Lieutenant Colonel William A. Bishop*

ACE OF ACES *by Captain René Fonck*

FIGHTING AIRMAN—THE WAY OF THE EAGLE
by Major Charles J. Biddle

FLYING FURY *by Major James T. B. McCudden*

WIND IN THE WIRES *by Captain Duncan Grinnell-Milne*

THE RED BARON *by Rittmeister Manfred Frh. von Richthofen*

ACE OF THE IRON CROSS *by Oberleutnant Ernst Udet*

UP AND AT 'EM

Harold E. Hartney
LIEUTENANT COLONEL, U. S. AIR SERVICE

Edited by
STANLEY M. ULANOFF
LT. COL. USAR

AIR COMBAT CLASSICS

Garden City, New York
DOUBLEDAY & COMPANY, INC.
1971

ACKNOWLEDGMENTS

I AM most grateful for the research assistance and help in obtaining photographs by Brigadier General Winant Sidle, the Army Chief of Information; Colonel Rodger R. Bankson of the Directorate for Defense Information; and Lieutenant Colonel Gerald M. Holland, Chief Magazine and Book Branch, Department of the Air Force.

I must also acknowledge with appreciation the permission to use the excellent box cover aircraft illustrations given by Renwal Products Inc. and Revell, Inc.

Bill Zider and Ray Kessell of Xerox were most gracious with their help and advice in copying valuable documents, and I offer my thanks to Linda Cohen and Raoul Holly for their assistance with the typing chores.

STANLEY M. ULANOFF
Editor

DEDICATION

IF I YIELDED to my heart's desire, I would dedicate this volume to my wife, Irene, whose steadfast patience through the shocks of each new wartime death list has been still outmeasured by the wealth of her sustaining love. If I followed the strong urge of grateful friendship and obligation, I would inscribe each page to George W. Sutton, Jr., overseas U. S. Tank Corps and Air Service Officer, my collaborator, who has worked his head off for many months in helping me prepare this volume.

On the other hand I have a strong inclination to dedicate it to the American Legion, of which I am a loyal and enthusiastic member, past commander of the Aviators' Post, New York. I consider the Legion one of the most substantial organizations in America and one of the strongest factors for peace. The Legion boys know war—too well.

But the long threads of poignant memory bind me to a duty. Filling it is a pleasure and a satisfaction.

It is both pleasure and satisfaction to dedicate these chapters to "Winged Warriors," especially to the men and officers, living and dead, of the Air Forces whose planes carried the insignias of Great Britain, France, Italy, and the United States of America over the battlefields of the World War. They sent down the roots of a great tradition. But for their kind, the role aeronautics is destined some day to play in the stabilization of all civilization would never become a reality.

HAROLD E. HARTNEY

NOTE

THE following excerpt, taken from the official history of the 1st Pursuit Group, U. S. Air Service, AEF, written for official purposes immediately after the Armistice and never published, is inserted here without the author's consent.

"THE 1st PURSUIT GROUP"

"No history of the 1st Pursuit Group can adequately express the secret of its unusual efficiency without the fullest acknowledgment of the debt it owes to Major Harold E. Hartney. Every officer and every pilot in the group feels indebted to the commanding officer for his personal attention to their needs. His extraordinary capacity for the details of every phase of the day's work, his thorough study of the science of combat fighting, of night flying and of air tactics were not only explained to the pilots under him, but were continuously demonstrated by Major Hartney in flights over the lines, both by day and by night.

"The commanding officer of the 1st Pursuit Group led his pilots by example as well as precept. His first care has always been to see that his men were made as comfortable and happy as the circumstances of war permitted, thus he was enabled to heighten the spirit of his pilots and give them an example in his own conduct which every officer in the group appreciated and strove to imitate.

"The secret of the 1st Pursuit Group's success is herewith gratefully acknowledged to be in the magnificent leadership of its commanding officer, Major H. E. Hartney."

CONTENTS

LIST OF ILLUSTRATIONS

INTRODUCTION TO NEW EDITION

THE 1st Pursuit Group was the finest air combat force put into the field by the fledgling U. S. Air Service to face the "Red Baron's" *Jagdgeschwader* and the cream of the German "Flying Circuses." It consisted of the famous 94th "Hat-in-the-Ring" Squadron, the 95th, 27th, and 147th, Aero Squadrons. These were later joined by the 185th Night Fighter Squadron.

In the short period (little more than six months) that the 1st Pursuit Group was on the Western Front it racked up a distinguished record. On its roster was the American Ace of Aces, Captain Eddie Rickenbacker with twenty-six confirmed victories, and Second Lieutenant Frank Luke, Jr., the Arizona "Balloon Buster," with eighteen enemy balloons and planes to his credit. These two were also the only fighter pilot recipients of the Medal of Honor awarded in the First World War. In all, the 1st Pursuit Group boasted of more Aces, saw more action, and gained more confirmed victories than any other American fighter group. In short one could say that the "First" was the pride of the American Expeditionary Force (AEF) in France.

Commanding this elite fighter group was Harold E. Hartney, a Canadian who had flown with the British Royal Flying Corps (RFC) earlier in the war. Hartney, an attorney, had been an officer in the Canadian militia, the equivalent of the American National Guard, and was mobilized with his regiment in 1914, shortly after the start of the war. While undergoing infantry training in England he requested transfer to the RFC. Following flight training he was posted to Number 20 Squadron.

Hartney flew the F.E. 2b, a two-seater pusher-type aircraft which had the propeller behind the pilot leaving the front cockpit free for an observer with a flexible Lewis machine gun to deal with the enemy Fokker *Eindekker* fighters. On a mission over the Ypres battlefield, in February 1917, in a battle with German fighters his plane was badly hit but he managed to crash-land on the Allied side of the lines.

Following hospitalization and recuperation, in one of those strange moves that sometimes occur in wartime, Hartney (then a captain in the RFC) was commissioned a major in the U. S. Air Service and given command of the 27th Aero Squadron. I say *strange* because, whereas Americans who had served with the French Lafayette Escadrille before America entered the war were commissioned in the U. S. Air Service, such as Major Charles J. Biddle who was given command of the 13th Aero Squadron and then of the 4th Pursuit Group, and Major Raoul Lufbery who was assigned to the "Hat-in-the-Ring" Squadron, *they had requested the transfers and commissions*. Hartney was a Canadian and had made no such request, but he accepted it with great delight and glee, looking forward to being an American. (He became a U.S. citizen in 1923.)

At any rate he assumed command of the 27th and led them through training in Canada, the United States, England, and France. On August 21, 1918, Major Hartney was appointed Commanding Officer of the 1st Pursuit Group.

Up and at 'Em, a truly great Air Combat Classic, tells the exciting story of America's participation in that First War in the Air—in Colonel Hartney's own words.

STANLEY M. ULANOFF
Editor

FOREWORD

COLONEL HARTNEY has written a most remarkable book. In it he catches the spirit of the aviation of the Allies during the last war. It is not the history of one man or of one unit, or even of one phase in that great struggle. It covers all, and therefore stands in a class by itself. Better still, it covers all without losing personality and color.

Colonel Hartney himself is certainly one of our best known fliers and though we think of him as an American, he was when the war started a Canadian. He was commander of our 1st Pursuit Group, which numbered among its membership Raoul Lufbery, Eddie Rickenbacker, Frank Luke, and my brother Quentin.

We who have "drunk delight of battle with our peers, far on the ringing plains of windy Troy," are apt in memory to endow the dim shapes of those peers with gigantic and godlike proportions. Colonel Hartney does not do this, but even if he did he would not have been far wrong, for those who composed the group were exceptional men; most of them were in the first flush of golden youth, reveling in just-attained powers. Their strength was at its prime and their ideals were untarnished.

The quarter of a century that has passed since those days has been a bitter disillusionment to us in America, so bitter that we tend to forget and discredit the ideals with which our country was then aflame. It is the truth, nonetheless, that we, the young men of America, went to that great war convinced not merely that our cause was righteous but that by winning the victory we were going to bring new and better days to the world. We felt we were fighting "a war to end wars," "a war to make the world safe for democracy." This was particularly true of the young aviators, in their joyous venture to battle in a new element. Colonel Hartney has been most happy in recapturing this spirit by the very self-restraint of his writing.

Moreover, this book not merely does this, but much more, for its author is one of our foremost aviators and knows flying thoroughly. The book therefore gives an accurate picture of the organization, tactical work, etc., that was necessary at those times. He and those who surrounded him were pioneers in aviation. In the use of airplanes as a weapon of war they were treading where no one had been before.

There is a chapter in the book that no one should miss. That chapter deals with the way we have treated the inventions offered to us as a nation by American citizens. The truth is that in most military services a new idea has as much difficulty gaining acceptance as the proverbial rich man had in getting into heaven. I recall reading a speech by a distinguished old British admiral at the time when steamboats had just been invented. He closed his impassioned remarks with the statement that he hoped he would "never live to see the time when an English line of battle was led by a floating teakettle."

The list of inventions originally refused by our government is appalling, ranging as they do from rifling in gun barrels to smokeless powder and airplanes.

Colonel Hartney is a gentleman of notable achievements and this is a notable book.

THEODORE ROOSEVELT, JR.

January 31, 1940.

UP AND AT 'EM

CHAPTER 1

War Comes to Canada

SOMEBODY once said, "Coming events cast their shadows before." This may be so. There was nothing, however, in my early life to indicate that some day I would be a military officer in command of several hundred aerial warriors engaged in shooting human beings down out of the sky. As I look into the mirror I do not see reflected the image of a warrior as it exists in the popular mind. Something under average height, with a face anything but ferocious and warlike, and now equipped with a permanent limp from a peacetime flying misfortune, nobody would point me out in a crowd and say, "There goes a soldier." Yet the transition from a peaceful and normal youth to the roaring, flaming daily contact with violent death seemed a gradual and natural one, always in a rising cadence of exciting changes and events.

In my childhood and early youth my winters were spent on the western Canadian prairies and my summers on the beautiful northern lakes of Ontario, with occasional periods of residence in the United States. There were six of us young Hartneys, a half sister, daughter of my father's first marriage, three older brothers and a younger sister—children of a pioneering family which always lived more or less away from the thickly populated centers. We were happy, carefree, and grew up with a love of the outdoors and an intense loyalty for our democratic form of government. It was as a gangling youth of twenty-three that I stepped out of the halls of the

University of Toronto, in June 1911, a graduate in Arts with a two-year dash of engineering, and began to ponder what to do with the rest of my life.

A brother who had become a lawyer directed the first stage of my post-college career. He wrote me from Saskatoon to join him out by the Saskatchewan where opportunities were unlimited, where the enormous acreage of undeveloped land was just beginning to be exploited, where the public was of a gambling nature ideal for real estate purposes and where lawyers were at a premium. I accepted his invitation, made a small but sufficient living as his "articled clerk" in law while taking a graduate degree "ad eundum gradum" at the University of Saskatchewan. And presently I was a lawyer preparing briefs, collecting bad accounts, approving loans and going through all the humdrum of a busy law office in a young country. This training came in very handy later on in meeting the complexities of military life.

Two other activities of mine in Saskatoon afterward proved of great wartime values—cornet playing and rifle shooting. In college I had eked out my allowance by tooting at the Wa Wa Hotel, Muskoka, for their dances and other festivities. I did the same in Saskatoon when fees were low and board bills high. I adopted rifle-shooting as a hobby, joined every rifle club in sight and finally, purely for the shooting, became a private in the Saskatoon 105th Fusiliers—a militia organization similar to the National Guard in the United States. This was from 1911 to that fateful August of 1914. I learned to drill but secretly hated it and, although I rose rapidly in the ranks and finally became a first lieutenant, I managed to spend most of my spare time tooting the cornet in the village band and battalion and engaging in target practice whenever I could get hold of some government ammunition. I got to be quite a good shot. I had purchased a special Ross target rifle. This was a duplicate of the arm then used by the Canadian Army. I thought it a wonderful shooting iron but it was destined to tragic failure and the blasphemous condemnation of the Dominion's soldiers a few months later.

It was about this time that my mother came out from the east to visit my brother and me. It was on the night of June 27, 1914, that she and I were walking along the banks of the Saskatchewan. That evening there was a brilliant display of the northern lights, streaking across the wide sky in long flashing streamers. We stopped to watch them. Said my mother, as if in clairvoyant mood, "That portends a great upheaval in this world. The years that are coming will be the most eventful in all civilization. I think there will be a world war." Said I, half in jest, "If war breaks out, I'm going to get Aunt Bella to buy me an airplane and I'll fight from the sky where I can see everything that's going on." I had never been in an airplane.

The next day the Archduke Ferdinand was shot at Sarajevo.

To me it meant nothing. I accompanied my mother on a pleasure trip to the lovely salt lake at Watrus and arranged for a very important personage to be there—a girl six years my junior to whose notice I had first come in Toronto while blowing the cornet in a Sunday school orchestra several years back and in whom I had since become very interested—by mail.

Our vacation trip, except for one thing, was a fizzle. That thing was the verification by Irene and me of our postal interest in each other—an interest that is as keen today as it was then. I was too busy enjoying the summer life and playing cornet serenades at night from a canoe on Lake Watrus to read the newspapers. In the rest of the world, however, great events were moving to swift conclusions that were quickly to engulf me along with millions of other peace-loving boys the world over.

Before I realized what was going on, England had declared war. And here I was, a lieutenant in the Canadian militia, whiling away my time at a pleasure resort. Hastily I telephoned my brother for news. The German Army was already on the march. The British Navy had put to sea. Sam Hughes, Minister of Militia at Ottawa, was mobilizing. In a matter of hours I was on a train back to Saskatoon.

Sam Hughes was the first dictator with whom I ever came in contact. And he was a corker. Slashing red tape right and left, through forms, orders, even laws, and sidestepping all the labyrinthine channels of military communication, he built Camp Valcartiers in a few days and did a wonderful emergency job.

Oh, the innocent excitement of those hectic days! We didn't know war then. Now, we'll still go, but even the kids have a sense of the reality of modern combat which will give every mobilization from now on for a long time a background of sober thought and doubt very different from the adventurous delirium of 1914.

Ordinary civilian work stopped in its tracks. Political differences were forgotten. Patriotism boiled over everywhere. Everybody was sure the war would be over before he could take a glorious part in it and collect his medals. A lot of us did foolish things. Disregarding all rules of military procedure I wired Sam Hughes direct for permission to go over with the first outfit, the wonderful Princess Pats. In addition to being entirely out of order, I was also too late. The Pats were already on their way.

I moved heaven and earth to get in the first contingent. I was glad I was a bachelor. I thought it would help me to get into the war faster. But I had already decided to get married after my military status was established. Two reasons impelled me. I felt a romantic need to leave some loved person behind to carry on for me, some relic of me if I failed to return. And then I had heard that, as a soldier, I could file claim to several hundred acres of public land which would go to my widow if I were bumped off. It was a definite something I could do for the little girl I loved.

After agonizing delays which, of course, were necessary to the gathering of even a semblance of military equipment and supplies, we got orders on October 1, 1914, for the already greatly augmented 105th Fusiliers to leave our little town and proceed to Winnipeg. We piled into the trains in a blinding snowstorm, young, enthusiastic, foolish. And at Winnipeg we lost our military identity. We became part of the 28th Battalion, Canadian Infantry, 5th Brigade, 2d Contingent, 640 fine, clean, rugged boys with a precious sprinkling of old British veterans and not a few Americans. I could write many pages about that ill-fated battalion. But Ian Hay's *The First Hundred Thousand* tells the same story. So does *All Quiet on the Western Front,* or any other book telling of human beings being regimented for war. Every thousand men throughout the world are about the same as every other thousand—so many of this type, so many of that. Education, background, home training, environment will differ. But the human impulses and their results in conduct are pretty uniform, thousand for thousand, in men.

I learned later, however, that there is one factor which calls for a difference in leadership. If your thousand men have become accustomed to discipline and routine, in their civilian work or in previous Regular Army service, their commander should be a driver and a disciplinarian even to the point of being a martinet. If, however, the majority have been independent businessmen, or other types of individualists who have always done their own thinking, they cannot be successfully driven. They must be led.

Luckily, I guessed correctly on this point when I got aboard that train at Saskatoon in my nice new first lieutenant's uniform. It was my first real experience in handling men. It was an opportunity to strut, a temptation to wield the authority of my then unearned insignia. Thousands of officers in all the Allied armies yielded to this vain weakness, to the great detriment of themselves, their men and the service. It is one of the penalties of democracy. In dictator countries the ranks are made up of men who have never known even peacetime freedom. In those armies the officers must bluster, bluff and strut. It is correct and necessary. But something told me it would not work with those high-minded, patriotic, intelligent Canadian boys. And it wouldn't.

As a lieutenant (pronounced "lef-tenant" in all British services, "loo-tenant" in the American) my job was to equip and train a platoon. In a Canadian battalion at that time such a unit consisted of forty men and was one-fourth of a company. There were four companies in the battalion and the head of the whole works was a lieutenant colonel. Our first billet at Winnipeg was the Old Horse Show building. The town welcomed us with the well-bred enthusiasm of all truly British communities, especially when we paraded with our band—a darn good one.

Hard work—long marches—digging trenches on neighboring farms—drilling—studying manuals—tactics. At last a leave of absence. And what a leave—what a tremendous event for me! I discussed it with Colonel Embury, my commanding officer, a fine fellow who afterward became one of the most efficient General Headquarters staff officers on the western front, and got his blessing. So back in Saskatoon, on November 11, 1914, there was a military wedding with the girl who had inspired me to win that gold medal in the cornet contest. Armistice Day has a double meaning for me now.

Back with my bride to Winnipeg for more work. By January 1, 1915, we were all convinced the war would be over before we could get into it and some of the boys actually consulted me on requesting their discharges because they felt they were wasting their time. Little did they know! It was one of the pleasantest periods of my life. That New Year's Eve, as the bells tolled the passing of the first war year, my batman solemnly handed me a silver United States dollar and told me to preserve it carefully because it would bring me home safely. Perhaps he should have kept it. Before that year was out he was blown to bits in a mining operation at St. Elois, France. I carried it through four years of active warfare.

At last we moved eastward. By this time the 28th Battalion, Canadian Expeditionary Force, was a unit to be proud of. The Duke of Connaught inspected us and said so. With officers competent and men keen and well trained, I really think it was one of the best trained infantry units that ever went to meet its doom in France. I am proud of my association with it.

Montreal—on to a big troop ship, a Cunard liner, in normal times a peaceful passenger ship.

I had arranged to have my wife chaperone a little girl, Margaret Le Grand, who danced at the Fort Garry Hotel in Winnipeg, across on the troop ship. They were already on board ship asleep in their cabins, which some of the officers had given up to them, when Major Ross, second in command, heard of them and refused to sail "with two women on board." It was against all rules, King's regulations and orders. After going to bed twice they were finally put off the boat at Montreal at 3 A.M. Margaret sailed the next week and, as Margaret Bannerman, eventually became a famous actress.

Our ship slipped out to sea May 28, 1915, at 4 A.M.—mysteriously, in complete darkness—off to the jolly old war.

CHAPTER 2

A Taste of the Real Thing

WE LANDED at Liverpool and sped by train to London. I had never seen England before—a gorgeous, green land with rich fields and closely cropped grass like an immense golf course—rabbits, thousands of them, pheasants, sheep, quaint houses, little trains with squeaky whistles. Then down through Kent to Dibgate Plains, not far from Dover.

Our battalion was in fine fettle, the men well fed and full of pep. The officers had not even begun to get on each other's nerves. Officers in British forces, I realized later, are not individually so political and ambitious to win promotion or push ahead of a brother officer as they are in some other armies. They bury their personal aspirations in a greater regard for the main cause. This does not indicate regimentation or lack of initiative. It is rather the exemplification of the oft-heard "doing my bit" philosophy of the whole race, which has been responsible for many outstanding victories for British arms.

During the busy weeks of drilling on Dibgate Plains there was awakened my first practical interest in flying. I suppose it first came from watching an occasional plane drone by overhead while we were slogging through the dust of the drill field. One day I stole away to an airdrome near Folkestone.

The sight of the airplanes—rickety old Maurice Farman longhorns and one crude ancient Blériot—I thought they were wonderful then—and the flying officers and busy mechanics touched off something inside of me and gave me a sudden yearning to be part of this new picture. The matter was settled by a smart-looking flying officer who recognized my uniform of a Canadian colonial lieutenant and gave me a snappy salute. With his two decorations for outstanding exploits he epitomized to me the highest class in this man's war and I determined to do something about it at once. That evening, as if to further lure me, Billy Bishop landed on Dibgate in a B.E. 2C, a dashing officer but little did we dream that he was destined to be the world's leading war ace.

Back in camp on a little portable typewriter I carefully pecked out, in my best military phraseology, an application to be transferred, attached or in some way connected with the Royal Flying Corps. Of course, this had to go "through channels" like all military communications and had to be endorsed by each superior officer on the way up to the top. Today, looking back, I am appalled at my gall in asking to leave my men and the battalion in which I had trained for so many happy months. I avoided the men and that night went to see the commanding officer about it. I was afraid that if I got back with the officers and men with whom I had developed such close bonds of friendship my sudden but powerful enthusiasm for flying would die and I would chuck the application into the fire.

You, with your present-day familiarity with aviation, will have difficulty appreciating the attitude of Army officers toward it in those early days of the war. To them flying was still in the "doodad" stage, a passing fad. It never could be more than a moderately useful "eye of the troops." Anyone connected with those dangerous heavier-than-air machines was plain crazy and the enthusiasts of lighter-than-air flying were just about as dizzy for only Germans could build Zeppelins and the smaller blimps were only good for patrol work near home shores in good weather.

My commanding officer was different. He was a citizen-soldier, a famous lawyer, a man of perception and progressive ideas. He agreed with me that flying was a coming thing but he believed the air service then was a suicide squad, equipped as were all its units with planes powered with engines that quit cold on an average at least once in each hour. He tried to discourage me from leaving the battalion —told me I must not forget my little bride back home and that I would be much safer to go ahead in the infantry and trot over to France with him, at the head of my platoon.

All of our officers and most of the men had spent some time making their wills. It seemed a sort of appropriate formality to us, engaged in a war. But, except for a coward here and there, I have never met a soldier in camp who felt that death would ever catch up with him on the battlefield. The supreme moment in any man's emotional life must be when he clambers out of a trench, goes "over the top," into the face of the artillery that has been trying to blow him asunder and into the hail of rifle and machine gun bullets that he has watched kicking up the dust above the fire step. At such times every man knows he is looking into the very eyes of death. But behind the lines, in camp, the Grim Reaper seems very far away indeed. And that's how I felt toward the colonel's fears for my safety should I go a-flying.

For a few seconds my mind went back to those airplanes at Folkestone and the significance of the colonel's next words came to me slowly.

"Why don't you bring her over?" he was saying. "And forget this flying thing. We'll be off for France soon."

Bring her over! I had given up the thought since they had thrown Irene off the boat at Montreal. But now, with my colonel as godfather, the idea was reborn in full vigor and,

in spite of the increased danger from submarines, the deed
was as good as done. But nothing else Colonel Embury said
chilled my enthusiasm for my other idea—flying. I determined to go on more actively than ever with the work of my
platoon but to redouble my efforts to get into the Royal
Flying Corps.

I had been writing Irene every day. Now I sent off a cable
(July 6) that must have knocked her off her feet. And I
made a strong official application for transfer to the RFC.
It never occurred to me that my regiment might be ordered
to France while Irene was on the ocean or before my application could go through. But there was a war on and things
were moving fast. The very next day the colonel's orderly
saluted at my tent and I was ordered to headquarters. Perhaps, I thought, I will be sent to a distant training camp of
the RFC and will have to get somebody else to meet my
wife. These thoughts were running through my mind when
I arrived at headquarters and prepared my snappiest salute
for my colonel. But it was not the colonel I met at all. It
was the second in command, the little strutting "Turkey"
who had caused us the trouble at Montreal. He seemed to
relish "riding" me again.

"Sorry, Hartney, but Brigade Headquarters has disap-
proved your request for flying. Now forget all about this
flighty business of being a soldier in the air and try to be
one on the ground. We'll be in the front line trenches before
another moon."

Outwardly he got my best military salute. Inwardly I
cursed him up hill and down dale. As I walked back to my
tent my feelings were all mixed up—chagrin that I was not
destined to be a flying man, excitement that we were so near
to actual fighting, worry about meeting Irene and having to
leave her so soon. A cable that day had told me she would
be on the SS *Baltic,* sailing for Liverpool July 14 from New

York. So I began to worry about submarines, which already were taking frightful toll of commercial shipping. After a rigmarole of red tape I got to Liverpool where I paced the dock one whole day (Saturday, July 24) and most of a night waiting for my beloved woman. Secrecy shrouded shipping in those days. Nobody could or would tell me when the *Baltic* was arriving. She lay in the Mersey that night. But next day into my arms she bore my bride and momentarily I forgot the war in favor of more tender thoughts. Three miles from Dibgate Plains, on a bluff overlooking ancient Hythe, at the place called Lympne I found a lovely little cottage and secured permission to spend nights there when not on special duty. And then my major, Charles R. Hill, third in command, seeing my luck, cabled for his wife to come over. Fine! Irene would have splendid company while he and I were in France.

The summer of 1915 wore on. General Steele gave the officers and their wives a garden party August 16 and Irene met Prince Alexander of Teck. The King and Earl Kitchener looked us over September 2. Still no embarkation orders arrived. The men were getting restless. No action. Then suddenly, one night all hell broke loose. Major Hill's wife had arrived and the four of us were enjoying dinner in a peaceful little Hythe restaurant. Suddenly our ears were split by the sound of sirens. The "Zepps are over!" yelled the waiter, and we all dashed to the door to peer into the blackness. Directly above our heads we could hear the telltale drone of those big Benz engines and the craft seemed so low that I was frantic because I didn't have a rifle to take a crack at it.

Straight on toward our camp the murderous visitor made her way. Then suddenly all was silent. Her motors had stopped. Some of our men, overconfident and forgetting their orders at Otterpool camp, had left their tent lights exposed. *W-h-e-e-e!*

It was the first enemy bomb I ever heard, whistling through the air. "Whee!" Another.

Then *Wham!* and the earth fairly trembled beneath us. *Wham!* again, *Wham! Wham!*—five times. Later, I became accustomed to these sounds from Hell. Now I would judge they were one hundred and fifty pound loads of flying death. Years later I was told by Captain Ernst Lehmann, a German officer aboard (later killed on the *Hindenburg*) that they were the biggest bombs dropped from Zeppelins up to that time and that they had been captured from the Russians on the eastern front.

Suddenly the Hun motors were heard again and she soared serenely off toward London, her work in our immediate vicinity done. It was horrible but legitimate work which no Zeppelin will ever do again in any first-class war. They will have another and more important mission in the coming conflict. Eighteen of our boys were dead, some of them absolutely obliterated. Where their tents had been were only gory shell holes. Many others were torn apart by bomb fragments but lived, after a fashion. By a lucky chance my platoon went off scot-free. We buried what was left of the eighteen the next day, eighteen flag-draped coffins in a row. It was the saddest military funeral I ever attended. It was my first, of many.

As tragic as it was, this Zeppelin raid had a marvelous psychological effect. Up to now the war had been a distant, vague thing to us, mostly a matter of newspaper stories, tales of survivors, and official communiqués. Now, with their buddies lying dead, our boys were seized with a fever of hatred and desire for revenge. As horrible as these thoughts are to normal, decent human beings they are vitally necessary to the soldier in the conduct of mankind's most asinine activity —war. Our boys were all hot now to get to France as soon as possible and to wipe out every filthy German in sight. Little good it did them! Four months later they themselves were wiped out almost to a man.

The raid was a great help to the Allied cause. It aroused the British colonies to the dangers threatening their mother country and caused the quickened enlistment of thousands of men and millions of dollars worth of equipment and supplies. It sent a shock of intensified effort and patriotism through every British subject, especially those in England itself, and undoubtedly hastened the end of the German dream, all in exchange for the lives of eighteen Canadian boys.

I take my hat off to the German efficiency. But that is all at present. The German people are brave, vigorous, brutal, stubborn, and loyal. Mentally they are astoundingly alert, inquisitive, and progressive. But in their dealings with other people, and with themselves, they are the stupidest race on the face of the earth. This has been glaringly true since, under Arminius the Great, they brought the first real defeat to the Roman Legions. Eventually, if they fail to join in human co-operation, this characteristic will destroy them, no matter what temporary victories they win. They are a doomed race unless their culture sends them into reverse and they abandon the vain dream of autocracy. The world has outgrown it.

One effect of the Zeppelin raid was the recognition by official England of the possible value of aviation. One plane and one aviator, with incendiary bullets, could easily have brought down that hydrogen-filled gas bag and, at least, traded her crew of eighteen or more Boche for the lost eighteen Canadians. Later that night I realized this, in the glow of French champagne and Gasper cigarettes, and my determination to be a flier was rekindled. And my wife said, "Put in your application again. Your heart is in flying. It is a call of some sort. Have a private chat with Colonel Embury and

Major Hill when you do it. And maybe this time will be the lucky one."

Then followed another of the great emotional episodes of my life. It was only a few days later, in a pouring rain, that orders arrived for me to be "seconded" to the Royal Flying Corps training camp at Norwich, and for the 28th Canadian Infantry Battalion to proceed to France. I felt like a slacker. I shall never forget my feelings as I said good-bye to my boys, all fitted up with new fighting paraphernalia. I took their pictures. I wept. Presently they were gone and the job of cleaning up their quarters for incoming troops delayed my reporting to the RFC for three days.

CHAPTER 3

A Flier at Last

OCTOBER 21, 1915, was a big day in my life. I arrived at Norwich to enter the Royal Flying Corps. Everything connected with RFC spelled efficiency and esprit de corps, even the snappy little Crossley station wagon that met us with the smart crew in their "maternity jackets." These, worn by officers and men, were a double-breasted affair, fastened well back at the side, with a high collar and no buttons showing anywhere. A dapper little captain, K. E. Clayton Kennedy, destined to become a big "brass hat," met us and escorted us to our billets in a charming private house. He was efficiency personified but intensely human. I have had pleasant meetings with him since in several parts of the world. He added to my admiration and pride that I was now in an Imperial outfit.

The next day—my first flight.

Why I am here to tell the tale I don't know. With five other "huns," the official nickname for embryo flying officers, we spent the morning checking over the types of guns and scanning through our complicated ground course curriculum. At four in the afternoon my big moment arrived. My pilot, Captain Anstey, was a heavy-set man with probably a hundred hours flying time. But he had his wings up and to me was a hero of heroes. The ship was a Maurice Farman longhorn, one of those early box kites with a control surface out in front as well as in the rear. It had a French Renault

air-cooled motor rated at 80 horsepower. The pilot and student sat up in front of the motor some ten feet off the ground
between the outriggers supporting the advanced control surface.

How sorry I felt for the small detachment of footsloggers
at one corner of the field, wearily drilling as I had done for
so many months, as we sailed off smoothly into the sunlight
on my first hop. We made several circuits over the airdrome
at about a hundred and fifty feet and at a speed of around
60 miles an hour. The approach for the first landing of my
life seemed so simple and easy but even I, a complete novice,
felt that we were overshooting the field. I was glad when the
pilot opened his throttle again to go on. Off we soared,
rising gently over some tents and small wooden buildings at
the end of the runway.

Suddenly the right wing went up in a vertical bank and
we did a quick spiral down from about a hundred and fifty
feet, landing squarely on the two sets of double wheels, perfectly and with hardly a bump. With my best manners I said
to my instructor, "Thanks, that was certainly fine." He looked
at me peculiarly and said, "Boy, you're damn lucky!" It was
not until weeks later that I found out he had stalled the
plane, it had spun out of control and I had safely come
through the one thing that has killed more students than all
other causes combined—a spinning nose-dive from low altitude. This began my luck which stayed with me throughout
the entire war.

Intensive ground school work followed for days and days,
with a few flights with dual controls. And with each day
my admiration for the RFC and its members increased. A
colonial officer was quite a novelty with them and for some
reason they called me "Yank"—a name I carried through all
my units in the British service. The only serious argument
I had was a silly one, with Lieutenant Albert Ball, later to

be the first British ace, over the relative merits of the American Indian motorcycle and the British Triumph. But we remained good friends. Incidentally, let's mention right here that in aviation an ace is a flier who has officially brought down five or more enemy machines. The word has been horribly misused since the war, especially by newspapers, and is now applied indiscriminately to any aviator, even if he has been only ten minutes in the air.

A few days later, November 24, Irene and I had to move again. I was ordered down to a new airdrome at Thetford in Norfolk. November, in Norfolk, is a clammy, dreary thing. And here I fell victim to the rigors of the wet English climate. Riding a bicycle to camp in the pouring rain and waiting around outdoors for hours for a chance to fly during a plane shortage I managed to catch a really first-class cold. I paid little attention to it but went on with my learning. And my, how much I learned! I made my solo flights. On December 13, after four hours and ten minutes solo, I earned my Royal Aero Club license and, finally, got my Fédération Aéronautique Internationale license. From Maurice Farman longhorns I graduated to shorthorns. I thought the absence of the outrigger sticking way out front would be fatal but it proved to mean nothing. My next step to the most maneuverable Henry Farman was an easy one. The rotary motors were difficult to handle but, after all, flying was more or less "tightrope walking"—and still is in military craft. Altogether I had had four hours dual instruction and eight hours solo work and I had actually taken off a real service machine, an F.E. 2B, a big pusher with a 160-horsepower Beardmore stationary water-cooled motor.

Then another horrible thing happened that blighted my life for months—the sudden killing of a close comrade. It happened countless times later and always caused me keen suffering. It was here, too, that I saw a dull student accidentally make a flying discovery that saved many lives from then on. I was standing by his instructor, Lieutenant D. M. Wynne, on the ground and we saw him go into that usually fatal spin, pull out of it smoothly, go into another on the other side, pull out of that, and repeat the performance several times. When he landed the mentor said, "What the hell are you trying to do? Kill yourself? How did you get out of that first spin and all the others?" His reply was a classic, "Put my controls in neutral, trusted in the Lord and slowly pulled out of it." And that was the solution of spinning thereafter.

And then they carried me off on January 17 to the military hospital in Cambridge, 35 miles by ambulance. My neglected cold had carried through my whole system and I had a very bad case of the most painful malady I have ever experienced—rheumatic fever, known in America as inflammatory rheumatism. For weeks I was in agony. I really believe if my wife had not been there I would have passed away. When I was somewhat better seven of my student pals came to bid farewell. One remarked that I would be in the hospital until spring (1916) and by that time the war would be over. When I did arrive in France a few months later only one of that group was living.

While I was still laid up I had another terrible shock. I had run low in funds and my pay orders were slow in arriving. I wrote to my old commander, Colonel Embury, in the 28th Battalion, requesting that my pay, coming as it did from Canadian funds, be deposited monthly in the Bank of Montreal in London, so I could draw on it. His short note, acceding to my request, conveyed news which actually gave me a relapse. "You'll have heard by now about your old platoon. We weren't in France but eight days when they moved us into the line at St. Elois. We could hear German sappers all night. We were told they had been working for months. Next evening about six, just after supper, while I was trying to catch a shave, the whole earth let go. You'll be verifying wills until doomsday. There were only twelve survivors of your company, none of your platoon. You would never know the gang now."

CHAPTER 4

Off for La Belle France

ALL MY BRIDGES were burned behind me. The platoon that still stayed in my mind as my Army home was wiped out—all the boys I had trained and whom I had grown to know so well. I thought of their parents and what I could say to them to comfort them when we met.

To offset my loneliness, I called up the flying camp at Thetford, my other Army home. Another shock. War seems just a succession of shocks. A new service unit which had come in since I was stricken was about to leave for France after being fitted out with so-called Vickers "gun buses" which I had never seen. There was not a soul there I had known just four months before.

Somehow all this personal grief helped to raise my already high admiration of the British people. The country, unprepared for war, was going through a terrific test. Only a superb sense of organization, a united opinion and a proved psychological system could have produced such results. Breaking new ground at every turn, with new equipment and new ideas and discoveries, those early pioneers of wartime aviation did a noble work. The one thing that struck me most forcibly, in contrast to conditions I met in the United States Army later on, was the absence of selfishness, politics, and bluff. These items cost America many valuable lives and a fortune in money and must not be present in places of authority the next time the United States is called upon to jump into uniform.

It was already apparent to me that if I ever did get out of the hospital I would have to start all over again with my flying work. Presently, as the beautiful English spring brought life back to the land again, I began to snap out of my misery and was able to take short walks through the lovely countryside. My strength returned quickly. Long before I was ready to resume the hurly-burly life, however, I received an order—after a short leave at Bournemouth and on my return to Thetford—to report immediately to Narborough Field.

From No. 12 Squadron I was officially transferred to No. 35. Instead of going backward they were pushing me forward, for this was an advanced school. A cynical old Army sergeant said, "Don't take your wife up there. You'll go through that school like a dose of salts and get overseas in a few days. If you don't you'll be bumped off anyway because that's the place they do the real stuff and few survive." Cheerful bloke! We started at once.

At Narborough I was marked for "light duty." It meant nothing. Instead of taking things easy I plunged into the intricacies and hazards of stunt flying. And up there they had the machines that could do it—Avros with 120-horse Le Rhone (rotary) engines and two-seater Vickers gun buses with 100-horse Monosoupapes (rotary), the latter a very good pusher-type machine doing fine service on the front at that very moment.

The composure of the British people was amazing. I shall never forget one family Irene and I visited at their old estate. Their serene but sophisticated acceptance of wartime conditions, the unanimity of their viewpoints, the beauty of their home life, their complete, unreserved hospitality made a profound impression on us. The husband of our hostess had been killed by a bullet in one of the earliest encounters of Kitchener's First Hundred Thousand. His wife's attitude of pride and sensible resignation to her awful bereavement is still a source of stimulation to us in our own trials and misfortunes. She had only five gallons of petrol for her little Daracq car but insisted we use it touring the nearby country, Stratford-on-Avon, Birmingham, and Coventry. While we were there she wrote up to the War Office and offered for airplane construction the fine old oaks on her place. Almost immediately a man was there inspecting the trees and some were on their way to the sawmills before we left a few days later. She was typical of the entire English population—a united people—during that particular war. And they're like that again in the new war in which they are now engaged.

Prince's Gate was owned by a rich American, J. P. Morgan. It was a gorgeous place almost in the grounds of Buckingham Palace itself. The owner had loaned it to the government as a nursing home. Here the wives of Canadian troops were allowed to go when the old stork put in his appearance and presently my bride was among its patients, May 29, 1916.

What a strange sequence of days! As I stepped out of the hospital after my first visit to Irene the newsboys were out with their big banners so unique in England: GERMAN FLEET DRIVEN BACK!

Rumors had been flying around all morning that a terrific naval battle had taken place. The populace was tense and eager. They could take it, whether victory or defeat. But instead of the big story they had a right to expect there was just a box on the front page with about a hundred words in it: *His Majesty's Government announce a very severe naval engagement off Jutland. Part of our fleet engaged the enemy's battle fleet about to come into the North Sea. His Majesty's Government regret to announce the loss of* (here followed the names of some of the most famous battleships afloat, belonging to Great Britain). *Casualities were heavy. The Admiralty has reason to believe that the enemy losses were very considerable for the foe retired to its base.*

That was all. The greatest naval battle in all history! The most decisive fight in the whole war, told to the people in a few guarded words. Can you imagine how the American papers would handle such a story, and the hell they would raise if they couldn't get more information on it!

Back to my work I went, awaiting the blessed event. Thirteen—fourteen—fifteen hours of solo work—still in the teens of my flying time. As I landed that afternoon, June 7, an orderly was waiting for me. I rushed to the telephone, "It's a girl! Both doing well. Hope you're all right." And thus arrived June, as beautiful and peppy as a war baby should be.

I galloped over to astound my instructor, Captain Aizelwood, with the momentous news. He was hard to find. I discovered him finally, dashing about like a beheaded chicken, and blurted out my tidings. I don't believe he even heard me. "Look here," he said. "I've got orders for France. I'm ferrying the very latest thing in ships, our hush-hush battleplane with the biggest plane engine yet—a Rolls-Royce—across the Channel in the morning. Will I give those Huns something to think about!"

He certainly did. Within thirty minutes he was packed and on his way to the station and I didn't hear from him for two days. Then astonishing word came back. He had sailed over to France, straight as a beeline, over the very trenches where earlier in the war he had groveled in the mud as an infantryman, on to the city of Lille and out to the airdrome where he set the beautiful machine down in a perfect landing—right in the middle of the entire German Army.

It was a gift from the gods for the Huns—the very last work in British battleplanes, because Aizelwood had made an error in navigation and had mistaken the captured city of Lille for his real destination. Imagine his blushes as he was led off to prison camp "for the duration!" That costly blunder, however, had two good effects, one on me, one on the Germans. This gorgeous big plane with its 275-horse-power motor and its three machine guns was an awful shock to them. They didn't know there was such an aerial fighter in existence and it damaged their morale for a long time. As for me it was a lesson which I took to heart. It made me realize that this flying business was one to pursue with greatest care—bravely but wisely—*fortiter ac sapientiter*—the old motto on my family tree, and I never forgot that lesson which has saved my life a number of times.

Pilots were badly needed in France. Trench warfare had set in all over the place and had to be busted up. A war of movement is the only one in which decisions can be made. Both sides agreed on that. And here I was, still on "light duty." That was my official status and I had no chance of getting to France until the ban was lifted. I felt fine and was actually, from the beginning, doing everything anybody could on "heavy duty." My ground course was complete except for my Morse. I could receive about thirteen words a minute in code but I had to get it up to fifteen.

All of a sudden, on June 12, 1916, orders came through for me to go to France as a pilot and report to the pilot pool at St. Omer. Light duty? I guess they forgot all about that. What a thrill! What a mixture of emotions! That day Irene's little Pekinese dog, which I was keeping in camp, was killed by a truck, adding its substantial bit to my confused feelings. Funds were low in the Hartney family but Irene was receiving gorgeous care at Prince's Gate at practically no expense. I was not getting my extra flying pay on account of some complications along the line, since I was only being loaned or seconded from Canadian to Imperial forces. I dashed in to London and spent a few hours with Irene and my six-day-old war baby, June—my second glimpse of her.

Between tears Irene and I settled matters of money, future correspondence, the home in Thetford where she would stay. The minutes flew. And before I knew it I had parted from two most beloved people and was off, by secret embarkation, to La Belle France, June 15, 1916.

CHAPTER 5

I Kill Some Men

THE HUMAN BRAIN has only a limited capacity for absorbing things. Active retentive memory is in a direct proportion to the combination of events plus the time which transpires while they are happening. The fewer the events the clearer the memory. That is why I cannot recall all the small details of the next day or so after leaving my little family and the nurses who wept when I was separated from my wife and baby.

Folkestone, a funny little steamer, the usual mixed crowd of Allied officers and men. France, for centuries the battlefield of Europe! One thing does stand out vividly in my memory—an American flying officer, trained with the British and blessed with about the same amount of solo flying time as I—nineteen hours.

"Listen," he said. "This is just madness sending us over here to fly in old untried kites, with only nineteen hours solo. It's murder in the first degree. If they try to put me in one of those suicide outfits, I'm going to crash 'em, crash the first ship on my first flight and I don't mean maybe."

This was the first of a brand of yellowness I encountered every once in a while in all the armies I contacted. Men like this do a lot of harm. I wondered about him and his future.

"If they should assign us to that squadron with those new Rolls-Royce engines, we might just as well write our epitaphs right now," he rattled on. "That company can build good

automobiles but their flying engine is lousy—too heavy. You
and I have been lucky enough to ride engines that quit cold
every hour. This one quits every quarter hour and when you
land a crate with one of those heavy babies you dig your own
grave and pull it in after you, you hit so hard."

The boy was plain scared and was airing his opinion on
something about which he knew absolutely nothing. His
chatter had a momentarily depressing effect on me but I
snapped out of it almost immediately.

My morose acquaintance said we'd be stuck for weeks at
the pilot pool at St. Omer. We were there twenty minutes.
Within that short space of time I had reported and was on
my way to the 20th Squadron, Royal Flying Corps, British
Expeditionary Force, France—a full-fledged war aviator—
my dream come true. And in the very next seat to me on
the funny, rickety little French train, en route to the only
squadron in France equipped with the new Rolls-Royce
engines, was my rebellious young palsy-walsy. He was most
unhappy.

I was in a state of most interested excitement as we arrived at the front. The 20th Squadron was stationed near a
little forest in Belgium, the Forêt de Clamarias, not more
than eight miles from Cassel, where, on top of a hill above
us, the headquarters of the First British Army was located.
It was a quiet spot. Most wartime airports are. It takes time
and distance to climb to the necessary altitude and it would
be uselessly risky to place the main airdromes near the front
lines. In any coming war the main airports will be even farther back. They'll be permanent ones with big concrete and
steel underground hangars. But there will be small "interceptor" fields almost in the front-line dugouts. This is usually
the case with British, French, and German aviators right
now.

I arrived at the front on June 16, 1916. It had taken me

twenty-two months from the time of my summer vacation at Lake Watrus, Canada, and already most of the men I had trained with in infantry and air force had been killed. The 20th Squadron, composed of three "flights" of eight pilot officers each and an equal number of observer officers, was equipped with cloth hangars with wooden frames and several hastily built wooden dormitories and three separate officers' mess houses or clubs, wherein was an atmosphere something like that of college fraternities. We were greeted with great courtesy but with a peculiar kindly derision, which I found was the custom with "huns," new untried arrivals. While waiting to report to the CO I wangled a glimpse at the machines in which we were to ride to glory. In the hangars I found the F.E. 2B, the slow but efficient pushers mounting two machine guns and the 160-horsepower Beardmore engine, being supplanted by the same plane beefed up and fitted with the 275-horsepower Rolls-Royce, about which I had heard so many rumors, good and bad. That engine was miles ahead of anything in the world at that time. One look at it and my morale went scooting up. It had three machine guns, one of which was a pilot fixed gun but readily usable by the gunner if needed.

My strange friend of the train journey, the one who was going to "crash 'em," was in the offing somewhere, waiting to pay his respects to the commander. I purposely avoided him until word came to report next morning at ten. Then I met him outside the headquarters hut and followed him into the presence of Major Malcolm, as fine a soldier as I ever met, a six-footer from the Regular Army and every inch a man. Bush with another officer as we came in, he promptly rose to greet the two green lieutenants. Extending his hand to my companion he started to welcome him but before he could utter a word the young man blurted out,

"Major, I'm sure glad to meet you, sir, but I'm afraid I'm in the wrong church. You know, I'm a scout pilot."

Such a statement, coming from a scared tyro, seemed to hit the gallant major right between the eyes. He paused and I saw the color mount in his face. Then, in a voice which must have been heard down to the farthest enlisted man's tent, he yelled, "What's that? Why, God damn you, you're nothing—nothing. A scout pilot and you haven't even seen a Hun! Young man, I just don't like you or your attitude. Will you please arrange to get out of this squadron at once. You're nothing—nothing. On your way!"

This was mighty embarrassing to me but secretly I rejoiced over the fate of the youth who had threatened to crack up his first machine, when planes were so scarce and, to me, so wonderful.

With the snappiest salute and sharpest heel click in my repertoire I stepped up as the other boy departed and said, "Reporting for duty, sir," as the adjutant stated my name.

"Glad to meet you, Hartney," said the major, shaking hands. "Happy to welcome you to the best outfit in France. You have nineteen hours solo, I see, but hours mean nothing. All you'll need are guts and loyalty. Forget that bird I just bawled out. There is no prejudice in this squadron. I suggest you get a ship out there at once. Fly it as much as you can. The commander of Flight A, to which I'm assigning you, is your best friend. Better find that out right away. Remember this is war. School is over. I'm here to help you at any time and you'll come to my mess one of these evenings when we can talk more freely. Good luck!"

Checking in with the flight commander was like joining the fraternity. The whole idea of a flight in a British air squadron, a type of organization I was later to help establish in the American squadrons, was to have the officers live closely together and associate closely at all times and to instill a sort of "single mind" unity into the entire group, on the ground and in the air, with a smooth chain of responsibility from the top down to the newest officer. We were to learn each other's methods of thinking so that, while the flight commander's ideas would prevail, we could know just what the others would be most likely to do in the various problems of aerial battles. In this way, in actual training maneuvers and over the whiskies and sodas in the evening (I was a teetotaler), we acquired an understanding that often saved our lives and cost the enemy plenty of men and machines.

In this atmosphere, with eight pilot officers and eight observers who were combined gunners, observers, and aerial photographers, all pledged to be "pukka scouts," I soon found myself smoothed out into harmony and team work. One flight consisted normally of eight planes. My flight commander promised me a plane as soon as another Rolls came along. Then, being the junior in the flight, I would inherit the oldest of the F.E.s with the 160-horsepower Beardmore motor. It would be my very own, with four ground men to take care of it.

For two days I worked my head off studying and tinkering in the flight machine shop, squadron machine-gun range, working out aerial tactics, memorizing maps, identities of surrounding troops, enemy situation and countless other vital items. The airdrome itself was a puzzle to me—and still is. A tiny place, not more than twenty-five acres, it was bordered on two sides by woods and, what was worse, it was the shape of a saucer "right side up." An airport, if not level, should be like a saucer "wrong side up," sloping downward at the edges. Another hazard, at the end farthest from the hangars, was a small lake which we used for machine-gun target practice from the air. Something began to worry me. In training nobody had seemed to consider the difference between peacetime and wartime loads. This is dangerously true in peacetime in all countries today. I wondered how we would lift those planes off that small "upside down" field with warloads of guns, ammunition, cameras, and full tanks.

My first flight was to make or break me. I was to take up "A 9" Rolls at 3:16 P.M. June 20 with A. M. Stanley as gunner. It was a dizzy affair, right in front of my flight commander and the squadron CO. I had studied all the plane's instruments and gadgets and could have located them blindfolded. I had checked and double checked gas, oil, temperature, and other items and bumped off down that awful field for a take-off. Rising nicely and not too abruptly I was beginning to pat myself on the back when—*whang! bang! bang! whang!* The engine was quitting—one bank of six cylinders cut cold. Down went the nose like a bullet and in the steepest bank I had ever made in my twenty-odd hours of flying I turned abruptly and glided back to the field with a dead engine and landed back on the runway downwind with scarcely a bump.

Any flier today knows that such a maneuver is practically fatal. It is the way Hobey Baker and countless others have been killed. Hardly anyone ever gets away with it today but I was fortunate beyond words. I lived and was actually complimented because the last boy trying it had been killed only the week before. The order "land straight ahead if your motor quits on the take-off" had not yet been written. Flying was too young.

Within a few minutes I had made another and completely successful take-off and did a little overhead sightseeing around Clamarias and took a short circle over St. Omer, the air depot nearby. The next morning I was allowed to take my "Cook's Tour"—a peep at the front lines with an escort plane to show me the way. Lieutenant Dewar was my observer-gunner. Up north as we climbed in the bright summer sunlight I could see the North Sea even as far as Holland, to the south the winding trench area came into view. I could see far over into enemy territory and, by turning my head a little, several of the largest industrial cities in Belgium became plainly visible. My escort had mentioned a number of points of interest to watch for. The three-cornered lake at Zillebeke, southeast of war-torn Ypres, was one. It came in very handy later in aerial combats because I could catch the flash of the sun on the water without even looking down and thus know my exact position.

Not an enemy ship flecked the sky. I was surprised at the clear way in which the trenches stood out for miles and miles with here and there an immense mine crater to tell of swift and awful death from beneath. My first sight of the trenches and my realization that they were inhabited by thousands of human beings bent on destruction was a powerful mental experience. Frequently a big puff from a bursting shell reminded me that this was real war and not just a picnic sail in the sunlight. From then on I always felt sorry for the boys groveling in the mud of Flanders and France. I was astonished by the activities behind both lines. Everywhere I could see the smoke from railroad trains. But from two and a half miles up I could not see human beings or automobiles. It all looked quiet and peaceful. As promised we went a little over the lines and into enemy territory, at a lower altitude. *Wuff, wuff-wuff-wuff!* Black and white bursts of antiaircraft fire burst below us and I was having my first baptism from the futile old "archies." Our tour lasted eighty minutes. When we landed I felt already a seasoned veteran. And, strange to say, I was so considered and so treated.

June 30, 1916, of all the big days in my wartime life, was probably the biggest. When I returned from my "Cook's Tour" and put in some more time over the lines, in the Beardmore powered F.E. 2B, my superiors made a report on me and I was labeled a regular. At mess that night I almost jumped

out of my skin when I was informed that I would be permitted
to go on an extraordinary mission the following morning,
June 30, in Rolls A9, as part of the protection to a balloon-
strafing expedition covering the whole front. Corporal Hodder was my gunner. This turned out to be one of the choice
"boners" of the brass hats but if you don't think it had me
excited you are mistaken. I didn't sleep five minutes in succession that night.

The big German observation balloons had become quite
bothersome. When none of our planes was about they would
bob up into the sky and pick up a lot of valuable information. When the air was full of planes they would be pulled
down until a quieter moment. The idea this time was a
sudden surprise mass attack with phosphorus bombs. It was
a good plan theoretically. Already the home defense units
had discovered that the flaming bullet was the only practical
missile against the lighter-than-air craft. But one lucky British flier, Warneford, had brought down a Zeppelin in flames
over Dunkirk with a phosphorus bomb and the high command became temporarily mad on them.

Up to that day I had not been assigned to even one of
the old F.E. 2Bs. Eight Rolls-Royces had arrived but so far
no plane of any kind had been ticketed for me. To my
amazement, the next morning at eight o'clock, I was presented
with one of the new Rolls-Royce ships, A9. I couldn't have
been prouder if they had offered me the British crown. At
the front but a few hours, here I was the proud possessor
of one of the finest two-seater fighters on the whole Allied
front. My morale went sky-high. I, the little mouse, began to
yell, "Bring on them cats!"

We were detailed to fly down the line and land alongside a
canal a few miles south. There we were to gas up and escort
thirty of the special bombers, "quirks" as we called them, over
their targets. We were told that other units along the whole

front would do likewise and certain pin points were given us indicating the positions of the balloons. We were to keep our altitude and come down only if the slow-moving bombers got tangled up with enemy fighters. The idea may have been good but it went "blooy."

Landing at the post of the "quirk" squadron, by the canal, the pilots almost went crazy over our beautiful machines. It gave them a sense of complete security. Were they not being escorted by ten of the best fighting planes in the whole war and by seasoned pilots of the famous 20th Squadron? I didn't mention to them that my flying time over the front was one hour and in my whole life but twenty hours. With their ground officers they gave us a grand luncheon on an old scow, while outside was the bold evidence of their intentions. Underneath each "quirk," on racks hastily constructed, were two phosphorus bombs per plane, each weighing about sixty pounds but as big as hundred pounders containing high explosive. After luncheon each of our pilots, with his gunner, had a chat with the pilot of the individual plane he was to escort. They knew their maps by heart. We were supposed to know them only cursorily. For, after all, weren't we supposed to spend our time clearing the skies of Huns and know the terrain only well enough to get back home after each patrol? More baloney!

The zero hour, as I recall it, was one o'clock. At that instant the attacks were to occur simultaneously all down the line and by 1:05 all balloons from the North Sea to Strassburg would be aflame and every German balloon company would have to write in its report *"Drachen gerflachen."* Some of our bombers had to travel as much as fifty miles to reach their objectives so at twelve o'clock we all strolled off the barge to observe their take-off with their heavy loads and start their climb. We, with our superior speed, would overtake them at the precise moment of dropping—one o'clock. Vain thought!

As the first plane moved slowly down the field for the take-off and the second was taxiing into position there was a blinding flash of flame and the air was suddenly rent asunder. *Wham!* went one of the phosphorus bombs on the first machine. It had tripped itself bumping over the rough ground. *Wham!* went one on the second plane. Instantly those two ships and all others near them were in the center of an appalling hurricane of flying phosphorus, streaking every which way, like giant chrysanthemum bursts of rockets.

Like a scared rabbit I dashed for my new ship. Our planes, by a rare chance, were not parked close together. *Wham!* went more explosives as the spreading flames and flying phosphorus did their bit for the enemy. When the excitement died down we counted up the damage—two hangars and five airplanes destroyed including one of our Rolls-Royce beauties from the 20th Squadron. But my precious plane, A9, was safe.

Even a dizzy experience like that could not be allowed to interfere with military plans and our part of the ill-fated balloon-strafing expedition went right ahead. Whoever figured out this big stunt forgot that low scudding clouds might render the whole scheme null and void. Thanks to a keen gunner, who knew his navigation perfectly, we arrived at our designated spot exactly on time—one o'clock. Through a network of small clouds under us I got glimpses of phosphorus bombs bursting and streaming earthward from the air all up and down the line. Many of them seemed to be missing their marks by a good five miles!

Bombs bursting in the air are terrifying from below, whether one is on the ground or flying, but viewed from above they look insignificant and puny. I was watching them intently when there occurred an incident so startling to me that I can only express it in the stupid movie word "colossal." In short, I saw my first EA—enemy aircraft. Remember those initials. You'll run into them frequently from now on. I was cruising along at about eight thousand feet in and out of muddy, well-defined cloud banks. And suddenly, a hundred yards ahead of me, was a flimsy-looking ship with two black Maltese crosses on the white under surfaces of the lower wing, a German Rumpler two-seater, black and foreboding beyond words —diving in a steep vertical bank, hiking for German territory for all it was worth.

I frightened my gunner, Hodder, more than myself as I leaned forward on the controls and to my surprise found myself overtaking the enemy ship. I was about on his tail, close enough to do business when my gunner signaled "washout" (jammed guns or something else making it inadvisable to continue the combat). Being much his junior in minutes in combat over the front (this being my very first second) I slowly broke away but as I did so, our momentum carrying us almost even with him, I could see the trouble. From the rear cockpit of the German biplane ship an enemy gunner was working his Spandau and bullets were flying past us plenty. The Spandau's cadence of firing was considerably slower than ours. I had lost altitude so much faster than I had been told I would, I had caught him so quickly, I had forgotten about that Boche gunner in the rear cockpit. I had not co-operated with my gunner. I had risked his life and mine unnecessarily—a dozen things made me ashamed of myself and I felt my whole mission had been a terrible failure and that, when I got back, my commanding officer would take my plane away from me.

On landing I made out my first combat report. It should have been a proud moment. Evidently I was the only escort plane of some fifteen up and down that long line that had actually encountered the Boche. I was "some punkins"—in dispatches. In reality, especially in my own mind, I was a complete flop.

The entire bomb-dropping expedition had destroyed exactly zero balloons. I doubt if it was tried more than once again. One evening four days later a similar but smaller attack was made at lower altitude but this time the bombs missed their small targets by even wider margins—sometimes as much as eight miles.

Work, work, work. Patrol after patrol, sometimes alone, sometimes with a group. Plenty of antiaircraft fire but no enemy planes except a couple diving away and too far off for excitement. It was indeed a quiet sector. One day I thought of my old 28th Infantry Battalion, which I had heard was operating down around Kemmel. For amusement I painted on the nose of my nacelle a fine replica of the 28th's maple leaf collar insignia, two feet in diameter, and flew extremely low over their position. I never did it again. It gave some of the high staff brass hats the jitters and an order came through forbidding any markings on planes which would identify the units on the ground below. One thing for which I have to congratulate myself was that none of the few enemy planes I saw succeeded in making a surprise attack on me. So I lived on. Most green pilots at the front live about five days, are surprised in an attack and die before they get fairly started or get such heart failure that they are never any good again.

July 1, 1916, Canada's famous Dominion Day, was to mark the first real Allied offensive. Surely the war would not last long after the Allies got under way that day, in the first battle of the Somme! The main theater of operations adjoined us to the south but to fliers in the air, naturally, there is no clean-cut line anywhere. Fifteen miles or so one way or the other makes little difference. On the night of June 30, about ten o'clock, our big Scotch flight commander called us all to the officers' mess hall. Combat orders for the big push had come through and we were to do our part with the whole squadron. I had done well with my Rolls that day so I was switched to another one, A3 and was to take along First "Ack Emma" Stanley, the best gunner in the outfit.

"No more patrols on our side of the lines. From now on it's fifteen miles over and we'll sink everything in sight. This war's got to end. We must knock the Germans out of the air, especially over a couple of airdromes, near Lille. Big doings down south and the show is over!"

Thus spoke our squadron commander and in turn my flight commander in June 1916. I should like to have argued about some points in those orders but one thing I had learned and, although difficult for men coming into the Army from the freedom of civilian life, it must be learned thoroughly by every soldier from private to general—an order, especially in wartime, is an order. It is inflexible and must be obeyed to the letter regardless of consequences and personal opinions. Ignorance of this basic principle is one of the great obstacles in training a democracy for war.

"Be in your planes with the engines ticking over at 4 A.M. and be ready to push off promptly at 4:15. You will cross at Armentières, proceed climbing directly to the airdrome south of Lille, back to Armentières, on our side, and then back over. Keep doing so. Strafe everything in sight."

Our five-plane formation was quite distinctive. It was the first real formation wartime flying, for which the 20th of the RFC must get the credit. Hitherto it had been impossible everywhere due to the lack of sufficient planes of any one type. Groups had gone out helter-skelter but controlled echelons were a curiosity. In the coming aerial war almost all combat flying will be in controlled formation, in fact, in hitherto unbelievable waves of planes but not necessarily "tight" formations. With us, the flight commander was in the center, one plane on each flank slightly ahead and above and two others considerably higher and back some five machine lengths. The theory was that the gunners in the two front planes would watch the higher rear planes and transmit their signals to the leader in the lowest center plane. With pusher-type machines this arrangement was ideal and gave plenty of gunplay in every possible direction from which an attack might come, and, in turn, afforded a good field of fire for us in pouring bullets from our side.

This was the first dawn patrol and everything worked perfectly. Thanks to fair weather, we formed up quickly over Cassel at 4000 feet and began a steady climb to the lines east and slightly south. I shall never forget that climb in formation. My position on the left rear I knew was the one always assigned to the newest arrival in the squadron and was invariably the plane first attacked by the enemy—frequently picked off at the very beginning of the battle. I did not worry whatever about that but there was plently of excitement in me as we roared forth into mortal combat. Ahead and below me over the top wing of the left advanced plane I could see the gunner in the cockpit with his eye on me and he, in turn, was in line with the other front plane and closely watched by the flight commander in the middle ship. I felt entirely safe with such protection in addition to Sergeant Stanley, my own veteran gunner.

We crossed the line at 10,000 feet at 4:55, exactly over the spot where I knew the "archies" were lurking. Sure enough our crossing tripped their fire. *Whoof, whoof!* All around us puffed their soft blossoms of lethal smoke but none nearer than four hundred yards. In a few seconds we were safely past them, knowing the guns were tied to their emplacements.

There was a slight breeze blowing from the west, a dangerous thing when your home base is west. Presently I could make out the big industrial cities of Lille, Tourcoing, and Roubaix, standing out clearly in the morning sun. I could see two enemy airdromes and even from ten thousand feet I could discern several planes taking off to come up after us. Once in the air they seemed to disappear but I knew we would have some fun with them. About five miles south and east of Lille, on signal, we made a slow turn to the left, my machine acting as a pivot, high above the others. Back to Armentières we sped, in perfect formation, climbing steadily up to 12,500 feet. We got another greeting of "archies" falling far short, as we scurried over the lines, then freedom for a few minutes as we sailed over our own territory, then around in a turn to go back at them again.

Memory tells me it must have been 5:35 A.M. when we were back over Lille, making our next turn on what the flight commander obviously felt was a bold challenge to the enemy—a regular parade, Armentières to Lille, back and forth, at 13,000 feet. In war the turn is the vulnerable maneuver. Away up and off to the east I could see two little specks—enemy planes watching us as they circled and climbed. Again, I was the pivot, as Callender, in the right rear ship, opened up his throttle for a sweeping turn. With a swoop the two little specks wheeled and came at him in a flatish dive.

Bang! went my Very pistol, spouting a smoking rocket to warn him and the others that we were being attacked. My flare just about coincided with two smoky streaks of tracer bullets from the Boche ships. The two planes zipped past Callender, almost as if they were going right on through him, brave men, then turned above and behind him. Two on one! With the flight commander's words, "Strafe everything in sight!" ringing in my ears and without any further co-ordination from him, I swerved for the attack—to shoot them off Callender's tail.

Like all fresh pilots I was quivering with anxiety to land my first quarry. He saw me first, however, and veered sharply away, scooting straight north. Callender, still unhit, did an Immelmann turn and was soon mastering the other plane. I was fascinated watching my gunner on the one hand and Callender's scrap on the other. Handling his Lewis machine guns with wonderful coolness, holding his fire when useless, giving short, quick bursts when it seemed likely to be effective, Callender's gunner literally butchered that poor single seater light rotary-engined Fokker monoplane. In a few seconds the Hun was belching smoke and flames and was on its way to the ground. It was a clean-cut victory, the first I had ever seen.

Watching that battle, however, had cost me precious altitude. I had gone too far north and was down to 8500 feet. The rest of the flight was nowhere to be seen, nor was there any sign of enemy ships. But I knew that was no assurance that there weren't any around. Stanley signaled me that both his guns were jammed and his head disappeared in the front cockpit, which he called his "office," as he bent over to fix them. As we climbed I looked at the speed indicator. We were making only 60 miles an hour and the altimeter was rising with agonizing slowness. Just then I got a hunch. "Things are suspiciously quiet around here," I said to myself. Unfastening my safety belt, I grasped the radiator behind me, took hold of the radiator cap, let the joy stick go so the plane would fly free, and lifted myself up to peer over the tail.

Crack-crack-crack-zip-click-click! Swarms of bullets came snapping past my ears on both sides—smokers and clear ones. And as I looked up quickly there was a Fokker monoplane diving straight at me from above. To this day, all I have to do to bring that awful sight back is to close my eyes—it appears before me instantly like the black spots you see after looking at a welding torch—a simple, straight, oncoming black mid-wing monoplane with a rounded cowl hurtling through the air at me is engraved forever on my retina.

Stanley, busy with his guns, did not know what was going on. He did not even look up. With safety belt still unbuckled I threw myself back into my seat. Frightened out of my wits, I leaned over and hit Stanley a vicious clout on the head. And then I had my first real lesson in aerial acrobatics. Holding the left wing slightly depressed, I slammed my foot down on the right-hand rudder. I thought that big plane would tear itself to pieces as the resulting side-slip skidded us downward to the left in a wild partial corkscrew lurch. All I could see of Stanley was his hand in front of me, clinging tensely to the nacelle ring. Now the other wing down, stick back, nose slightly up and a momentary kick on the opposite rudder. A quick glance, both sides—no sign of the Hun. So get ready for a gamble and a blind Immelmann. Swiftly, after a short preliminary straightaway dive, I leaned forcibly back on the stick. Then, as all controls become flabby and we are poised momentarily in the air, crash with the right foot down on the rudder and in a split second, out of control, we reverse direction. Now we are headed back for enemy territory again in complete control. And there, right in front of me, streaking like hell, and slightly below is my German friend.

The black-helmeted begoggled pilot, alone in his rickety little plane, bent over his windshield, then slowly turned his head to look at me, as my 275-horsepower whipped me up close to his hundred ten. *Putt-putt-putt-putt.* Stanley was again on the job. Tracer, ordinary, armor piercing and incendiary bullets in five bursts of four each, went screaming at the enemy ship, all over it, through it and through its driver. He was doomed. His tank ablaze he pulled up almost directly in front of us, then whip-stalled to Eternity. I once saw a kitten, its head run over by an automobile, jump straight up in the air, then dive to the ground and roll over and over. Our enemy was doing just this. In addition, he was afire.

As the poor fellow went down, Stanley turned around to me with a sickly, half-guilty but triumphant smile below his leather-rimmed face mask and goggles. With one hand he signaled "thumbs down" for the fallen enemy—a traditional gesture with all war aviators. I banked up and looked over the side for a moment to see where the Fokker hit. Then I came to my senses. We were much farther over the enemy lines than we should have been, our gas was running low and we had a nasty head wind to buck. It was time to scuttle for home—a mean job well done. I had killed, or helped to kill, my first German. I could feel no exultation. I could only think of that black clad flier in flames—and his family.

I leveled off and started back for the nearest point westward on our side. Stanley glanced about once, then busied himself with a couple of fresh trays of ammunition. I had learned, or rather relearned in actual combat, two of the war flier's most vital lessons—watch over the tail and never hesitate to turn back into enemy territory. In a minute or less a couple of short bursts showed Stanley both of his guns were in working order. Cupping a hand over his eyes like a sailor he gave the horizon and the sky a thorough going over. Suddenly he pointed way upward and southward. "Archies" were bursting, enemy "archies." And there above them were the three front ships of our patrol, still wheeling along in formation but seemingly miles above us—specks in the blue —and completely out of touch. To climb and join them appeared a foolish thought. But where was Callender?

Just as the question formed in my mind, Stanley came to life excitedly. Pointing over the tail he began to shake his fist madly. It was the official signal for enemy aircraft and was wholly unwelcome at this moment. At only 7000 feet altitude and ten miles over the enemy lines with only a little gas left we were in no shape for a long combat. But there was no help for it. In fact, this was just the beginning. It was the Fokker which had run away from us, the second speck, and he had almost succeeded in pulling a surprise attack on us. Stanley touched the telescope rear mast mount, which meant he could not bring his guns to bear on the enemy, and pulled his hand back into his stomach, thus telling me to stall the nose upward. I did so immediately and a few shots from Stanley went putt-putt-putting after the black ship with black crosses as it went over us from the rear after flattening out. We were after him instantly.

Some say that monoplanes can outmaneuver biplanes. This certainly was not true in this case. Perhaps on account of our power and the pusher weights concentrated amidship, we ran circles around that poor Heinie. He had altitude on us, the most valuable of all advantages in a sky battle. Putting my nose down a bit to gain speed, I slowly pulled back on the stick, with throttle wide open, and he just seemed to be sinking alongside of us as I soared for altitude above him. And right now I learned a third lesson which stood me in good stead many times afterward—always watch out for enemy reinforcements. Learning this nearly cost me my life that morning.

As I zoomed up after our quarry, who had disappeared for the moment, a sudden and serious pantomime took place on our ship. Stanley looked around to see me frantically shaking my fist to signal EA ahead. And he was shaking his fist just as furiously to tell me of EA to the rear. In a second we were all in a circus—zooming and diving, two to one—our two-seater against two single-seaters. But I was gaining altitude, they were both losing it. Finally, on insistent signals from Stanley, I steadied out and his cool eyes and flexible guns caught one of the Boche ships in a vital spot on a pot shot as it dived away from us. It was so close we seemed about to ride on its back. Crazily it started toward the ground while the other turned tail and ran, letting discretion be the better part of valor.

Now, however, we were in a pickle. The lines which hitherto we could discern plainly in the west had become invisible in a slight ground haze. I remember resigning myself then and there to landing in German territory, to be a prisoner for the rest of the war if I didn't get my head blown off. Could my family get photographs through to me? Such thoughts came to a sudden end, however, as we found ourselves again in a double attack. I began to get a little panicky but the cool, courageous Stanley calmly singled out the closer of the two adversaries and tried to bring his guns into action. He couldn't quite make it so he indicated his trouble by looking back over his shoulder and I went about correcting it. One of the two was very cautious and, even before coming into range, veered and zoomed away from us. The other crossed boldly in front of us but Stanley, not trusting a pot shot and running short of ammunition, coolly followed him with his guns but held his fire. I was fearful another jam had caused this but on getting a knowing "O.K." from Stanley I brought the ship around to get on the Fokker's tail. This worked perfectly and the lower of the two enemy fliers foolishly swooped away—a sitting shot—the crazy straightaway flight which has caused several breeds of game birds to become extinct in this country. With my superior speed and Stanley's cool judgment and skillful aim, another German ship went hurtling earthward—not in the familiar unguided spin but in a straight dive. There was no doubt about this victory. If he had tried to pull out quickly his wings would surely have kept going but not as fast as his fuselage. Smoke was streaking out behind him. Nothing could have saved him.

I shall pass over the repeated attacks we underwent that dizzy morning. Later we were officially credited with bringing down two enemy ships. I have promised myself someday to search the files of the local papers, if any, published in that great Belgian industrial area to see what the spectators thought of our antics up there above them. Between jammed guns, sudden double attacks and every acrobatic stunt in my whole repertoire we had recovered about five miles toward the lines but in doing so had been driven many miles too far south. The haze was lifting. Halfway between Lille and Armentières there came a situation which put an end to our exciting activities for the day.

Once again Stanley signaled "Hun on tail." Again I signaled "Hun in front." Before I could decide which to engage a ripping of bullets through the aluminum nacelle and cowling settled the question for me. I had no idea the man behind was so close. A startled glance at my instruments, a "shove-away" of Stanley's Number One gun, which was completely *hors de combat* and only a few bullets left for the second, two Boche pumping bullets at us, a rough engine, sputtering, quitting, a vain call from Stanley for maneuvers I couldn't deliver, a sudden but momentary revival of the engine, the "rev. counter" swaying madly from 10 to 1800, air pressure gone, the needle of the oil pressure gauge down to zero. A hell of a situation! Prepare to land, but dodge that last one if possible!

I had heard of fliers ramming the enemy. Wilbur White, one of the best pilots that ever flew for the U.S.A., actually did so later in the war in my outfit and died knocking a Hun off a comrade's tail. I have heard plenty of people say it is impossible and incredible. Nonsense! In desperation it is a natural instinct. One of the German ships was coming straight at us from the front. As Stanley signaled both guns jammed I steered straight for that oncoming ship. The only thought I remember was "I'll try to hit him with my heavy oleo under gear and there may be a chance for us to get down alive." Perhaps the German read my thought. Anyway, he swerved out of the way only a few feet in front of us and I never again aimed an airplane deliberately at another.

A quick vertical bank pointed our nose toward Amentières. Still 6000 feet up, with a few weak kicks in the motor, I tried to "ride her" and stretch the long glide for all it was worth. Looking over the side I was shocked at the absence of landing places in the pock-marked terrain. We were down to 1000 feet and suddenly I saw the trenches right below us. We were over! You have no idea what a feeling of joy seized us, although we were still in serious trouble. Here the engine stopped cold, with a last wicked kick-over of the propeller. I felt she would "burble" any second. How to climb down that thousand feet and land in one piece! Stalling over some high poplar trees on the road from Armentières to Bailleul, I very nearly slipped off on the wing. But another few seconds and the wheels actually touched good old terra firma and we landed in a pancake, not running more than a hundred yards on a funny little field moderately full of shell holes. Some troops in support trenches had tried to grow vegetables in it. I stopped a lot of that, or at least plowed it up for them for a few dozen yards. *C'est la guerre!*

Stanley and I jumped out quickly. "Right-o, that'll do!" he said and came over and put his arm around me. Then we began to inspect our plane. It was in horrible shape, riddled with bullets and how it held together is a mystery. The fabric in places was torn clear from the leading edge to the trailing. If we had tried to paint an Iron Cross on every hole, as we did later in the war, it would have taken all night. That motor should have been put in a museum. It had saved our lives but how it did it I don't know to this day. Seven bullets were actually sticking in the water jackets and in the plumbing. The cowling was almost a sieve. And here's gospel truth, although my word on it has often been doubted—four of the aluminum pistons, a secret Rolls-Royce innovation, had actually fused and were holding up four of the exhaust valves. There was no water whatever in the engine and practically no oil. For those last few minutes it had been doing its bit for old England metal to metal—at melting temperatures. I pulled out two of the bullets and kept them for souvenirs. Stanley, much more experienced than I, merely shook his head, mumbling, "A miracle! A bloody miracle!"

Suddenly we realized we were surrounded by soldiers—a new kind to us—Australians—grand fellows. They were much interested in us and in our war-wracked plane. Presently their captain came along and promised to get a message to our squadron. He told us the war was practically over—July 1, 1916!—that the operations adjacent to us to the south had been the fiercest to date, with the Allies' guns hub to hub. He left us on the run to try to get our message through.

And then, believe it or not, our nerves cracked. Stanley and I both lay down under the wing of Old Faithful, our heroic plane, and went sound asleep in the middle of the first battle of the Somme, with the roar of nearby artillery and exploding enemy shells down southward and east deafening our ears. The intense excitement of ninety minutes of bitter air fighting plus the reaction of a safe landing among friendly people was all our systems could stand.

My nap lasted about fifteen minutes. Something woke me—a sort of reverberating crash. It was an enemy shell about four hundred yards away. The Germans had a general idea of where we had landed and thought it would be a good idea to shoot for our machine—a futile thought but one practiced often in the early days of the war. I had no great fear of them, such was my relief at getting away from the rat-tat-tat of those Spandau machine guns. I feel the same about anti-aircraft cannon in comparison with direct machine gunning. "Archies" have their value, especially up to ten thousand feet, but it lies mainly in the job of keeping airplanes flying so high that their bombing accuracy is seriously impaired. Anti-aircraft has another good point—it raises the morals of civilians and troops in the immediate neighborhood. Although their record for bringing down enemy planes can never be high, the "archies" are worth having in large numbers for their value on the two points I have mentioned.

Presently an orderly brought instructions to call Cassel GHQ at 9:15 A.M. and ask for our commanding officer who would be waiting there.

"I wonder what he'll think," said Stanley. "We've done all right this morning and don't let anyone say we haven't."

Frankly, I was proud. I was filled with a peculiar mixture of exultation and regret. The latter was for the lives we had extinguished. The exultation had several reasons: the successful accomplishment of my first big assignment in this vital and gigantic game of war, landing my riddled ship safely and achieving several clean-cut victories which would be credited to our squadron and thus justify my membership in it.

"Stanley, how many times were we in separate fights?" I asked.

"We had eleven scraps," he figured, "but my guns were out completely on two and a half of them. We can claim nine victories because in one of the scraps I know we got two."

Even in my enthusiasm I knew it would be ridiculous to claim nine victories. Two in one sortie was the record up to that time. Anyhow, I sat down under the wing of our plane and, in my old Canadian infantry message book, wrote an official report of our experiences, letting the future take care of victory credits. I still have a copy. Eventually, as I have said, we were credited with bringing down two Boche planes that day.

At the appointed time I recognized the voice of Major Malcolm, CO, on the telephone. As usual he was brusque but fair.

"What's the damage?" he asked.

"Machine riddled and motor completely gone," I reported.

"If I send out an engine could you install it and fly her out?"

He was, of course, ignorant of our position so close to the enemy lines and of our pierced longerons, wingspars, and propeller.

"Absolutely no, sir," I replied.

"Then you've crashed your ship."

This was one right between the eyes. I hastened to say: "Beg your pardon, sir. That's not correct. The enemy has riddled it and burnt up my Rolls."

With quick decision he said: "A tender and dolly will meet you in the square at Bailleul at noon. Have the machine dismantled and be ready to haul the thing back by the tail when our camion arrives."

No praise, no congratulations. No wonder! There were only eight of these wonderful ships in all France. We followed instructions and began our journey home. At dusk the guns all along the front started up again. "Celebrating for you Canucks," said the truck driver. "This is the worst yet." And he pointed back to the star shells rising in glaring streaks along the entire line as far as the eye could reach north and south. Dragging the plane with its wheels mounted only on bronze bearings, we were soon in trouble. The bearings heated and seized. We had to pour water on them and stop and grease them every few miles. It was a slow all night journey.

Greatly delayed, we arrived at our camp at 5 A.M. as dawn was breaking. A morning patrol was just taking off. Filing my report with the adjutant, Stanley and I turned in for a sleep. But within an hour I was back to watch the second patrol go out. "Wish you hadn't ruined that crate of yours," said the adjutant. "We need it badly."

"*I* ruined it?" I exploded.

Just then along came Major Malcolm, the squadron CO. He greeted me warmly.

"Hartney, you did a fine job. In fact, you did exactly as I would have tried to do under the circumstances. But look at this letter from the wing."

Ah, thought I. Can this be a decoration so soon?

I read the letter. It said in substance:

"To the CO 20th Squadron, RFC. BEF:

"You will ascertain why Hartney and Callender left the formation this morning and report to this office. You will inform these officers immediately that a repetition will mean a court-martial."

I was speechless, aghast. Callender had left the formation because he was attacked by two enemy planes and I had left to save him, in compliance with our orders, "Strafe everything in sight." It was my first encounter with the Kiwis, those wingless birds of the air service, ground officers, with no knowledge of flying, some of whom, as every pilot knows, were forever issuing asinine orders like this one and generally retarding things and causing trouble in the early days of the flying art, in fact even up to today. Callender had not yet reported to the squadron. He had been shot down and crashed, was slightly injured and never reported back to fight in the 20th.

In the course of time, as in Germany now, all responsible positions in the aviation services will be filled by officers of long flying experience who know what it is all about. The absence of this policy in the United States has seriously affected her efficiency and has been the cause of great and unnecessary expense. Later, in the United States Army, another Kiwi issued an equally idiotic order which became a classic. Observing that planes usually bounced several times on landing, a matter determined entirely by the direction of wind, speed, condition of field, and other physical factors, the little Kiwi gave forth this military gem:

"Hereafter pilots must refrain from hopping their planes on landing like birds from place to place. They will place their tires firmly on the ground and make them run smoothly and without taking off again to a steady landing straight ahead."

The battle between the actual aviators and the ground officers without flying experience will go on as long as the condition is allowed to exist. Major Malcolm, himself a pilot, tried to cheer me up.

"I'd have done the very same thing under the circumstances. You put up a stout show. Don't worry about this letter. I understand."

I was highly discouraged. I had been taught that victory was glorious and here the glory was being destroyed by a witless ass of a Kiwi. An hour later something else happened that vastly deepened my gloom.

Lieutenant Chancellor, a fine young flying observer veteran, had returned from a patrol over the lines and told how his two guns had jammed at a crucial moment. He was right on top of an enemy ship, whose pilot undoubtedly knew he was on the brink of doom. When Chancellor sailed by him without firing and gave him a wave of the hand, the German, probably the most surprised man in the world, returned the greeting.

With Chancellor as gunner, Major Malcolm, who up to then had only flown the slower Beardmore powered F.E. 2Bs, decided to make his first solo in the new, faster Rolls F.E. They took off northeastward over the little lake and rose above the woods at the side of the field. Those of us watching were turning away to go about our business when bang-bang! Sputter—silence. Their engine had quit. Fascinated, we prayed they would not try to turn back onto the field. Instead came that awful, slow nose-dive, straight down, straight into the midst of the trees—both men dead.

With Malcolm gone, the man of understanding, the only one between me and the Kiwis of the wing, I felt as if I had lost my parents. Next day we laid both to rest at St. Omer. We obtained two plain pine boxes, wrapped both in Union Jacks, and put them sidewise and side by side into a trench and pulled some earth over them in the burial pit fifty yards long, ten feet deep and eight feet wide, which only filled up as bodies were deposited in it and a little earth pulled over them.

The following day Major Mansfield arrived to replace Malcolm. The new CO was the typical high type of regular British Army officer, the same caliber as Malcolm, just as understanding, fair, and helpful to budding young pilots.

The war went on.

Our superior planes, soon mounting three unsynchronized guns each, one a fixed but readily convertible pilot gun with a Bowden wire trigger control on the pilot's stick, held the supremacy in that sector by their formidable appearance and fine performance. Fights were many but nearly always the men of our squadron were victorious. In fact, our supremacy was so complete that patrols became boresome and we were constantly pushing them deeper into enemy territory. Occasionally we lost a plane when an EA would sneak in and effect a surprise attack on a new man. Sorties over the line meant the usual barrage of archie bursts, always futile, never touching us.

This gave me a brilliant idea. I was gaining self-confidence and was growing considerably bolder. So, about September

1, 1916, I put a proposition to my flight commander and he passed it along to the squadron CO.

"Those antiaircraft shells cost a lot of money and materials and take the time of a lot of people to make. Let me go back after patrols and present my machine as a target. They'll never hit me and we can put a serious drain on the German shell factories."

No sooner said than done. For several days after that, following every patrol, I went back and, flying at about 12,000 feet, let them fill the sky with black and white bursts, high explosives, and shrapnel. By simple arithmetic, we would count the little balls of smoke hanging in the sky each time, multiply them by their approximate cost and figure that the wastage in shells about equaled the cost of my plane—and we still had the plane. The many factors of possible error arising when firing at a plane 10,000 feet up are so great that antiaircraft fire is not accurate and probably never will be at that altitude or higher.

I know the German gunners thought I was a jackass, coming over there in the same place on the hour, every hour, after each patrol. But the scheme worked perfectly. It was not a question of diving, zooming, and climbing to dodge the archies. It was simply one of easing right, left rudder, sometimes twice in succession, sometimes quickly lowering my altitude, never the same, skidding and speeding up in the twenty seconds consumed by the shell in its trip from the gun to the approximate spot where I had been or where they hoped I would be. Meanwhile Stanley and my other gunners, Carver, Jourdan, and Wilkinson, son of a Toronto minister, killed in action later, and I did a lot of fancy bomb dropping which may have had some results below, always small bombs.

Our boldness prompted the enemy to adopt a new antiaircraft cannon technique which presently became the regular practice of all air services—bracketing. It took me by surprise. One evening, just as we were about to pull a couple of twenty-pound Cooper bombs after taking careful aim, my ears were discomfited by six explosions—above, below, in front, behind, and at each side. Thereupon we decided to go home. Somewhere in the records there is a photograph of an airplane with 416 patches on it covering tiny holes made by flying bits of shrapnel and not known to its crew until they landed. That was our plane and the experience marked the end of the little shell-wasting racket we had been working on the Germans.

CHAPTER 6

Things That Try Men's Souls

OUR SQUADRON did a lot of pioneering in formation flying. After our first successful experiment on July 1, 1916, we tried out a lot of other shapes and diagrams. Limited to our pusher-type planes we devised some which are impossible with the tractor planes now universally used. Up to the arrival of our Rolls-Royce powered planes the average rate of forced landings due to engine failure at the front had been approximately one for every two hours of flying time—twice as good a record as the training machines back in England. With our new machines, however, the rate came down to about one mechanical stoppage every ten hours thus allowing us greatly extended tactics with greater numbers of machines in the air at a time.

The heart of an airplane is its motor. Startling as it may sound, the airplane itself does not show any radical change aerodynamically from the original Wright ship flown at Kitty Hawk in December 1903. A plane is pushed or pulled through the air by its motor. As it pushes down a current of air which supports it slightly from below, it is sucked upward by the air above it, thus giving it a steady flight path. This was the scientific principle used by the Wright Brothers. With rigid wings, the modern plane is controlled, just as Orville Wright controlled that first plane (although he warped his first wings like a piece of cardboard) by simple levers actuating other plane surfaces. These cannot operate and the ship falls and does not fly unless it is being forced through the air at flying speed. The whole vehicle is still far from satisfactory. New plane shapes have brought greater speed and more pounds of lift per gallon of petrol expended, but nobody has produced a practical machine which can defy the limitations that were present in the Wright plane in which man made the first mechanical flight. Some day some man will and then— watch out. The helicopter looks much as if it might be the answer.

For a short time, after the war while we were still satisfied with wartime speeds, we did make airplanes a little safer inherently. But the demand for better performance, speedier climb, faster take-off and greater load capacity soon washed away the inherent safety aerodynamic features.

With the engine the story is vastly different. While some authoritative people believe the plane of the near future will be powered with safe, sure-running, oil-burning diesel engines, the normal military, commercial, and sport airplane of today is still propelled by a conventional engine of the automobile type (Otto cycle) valve-operated with spark ignition, cooled either by air or liquid. Progress in this type of motor has been nothing short of marvelous. In the 20th Squadron and in all the other squadrons with which I was connected from 1916 on, we were doing our share to improve engines.

We were the human guinea pigs. In the 20th, two Rolls-Royce engineers were on the front with us continuously, studying our problems and solving them for the makers back in England. Theirs is still the only correct policy. Today too many aviation experts sit in swivel chairs miles from any flying field and expect some divine guidance to enable them to solve problems without flying or even watching flying or listening to it in its flight paths of the three dimensions of space.

It is safe to say that had the things which we learned in

the 20th Squadron and which the British makers adopted in reduction gears, carburetion, lubrication, altitude adjustment, ignition, cylinders, pistons, and crankshaft and camshaft construction been embraced immediately in 1917 in all the American aviation engines, including the Liberty, many a man now dead would have been alive today.

We made rapid strides in instruments and in radio with the help of experts in each line sent out to work with us. In radios we had vacuum tubes with continuous wave operation way back there in 1916. I had one such set in my plane and operated it in conjunction with compass (broadcasting) stations. We developed trailing and fixed antennae which would make modern patentees' eyes bulge with wonderment. One day I discovered the possibility of compass radio direction finding and reported it. For blind flying we attempted crudely to provide either a vertical or horizontal fixed line on the dash which would be vertical or horizontal regardless of acceleration, slips, maneuvers, or dives. We actually worked on something I have yet to see perfected in this country— something very badly needed—an instrument to help the pilot to detect mountains or other high obstacles ahead in fogs or when he has his head in the closed cockpit.

About the first of September I became a casualty from an incredible malady—a frostbitten face. Yes, sir, I froze my face flying at 14,000 feet in the crisp autumn air. And this got me my first leave—a few days in nearby St. Omer. Shortly before that (July 21) I had come down with a bad sore throat which kept me in my bunk when I should have been flying. I heard my B flight patrol go off without me, trying to guess from the sound of each motor who was driving and who was the gunner. The fog was closing down and I thought it was a pretty thick day for patrol work. My throat grew more painful, sort of a quinsy attack. All morning I lay there in intense discomfort, wanting to kill the orderly in B flight mess who was playing *The Girl I Love Is on a Magazine Cover* over and over again on the wheezy phonograph and waiting to hear the boys come back.

Luncheon time came. I couldn't eat. The doctor fed me more Dover's powders. I was running a temperature and getting a little delirious. Damn that guy playing *Magazine Cover* all day. Someone brought me some tea.

"Where is B flight and Maxwell, their commander?"

"I don't know, sir. None of them have come back and the CO is worrying."

When I hear that *Magazine Cover* thing today the whole scene comes back to me. It was awful. By midafternoon we had the whole gory information. The ceiling had lowered and finally a fog bank had come right down to the ground at a hilly spot near the lines. Our fliers had become confused. One after another they followed Maxwell, crashing into the hill at a hundred miles an hour. Every machine—five of them—was smashed to smithereens. A minute later only Maxwell and two observers were alive. A whole flight practically wiped out. And I was lying there with a quinsy sore throat. Fate again had spared me for something.

September 10 I was ordered to England for a rest, my first in three months at the front, several days before it was due. Next day I was on a packet boat bound for Thetford and a few hours later I was again with my beloved Irene and our lovely fast-growing daughter. It was a joyous reunion. But once more the cruelty of war descended on me. I had been home only three hours. Irene had just told me of a sweet girl who had been living in the same house with her and had married one of the noncoms in the mystery-secret camp close by. An amazing development had been going on there. The local people thought it was the construction of a tremendous new explosive which would blow up whole towns and areas. One day men came to the house and took the young bride

JOIN THE
ARMY AIR SERVICE
BE AN AMERICAN EAGLE!
CONSULT YOUR LOCAL DRAFT BOARD. READ THE ILLUSTRATED
BOOKLET AT ANY RECRUITING OFFICE, OR WRITE TO THE CHIEF
SIGNAL OFFICER OF THE ARMY, WASHINGTON, D.C.

25. "Be an American Eagle." USAS

26. A DH 4, the only type aircraft built in the U.S. that saw combat in World War I. USAF

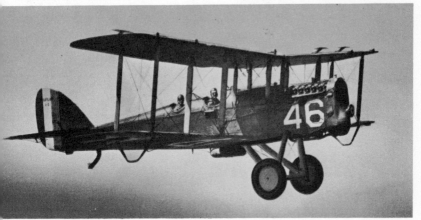

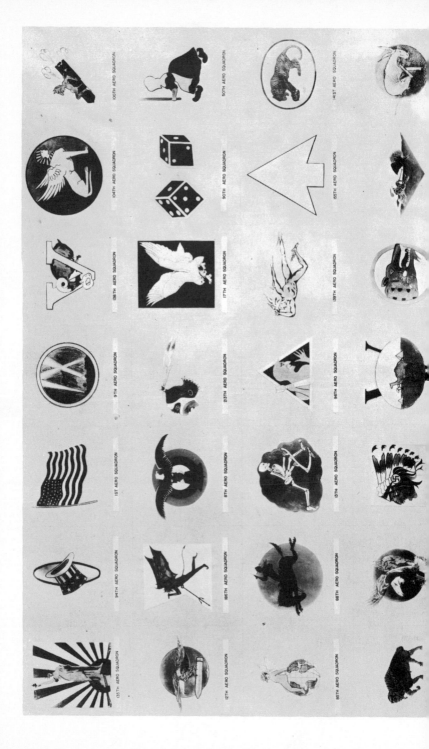

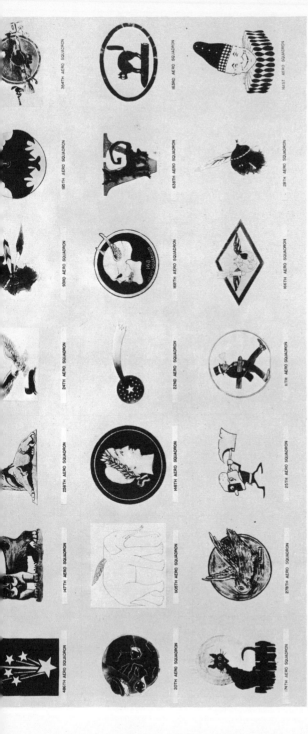

354TH AERO SQUADRON
163RD AERO SQUADRON
161ST AERO SQUADRON

185TH AERO SQUADRON
638TH AERO SQUADRON
28TH AERO SQUADRON

93RD AERO SQUADRON
165TH AERO SQUADRON
166TH AERO SQUADRON

24TH AERO SQUADRON
22ND AERO SQUADRON
11TH AERO SQUADRON

258TH AERO SQUADRON
148TH AERO SQUADRON
25TH AERO SQUADRON

147TH AERO SQUADRON
1005TH AERO SQUADRON
278TH AERO SQUADRON

486TH AERO SQUADRON
20TH AERO SQUADRON
17TH AERO SQUADRON

27. U.S. Air Service squadron insignia in World War I

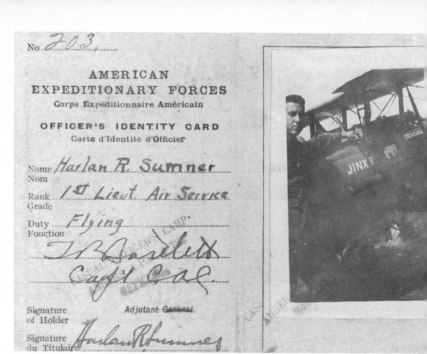

28. An AEF flying officer's identity card. USAF

29. Château-Thierry from the air. USAF

AIR SERVICE STATIONS ON NOVEMBER 11, 1918

		Max Cadet Capacity
Baker's Field: PG	Rochester, N. Y.	—
Barron Field (1): F	Everman, Texas	300
Bolling Field: A	Anacostia, D. C.	—
Brooks Field (2): I	San Antonio, Texas	300
Call Field (1): O	Wichita Falls, Texas	300
Carlstrom Field: P	Arcadia, Florida	400
Carruthers Field (1): F	Benbrook, Texas	300
Chanute Field (1): F	Rantoul, Illinois	300
Dorr Field (1): F	Arcadia, Texas	120
Eberts Field (1): F	Lonoke, Arkansas	300
Ellington Field (6): B & G	Houston, Texas	600
Emerson Field: A	Columbia, S. C.	—
First Reserve Wing	Mineola, L. I.	—
Brindley Field: A	Commack, L. I.	—
Henry J. Domm Field: A	Babylon, L. I.	—
Hazelhurst Field: A	Mineola, L. I.	—
Lufberry Field: A	Wantagh, L. I.	—
Mitchell Field: A	Hempstead, L. I.	—
Roosevelt Field: A	Mineola, L. I.	—
France Field: A	Cocoa Walk, Panama, Canal Zone	—
Gerstner Field: B	Lake Charles, Louisiana	600
Kelly Field (2): F	San Antonio, Texas	600
Love Field (2): F	Dallas, Texas	300
March Field: F	Riverside, California	300
Mather Field: F	Sacramento, California	300
Park Field (2): F	Millington, Tennessee	300

		Max Cadet Capacity
Payne Field (2): A	West Point, Mississippi	300
Post Field: O	Fort Sill, Oklahoma	315
Rich Field (5): F	Waco, Texas	300
Rockwell Field (1):* P & G	San Diego, California	400
Second Reserve Wing	Park Place, Houston, Texas	—
Selfridge Field: G	Mt. Clemens, Michigan	350
Scott Field (1): F	Belleville, Illinois	300
Southern Field (1): F	Americus, Georgia	300
Taliaferro Field: G	Hicks, Texas	180
Taylor Field (3): F	Montgomery, Alabama	300
Camp Dick (Cadet Gunnery Camp)	Dallas, Texas	4,500
Wilbur Wright Field (Armorers' School)	Fairfield, Ohio	600
Langley Field (Observers' School)	Hampton, Virginia	210

SCHOOLS OF MILITARY AERONAUTICS

University of California	Berkeley, California	1,200
Cornell	Ithaca, New York	1,000
Princeton	Princeton, New Jersey	1,200
University of Illinois	Urbana, Illinois	1,200
University of Texas	Austin, Texas	1,400

Note: The special functions of the different fields are indicated as follows: A, advanced flying; B, bombing school; F, primary flying; G, aerial gunnery; I, instructors' school; O, observers' school; P, pursuit flying; PG, photographic. Figures in parentheses after names of fields refer to number of auxiliary fields.

Source: USAF, Air University; Air Historical Division.

* Auxiliary field at Otoymoso, California.

OFFICIAL VICTORIES OF THE
FIRST PURSUIT GROUP

The following list is arranged according to rank. Attention is invited to the fact that in the case of officers who were transferred out of the organization, this record only covers victories they gained while with the First Pursuit Group or with our Allies.

Officers	Enemy Aircraft Brought Down	Squadron	Remarks
Maj. Harold E. Hartney (Note 1)	6	Group	Group Commander
Maj. John F. M. Huffer (Note 3)	4	94th	
Maj. Raoul Lufbery (Note 2)	17	94th	Killed in action
Maj. David McK. Peterson (Note 4)	5	95th	
Maj. Kenneth Marr (Note 5)	1	94th	
Maj. Maxwell Kirby	1	94th	
Capt. James N. Hall (Note 6)	3	94th	Prisoner
Capt. Alfred A. Grant	3 C.O.	27th	
Capt. James A. Meissner	8 C.O.	147th	
Capt. Hamilton Coolidge	8	94th	Killed in action
Capt. Edward V. Rickenbacker	26 C.O.	94th	
Capt. John Mitchell	3 C.O.	95th	
Capt. Reed M. Chambers	7	94th	
Capt. Alexander H. McLanahan	3	95th	

Officers	Enemy Aircraft Brought Down	Squadron	Remarks
Capt. Thorne C. Taylor	2	94th	
Capt. Douglas Campbell	6	94th	
Capt. Harold R. Buckley	5	95th	
Capt. Jerry C. Vasconcells	6	27th	
Capt. Edward W. Rucker	1	27th	
1st Lt. John A. Hambleton	2	95th	
1st Lt. Quentin Roosevelt	1	95th	Killed in action
1st Lt. Eugene R. Scroggie	1	94th	Missing
1st Lt. George F. Fisher	1	95th	
1st Lt. Edward Buford, Jr.	2	95th	
1st Lt. Thomas F. Lennon	2	27th	
1st Lt. Stuart E. McKeown	1	95th	Prisoner
1st Lt. Charles M. Gravatt	1	95th	
1st Lt. Wilford V. Casgrain	1	95th	Prisoner
1st. Lt. Herbert R. Hall	2	95th	
1st Lt. Waldo H. Heinrichs	2	95th	Prisoner (wounded)
1st Lt. John M. Jeffers	2	94th	
1st Lt. James Knowles	5	95th	
1st. Lt. Alden B. Sherry	1	94th	
1st Lt. William H. Taylor	1	95th	Killed in action
1st Lt. Fred W. Norton	2	27th	Died of wounds
1st Lt. Edward P. Curtiss	6	95th	
1st Lt. Wiley S. Sparks	1	94th	
1st Lt. Lansing C. Holden	7	95th	
1st Lt. Ernest W. Hewitt	1	27th	
1st Lt. George C. Waters	1	147th	
1st Lt. Edward G. Garnsey	1	94th	Killed in action

Officers	Enemy Aircraft Brought *Down*	*Squadron*	*Remarks*
1st Lt. Sumner Sewall	6	95th	
1st Lt. Joseph H. Wehner	5	27th	Killed in action
1st Lt. George W. Puryear	1	95th	Prisoner (escaped)
1st Lt. William J. Hoover	3	27th	
1st Lt. Donald Hudson	6	27th	
1st Lt. Robert E. Hill	1	27th	
1st Lt. Zenos R. Miller	1	27th	Prisoner
1st Lt. Harvey W. Cook	7	94th	
1st Lt. Ralph S. Schmitt	2	27th	Wounded
1st Lt. Robert Z. Cates	1	94th	
1st Lt. Grover C. Vann	1	95th	Missing
1st Lt. James P. Herron	1	147th	
1st Lt. Leo R. Dawson	4	27th	
1st Lt. Clarence S. Gill	1	95th	
1st Lt. Albert J. Weatherhead	4	95th	
1st Lt. William W. Palmer	3	94th	
1st Lt. William F. Loomis	1	94th	
1st Lt. Oscar B. Meyers	2	147th	
1st Lt. Samuel Kaye, Jr.	4	94th	
1st Lt. Walter L. Avery	2	95th	Missing
1st Lt. Thomas F. Butz	1	95th	
1st Lt. Henry J. Popperfuss	1	95th	
1st Lt. Ruliff Nevius	1	27th	Killed in accident
1st Lt. Alan Nutt	1	94th	Killed in action
1st Lt. James A. Healy	5	147th	
1st Lt. Joseph C. Raible, Jr.	2	147th	
1st Lt. George A. S. Robertson	1	147th	
1st Lt. Kenneth L. Porter	5	147th	

Officers	Enemy Aircraft Brought Down	Squadron	Remarks
1st Lt. Louis C. Simon, Jr.	2	147th	
1st Lt. Arthur H. Jones	4	147th	
1st Lt. Francis M. Simonds	4	147th	
1st Lt. Ralph A. O'Neil	6	147th	
1st Lt. Sidney White	1	27th	Killed in action
1st Lt. Samuel H. Colton	2	27th	
1st Lt. William F. Stuart	1	27th	
1st Lt. Robert W. Donaldson	1	27th	
1st Lt. Eugene L. McCubbin	1	27th	
1st Lt. Roger W. Rowland	2	27th	
1st Lt. J. J. Pegues	2	95th	
1st Lt. William Vail	2	95th	Severely wounded
1st Lt. Meredith J. Roberts	1	95th	
1st Lt. Victor A. Lyman	1	27th	
1st Lt. Corliss C. Moseley	1	27th	
1st Lt. Joseph M. Gwinn	1	27th	
1st Lt. John Dewitt	1	94th	
1st Lt. Leslie B. Cooper	1	27th	
2d Lt. Elmer G. Rhenstrom	1	95th	
2d Lt. Frederick W. Bailey	1	27th	
2d Lt. Kenneth S. Clapp	2	27th	
2d Lt. William H. Plyler	1	27th	Prisoner
2d Lt. John MacArthur	5	27th	Missing
2d Lt. Frank Luke, Jr.	18	27th	Killed in action
2d Lt. Granville Woodard	2	95th	
2d Lt. Ivan A. Roberts	3	27th	Missing
2d Lt. Frank S. Ennis	1	147th	
2d Lt. Cleveland W. McDermott	3	147th	Wounded
2d Lt. Tyler C. Bronson	1	147th	

Officers	Enemy Aircraft Brought Down	Squadron	Remarks
2d Lt. Wilbert W. White	8	147th	Missing
2d Lt. William E. Brotherton	3	147th	Missing
2d Lt. Maxwell O. Parry	1	147th	Missing
2d Lt. John H. Stevens	1	147th	Killed in action
2d Lt. Thomas J. Abernathy	3	147th	
2d Lt. Charles P. Porter	4	147th	
2d Lt. Alan F. Winslow	2	94th	Prisoner (wounded)

Note 1. This pilot gained five (5) of these victories while in the British Army.

Note 2. This pilot gained seventeen (17) of these victories while in the French Army.

Note 3. This pilot gained four (4) of these victories while in the French Army.

Note 4. This pilot gained one (1) of these victories while in the French Army.

Note 5. This pilot claims to have gained this victory while in the French Army.

Note 6. This pilot gained two (2) of these victories while in the French Army.

HOW THE U.S. CREDITED AIR VICTORIES
IN WORLD WAR I

The first aero squadrons of the U. S. Air Service that went into combat in France during World War I were under the tactical control of French and British units, and the victory credits earned by members of these units during this period were confirmed and recorded by the French or British. Later, after U.S. aero squadrons were operating under American control, the Air Service, American Expeditionary Forces, set up its own victory credits program.

Under the American rules, official credit for a victory won in aerial combat could be awarded to an aviator of the AEF if an enemy aircraft was destroyed over enemy territory or fell or landed within an area held by U.S. or allied forces. No credit could be awarded for an enemy aircraft that was forced down but made a normal landing in enemy territory. In practice these rules, in which the term "aircraft" included both airplanes and balloons, were expanded to give credit for destruction of balloons inflated in their beds on the ground.

A victory claimed by a member of the U. S. Air Service had to be confirmed before official credit could be granted. Confirmation could be provided by any person who witnessed the combat from the air or from the ground, or who saw the debris of the enemy aircraft at the place specified by the claimant.* After a mission a pilot or observer sometimes went out to try to find someone who could confirm his victory. Some units even established "confirmation teams" to obtain evidence that would

---

* A member of a pilot-observer team could not confirm a victory by the other member because a victory gained by one crew member would, when confirmed, be credited as a victory for each of the two men of the team.

support the claims of their members. But despite such efforts, many victories, especially those won far behind enemy lines, could not be confirmed. Thus, members of the U. S. Air Service undoubtedly won many aerial victories that could not be officially credited to them.

When a claim was properly confirmed, credit was awarded by a general order issued by the air service of the Army (U. S. First or Second) with which the person and his unit were associated. Credits awarded by French and British organizations to which members of the U. S. Air Service were attached, either individually or with their units, were recognized and accepted as valid by the U. S. Air Service but usually were not recorded in American orders.

The British divided credits so that each person who contributed directly to a victory received an equal fraction of the credit. The French and Americans, however, awarded a full credit to each person who contributed to a victory. Under the latter system, if two pilots in monoplane pursuit planes brought down an enemy aircraft, each pilot received one credit. If either the pilot or observer in a biplane airplane shot down an enemy aircraft, each received one credit, which resulted in credits for persons who, in fact, did not shoot down any enemy aircraft. Furthermore, the credits became rather complicated when several pilot-observer teams were involved in one victory. In two cases, sixteen men (eight pilots and their observers) were each given one credit for the enemy airplane they all helped to bring down.

The pamphlet* records 1513 credits for the destruction of 832 enemy aircraft (756 airplanes and 76 balloons). In each of 491 cases the credit was awarded to one person. The remaining 341 victories resulted in 1022 awards, with each victory being credited to two or more men. Three complete lists of the credits are presented: (1) an alphabetical listing of members of the U. S. Army Air Service with the credits awarded to each;

* USAF Historical Study No. 133, *U. S. Air Service Victory Credits, World War I,* Air University, Maxwell AFB, Alabama, June 1969.

(2) a chronological listing in which the persons who received credits for the same enemy aircraft are grouped together; and (3) a listing of credits by U.S. units, and by foreign services with which members of the U. S. Air Service served in combat.

LEADING ALLIED ACES, 1914–18

A total of 117 Americans shot down five or more enemy air-craft, officially confirmed, to become Aces. This list also includes victories gained while serving with the French and British.

	Squadron	Victories
Capt. E. V. Rickenbacker	94th	26
Capt. S. W. Rosevear	201st RFC	23
*Capt. William C. Lambert	24th RFC	22
2nd Lt. Frank Luke, Jr.	27th	21
*Capt. Frederick W. Gillette	RFC	20
*Flt. Sub-Lt. J. J. Malone	3rd RNAS	20
*Maj. Alan M. Wilkinson	48th RFC	20
*Capt. Frank L. Hale	85th RFC	18
*Capt. Paul T. Iaccaci	20th RFC	18
Maj. Raoul Lufbery	94th	17
Lt. Harold A. Kullberg	1st RFC	16
*Capt. Oren J. Rose	92nd RFC	16
*Lt. C. T. Warman	RFC	15
*Capt. Frederick Libby	25th RFC	14
1st Lt. George A. Vaughn	17th	13
**Sgt. Frank L. Baylies	SPA. 3	12
Capt. Field E. Kindley	148th	12

* Served only with the British Royal Naval Air Service (RNAS), the Royal Flying Corps (RFC), or the Royal Air Force (RAF).
** Served only with the French Air Service (and Lafayette Flying Corps).

	Squadron	Victories
1st Lt. David E. Putnam	134th	12
Capt. Elliot W. Springs	148th	12
*Lt. Thayer A. Iaccaci	22nd RFC	11
Maj. Reed G. Landis	25th	10
*Lt. L. L. Richardson	RFC	10
Capt. Jacques M. Swaab	22nd	10
1st Lt. L. A. Hamilton	17th	9
Capt. Frank O'Driscoll Hunter	103rd	9
1st Lt. Chester E. Wright	93rd	9
1st Lt. Paul F. Baer	103rd	8
Maj. Charles J. Biddle	13th, 4th Pursuit Group	8
Capt. T. C. Cassady	28th	8
**Adj. James J. Connelly	SPA. 163	8
Capt. Hamilton Coolidge	94th	8
1st Lt. H. R. Clay, Jr.	148th	8
1st Lt. Jesse O. Creech	148th	8
*Capt. John O. Donaldson	85th RFC	8
1st Lt. William P. Erwin	1st	8
2nd Lt. Clinton Jones	22nd	8
*Lt. Dean I. Lamb	4th RFC	8
Capt. Gorman De. F. Larner	103rd	8
Maj. James A. Meissner	147th	8
**Lt. Edwin C. Parsons	SPA. 3	8
1st Lt. Joseph F. Wehner	27th	8
1st Lt. Wilbur W. White, Jr.	147th	8
1st Lt. Howard Burdick	17th	7
Maj. Reed McK. Chambers	94th	7
1st Lt. Harvey W. Cook	94th	7
1st Lt. Lansing C. Holden	95th	7
Maj. John W. F. M. Huffer	93rd	7

* Served only with the British Royal Naval Air Service (RNAS), the Royal Flying Corps (RFC), or the Royal Air Force (RAF).
** Served only with the French Air Service (and Lafayette Flying Corps).

	Squadron	Victories
1st Lt. John K. MacArthur	27th	7
1st Lt. Wendel A. Robertson	139th	7
1st Lt. Leslie J. Rummel	93rd	7
1st Lt. Karl J. Schoen	139th	7
Capt. Sumner Sewell	95th	7
1st Lt. William H. Stovall	13th	7
1st Lt. Byrne V. Baucom	1st	6
1st Lt. James D. Beane	22nd	6
Capt. Arthur R. Brooks	139th	6
Capt. Douglas Campbell	94th	6
Capt. Edward P. Curtiss	95th	6
1st Lt. Murray K. Guthrie	13th	6
Capt. James N. Hall	94th	6
Capt. Leonard C. Hammond	91st	6
Lt. Col. Harold E. Hartney	1st Pursuit Group	6
1st Lt. Frank K. Hayes	13th	6
Capt. Donald Hudson	27th	6
2nd Lt. H. C. Knotts	17th	6
Maj. James Keating	139th	6
1st Lt. Robert O. Lindsay	139th	6
1st Lt. Ralph A. O'Neill	147th	6
Maj. David McK. Peterson	95th	6
1st Lt. W. T. Ponder	103rd	6
2nd Lt. K. L. Porter	147th	6
*Lt. Frank A. Robertson	29th RFC	6
Capt. Martinus Stenseth	28th	6
Lt. Col. William Thaw	103rd	6
Capt. Edgar G. Tobin	103rd	6
Capt. Jerry C. Vasconcells	27th	6
1st Lt. William T. Badham	91st	6
1st Lt. Hilbert L. Bair	24th	5
Capt. Clayton L. Bissell	148th	5

* Served only with the British Royal Naval Air Service (RNAS), the Royal Flying Corps (RFC), or the Royal Air Force (RAF).

	Squadron	Victories
Capt. Harold R. Buckley	95th	5
1st Lt. Lawrence K. Calahan	148th	5
Capt. Everett R. Cook	91st	5
1st Lt. Charles R. D'Olive	93rd	5
1st Lt. Arthur E. Easterbrook	1st	5
1st Lt. H. Clay Ferguson		5
1st Lt. George W. Furlow	103rd	5
1st Lt. Harold H. George	139th	5
Capt. Charles C. Gray	213th	5
1st Lt. Edward M. Haight	139th	5
Capt. James A. Healy	147th	5
***Lt. David S. Ingalls	213th RAF	5
1st Lt. J. Knowles, Jr.	95th	5
1st Lt. Frederick E. Luff	25th	5
*Lt. Alexandre Matthews	84th RFC	5
1st Lt. Ewart S. Miller	139th	5
2nd Lt. J. Sidney Owens	139th	5
*Capt. W. J. Pace	RFC	5
**2nd Lt. Norman Prince	N.124	5
1st Lt. Orville A. Ralston	148th	5
1st Lt. John J. Seerley	13th	5
Maj. Victor H. Strahm	91st	5
1st Lt. Francis M. Symonds	147th	5
Capt. William D. Tipton	17th	5
2nd Lt. Robert M. Todd	17th	5
1st Lt. Charles H. Veil	SPA. 150	5
1st Lt. Remington De B. Vernon	22nd	5
*Lt. F. Westing	RFC	5
1st Lt. Rodney D. Williams	17th	5

* Served only with the British Royal Naval Air Service (RNAS), the Royal Flying Corps (RFC), or the Royal Air Force (RAF).
** Served only with the French Air Service (and Lafayette Flying Corps).
*** U. S. Naval Air Service officer attached to the Royal Air Force (RAF), successor to the RFC.

FRENCH

There were a total of 160 Aces in the French Aviation Service. Following are those who head the list:

	Victories
Capt. Paul-René Fonck	75
Capt. Georges Guynemer	53
Lt. Charles Nungesser	45
Lt. Georges Madon	41
Lt. Maurice Boyeau	35

BRITISH

Some 550 British fighter pilots, including Commonwealth nations (Canada, Australia, New Zealand, Ireland, South Africa, etc.) downed five enemy aircraft each to qualify as Aces. There were also nineteen Americans in their ranks. (Officially, the British did not recognize the Ace designation and in fact considered 10 victories as the minimum.)
These are the top five:

	Victories
Maj. Edward "Mick" Mannock	73
Lt. Col. William A. Bishop	72
Maj. Raymond Collishaw	68
Capt. James T. B. McCudden	58
Capt. A. Beauchamp-Proctor	54

BELGIAN

Victories

Tiny Belgium produced a total of five Aces:

Lt. Willy Coppens	34
Lt. Edmond Thieffry	10
Adj. André de Meulemeester	10
Capt. F. Jacquet	7
Lt. Jan Olieslagers	6

ITALIAN

Among the forty-three Italian fliers who qualified as Aces were:

Victories

Maj. Francesco Baracca	36
Lt. Silvio Scaroni	26
Maj. Pier Ruggiero Piccio	24
Lt. Flavio Barracchini	21
Capt. Fulco Ruffo di Calabria	20

RUSSIAN

Because of the Russian Revolution and the loss and destruction of official records, the total number of Russian Aces will never be known. The following five head the list of those whose records remained or were reconstructed.

	Victories
Capt. Alexander Kazakov	17
Capt. P. d'Argueeff	15
Lt. Cmdr. Alexander de Seversky	13
Lt. I. Smirnoff	12
Lt. M. Safonov	11

LEADING ENEMY ACES, 1914–18

Heading the list of more than three hundred German Aces was Rittmeister Manfred von Richthofen, also known as the "Red Baron" because of his all red Fokker fighter. He was leader of the famous "Flying Circus" and was the ranking Ace of both sides—friend and foe—in the First World War.

	Victories
Capt. Manfred von Richthofen	80
Lt. Ernst Udet	62
Lt. Erich Lowenhardt	56
Lt. Werner Voss	48
Capt. Burno Loerzer	45

AUSTRO-HUNGARIAN

Like the British, the Austro-Hungarians considered only those with ten or more victories as Aces. However, some thirty of their pilots downed more than five enemy aircraft apiece.

	Victories
Capt. Godwin Brumowski	40
Lt. Julius Arigi	32
Lt. Frank Linke-Crawford	30
Lt. Benno Fiala	29
Lt. Josef Kiss	19

23. The U. S. Distinguished Service Cross. *20th Century-Fox*

24. Presentation of Medals.

21. Spads and a Nieuport 27 at an Allied aerodrome. USAF

22. An American two-seater squadron lined up in a review formation on a field in France. USAF

19. Lieutenant Ernst Udet beside his Fokker D VII. He ranked immediately after the "Red Baron" on the German Ace list. *National Archives*

20. The aerodrome at Tours, France. USAF

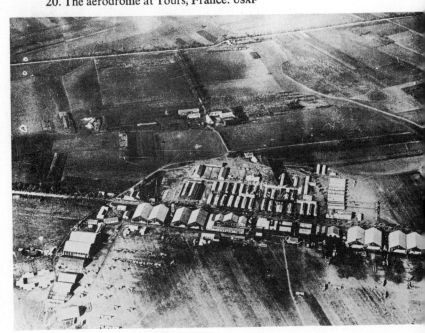

18. The "Red Baron" himself. USAAF

away and she was shot at 5:40 the morning before I arrived. The activity that had been going on was the first secret development of the first tanks and the charming German spy had been caught trying to transmit the news of it to her fatherland. *C'est la guerre*. It's a good thing she didn't get it through. Some claim she did. The surprise impact of the first slow tank attack was tremendous and the tanks had an important military and psychological effect in bringing about the end of the war.

And again *c'est la guerre*—three hours after I arrived, the knocker called the maid to the front door. A telegram: LIEUTENANT HARTNEY WILL REPORT AT ONCE TO HIS UNIT. LEAVE CANCELED.

It was cruel blow. By this time, however, I was becoming pretty well soaked in the routine of the war and more inclined to take things in my stride.

"If I can catch an airplane being ferried over to France perhaps I can delay things for a few precious hours," I said to myself. "There must be something big doing over there. Maybe that's why they let me go a little ahead of time."

I called Farnborough, the air depot south of London.

"If Lieutenant Hartney will report at 7 A.M. there will be a machine waiting for him to ferry over the Channel."

And at Farnborough I was assigned to a plane—not one of my beloved Rolls but an old Beardmore 160-horsepower. I found that a pilot who had lived through three months at the front was "some punkins" and I was treated with the greatest respect by everybody.

Just as I was about to take off, a pilot, arriving from France in his GHQ plane, rushed up with his reports.

"My God, man, you should have been over there a few hours ago!" he told me. "We've launched an attack, using those tanks developed at Thetford. The Germans are on the run. Never were cannon massed so close. It's the second battle of the Somme and it's on to Berlin by Christmas!" (September 15, 1916.)

Presently I was on my first flight over the Channel. It was beautiful that day but in almost no time I was across. I had a passenger in the front cockpit but I never met him, or even looked at him. But I should have. He was destined to have no small effect on the course of the war. He was one of the highest staff officers at Haig's headquarters.

Landing at St. Omer depot I called for a tender and reached my squadron too late for an afternoon patrol. Major Mansfield seemed highly pleased to see me. I was proud that nobody had used my plane during my absence. It was my third, A 30. Two had been "shot out from under me" and during my brief leave this one, a beauty, had been fixed up to a T. Sergeant Major James Allen, now an American citizen in San Francisco, had seen to that.

Next morning I went on an early patrol. The second battle of the Somme did not involve our sector, but later, partly for the excitement and partly to overlap on our co-ordination, I would wander off our little front and visit that of the Army to the south. Once I was mildly called down for this, but with a push on, it was generally overlooked and I think perhaps it was helpful.

By this time I was second in command of the flight. I was gaining self-reliance. I realized how quickly an enemy machine could pop up from nowhere. I had stayed alive three months on the front. I knew most of the tricks. But every day I had a few moments of downright cowardly jitters. It was that little period before I could sight any enemy ships on patrol when I knew full well they were about; I have the same feeling today just before I am to meet some big man in a conference. Once face to face, everything is O.K.

I could write a whole book about my experiences with the

20th, about the wonderful spirit of unity of officers and men, about the public school lad who got drunk one night because, as he told me, he knew he was going to die the next day and did. The observers were all brave men. They had to ride with some awfully dud pilots at times. Observers of the caliber of Dewar, Knowles, Chancellor, Hamilton, Hanshaw, Hoover, Scott, Stewart—where are they all now?

I must say something about the privates. A more loyal crowd never lived. To say that they worshiped their flying officers as heroes is putting it mildly. Every machine crew would have gone to hell gladly for the pilot whose machine they were tending.

Before I knew it I was within two days of the completion of my first six months on the front—an old graybeard of the air service. Through almost daily battles and hazards I had lived while my pals, dozens of them, had died. I seemed to be leading a charmed existence. On December 8, 1916, I was advised that I could leave the deadly danger of the front and take a long tour of duty in England, where I could be with my family—or become flight commander at the next vacancy, with a ten days' leave, starting December 10.

What a choice! A captaincy in the Royal Flying Corps, something for lords and kings, or the life of Reilly on home defense, a few Zeppelins probably, but a "cushy" job with little danger. Naturally, I chose the flight commandership on the front.

On December 10 I left for England, with orders to return on Christmas Day, the 25th, and assume command of A flight. That had been the "high hat" flight of the whole squadron. It had brought down more enemy machines than B flight, my outfit, and C combined. I was the fourth pilot in seniority in the whole squadron. All the others had been killed or invalided. I doubted my merit but I jumped at the opportunity. The reunion with my family was wonderful. My older brother Jim had come over and was training in the RFC to be a flier. He had brought my sister Kathleen over with him on September 17, and we spent a grand few days with my wife and daughter in their new apartment in London.

On January 1 I was given a fine dinner and toasted by my pals in A flight. It should have been a jolly occasion. But our thoughts were all back with our families—or with Lieutenant Johnson. He had gone out with his patrol that afternoon and hadn't come back. That night, my first in command of A flight, our mess hall, where I was supposed to preside at dinner every evening, burned down. Bad omen, that, for some one. In the ashes I saw the skeleton of our phonograph. No more *Girl on the Magazine Cover*. Good!

The war went along. One of the other two flight commanders was killed, the other transferred to another squadron and new ones stepped up to replace them. I was now senior flight commander, second in command of the whole famous 20th Squadron, BEF. I made some real friendships, a few of which have been spared me to the present day. But I am not sure it is a good thing for fighting soldiers to form close comradeships. The shock is too great when they are suddenly ended by a bullet or shell. Take my pal Stead, probably the grandest fellow I ever knew. A nephew of W. T. Stead, the famous writer who perished on the *Titanic,* he and I became buddies from the moment he joined the squadron. His character was like the Rock of Gibraltar. In battle he was a hundred per cent. I could always count on him and know what he was going to do.

One day in January, when I was off duty, he came in from a patrol, full of excitement.

"You should have been out there today, Harold. You'd have had Huns to your heart's content—bushels of them— new ones—little fellows all painted up like those American

Indians you've told me about—camouflage. They're like gold fish in a bowl. There are dozens of them and they're a real live bunch. You'll enjoy meeting them."

This was my first news of an important new development. The German General Staff had decided that airplanes really amounted to something in warfare. They had picked their best man and given him dictatorial powers. One type of fighting plane had been decided upon and put into heavy production. Theorists behind the lines—and let's remember this in any future war—had nothing to say about it except to engineer it in such a manner that it would give superb service for not more than fifty hours—"Because," said a captured German flier, "doesn't a plane get washed out on an average of every twelve hours anyway, so why build them to last forever?"

So along came the little Albatrosses in great numbers and took the air supremacy away from us and my three best friends away from me. They were very fast, with a swifter climb than ours and easily kept serviceable. With them the morale of the German fliers rose to great heights and we were in for a lot of trouble.

One day (February 1, 1917), we started out over Lille to get a vital photograph of Courtrai, timed for one-half hour after an aerial bombardment of the railroad yards. My second gunner, Hodder, had died that day when B flight smacked into the hill. My gunner in A flight was a crackerjack, Captain Carbert, MC. But this day Carbert went with Lieutenant Spicer and my second choice gunner, W. T. Jourdan, went with Stead. I took along a comparatively new man, Lieutenant Griffiths (South African), an expert photographer and promising machine gunner.

Quickly our five machines dodged the archies as we crossed above the graveyard of my old 28th Battalion at St. Elois. Over Lille we were joined by two other planes—enemy planes.

Never were we so bold. We paid no attention to them but flew right along with them far into German territory to get our pictures of the bombardment of Courtrai. The two strangers were about three hundred yards to the right of Stead and were climbing for height. Presently an enemy lone eagle appeared to the left of Spicer and slightly higher. We kept right on and got our shots of Courtrai, then started that long left swing for home. And here was where they jumped us.

A flare from Jourdan's pistol, another from Carbert's and we were in it. Back and forth, up and down, the usual acrobatics. A pause to stabilize the gun platform for my gunner, then more stunts. These Boche planes were different, like little bulldogs. Suddenly Griffiths accidently let slip an empty gun tray that hit me a mighty wallop on the shoulder. Momentarily stunned, I was down to 10,000 feet before I knew it and the jolly little Boche were right with me. I pulled back on my stick and went into a wishy-washy bank, then into a spinning power dive. When I came out of it there was not a machine in sight. Both enemy and friends were miles away and I knew I should cut for home, hedge-hopping the trenches. We landed alone.

Where were my pals? Fifteen minutes passed. Nobody arrived. Oh, where are you Stead, Carbert, Spicer, "Jock" Jourdan? Two hours went by. How I prayed that they were, at the worst, prisoners. Griffiths showed me a beautiful print of the bombardment. It failed to console me. Four agonizing hours. Eight o'clock. The telephone! It was the green pilot up top behind. He had been shot down and landed safely near Abelle. He would tow the ship back next day. He knew nothing about the others. At nine, ding-a-ling-a-ling. Jourdan, speaking from the Canadian Hospital at Bailleul. Stead had been shot through the calf of the leg. At 14,000 feet the blood spurted out like a fountain. A tourniquet was useless.

He had made a perfect landing on Bailleul, then collapsed. Three men carried him out of the plane, unconscious.

"I'll call you in the morning," said Jourdan. "It's serious. The doctor is with him all the time. He doesn't seem to want to come out of it."

It was with a heavy heart that I attended the conference that night and made plans for the morrow's work with reserve men and planes. All night I grieved over Stead—and Spicer and Carbert. Where were they? In Germany alive? Or where?

I intended to fly over to Bailleul after the first morning patrol. But the day dawned foggy and we had to stand by. The next day I made it about 2 P.M. Jourdan ran up as I taxied to a stop.

"Too late! A Canadian padre gave him blood for a transfusion. No good. Gangrene set in. Joy-boy's dead!"

Soldiers don't weep as a rule, but two did right then and there, copiously and unashamed. I shall never forget my old pal Stead. Jourdan and I fashioned a cross over his grave, made from his damaged laminated walnut propeller. We wrote *Ad Astra* on it and felt our buddy was at rest. Later, in 1918, when Bailleul was captured by the Germans after heavy bombardment nothing was left of that graveyard but shell holes, bones, mud, and tangled wire.

The following day along came my commission as captain. I was in no mood to celebrate my elevation. To me, with my new responsibilities, the war had become a frantic, grim routine of "Kill Boche, Kill Boche. That's the job. Keep machines serviceable, get the morale of the mechanics working at high pitch, keep patrols going, do the job until they get you." We worked like automatons in our hectic business of killing.

It was three months before we learned what had happened to Spicer and Carbert and it came in a report from the American Red Cross in Brussels. And here, in a few tragic words, is the end of two brave pals: Spicer was shot through the head and killed instantly at the very start of the combat. The plane was hit and it was necessary to bring it down far inside of enemy territory. Carbert tried a trick I had taught him. He got out on the wing to balance the uncontrolled ship and with one hand held back the stick. He came in to a landing on fairly smooth but frozen ground far inside of captured Belgian territory. His wheels hit a bump and the plane bounced high in the air. Carbert was thrown off the wing and landed on the hard ground with his head doubled up under him. His neck was broken and he died on the spot —a fine officer gone west in line of duty—one who had survived the awful infantry battle of Festubert, in which he won the Military Cross.

It was in that plane that our secret radio set was captured. We had always carried a heavy little hammer to break up the radio tubes, now so commonly used throughout the world but then known only to the Allies. The radio was used but only fairly successfully by our squadron and others for several months. Carbert's set was captured intact and after the war I read the Germans' report of its falling into their hands and the excitement with which it was received.

CHAPTER 7

I Meet Mr. Richthofen, Violently

AND NOW, ladies and gentlemen, I am about to leave the Royal Flying Corps in France—unexpectedly. My next patrol was my last for a long, long time. Why it wasn't my very last I don't know.

It was St. Valentine's Day, February 14, 1917, a day for the exhange of loving thoughts. The 20th Squadron had moved temporarily over to a little place called Boisdingham, about eight miles north and west of St. Omer. I had been with the 20th for eight months, all of it on the front and was one of the few survivors of the original squadron. Having risen from a green "hun" to senior flight commander, I had become a little too cocksure of myself, too full of that feeling "they can't hit me. I'm too good for them." I had been taking a lot of unnecessary chances and had tried in vain for days to lure one of the German ships across the lines so I could bring it down on our side.

But the enemy air service had been getting better. They were still afraid or too wise to come over the lines into our territory but it was no longer necessary for us to get radio information from the ground to help us find them and get a combat—behind their lines. And in the near-zero winter weather of northern Belgium their heavy conventional Mercedes, Benz, B.M.W., and Opel motors seemed better able to function than our delicately cooled but far superior Rolls-Royces.

Once we got our engines running they were superb but we were having a lot of trouble with freezing water jackets, water condensation in the carburetor, congealment of oil and other maddening things that happen when steel gets cold and sparks seem unable to ignite reluctant fuel.

We were still proud of our big Rolls-Royce F.E.s, but the Germans were creeping up on us with those snappy little Albatrosses, which, although lively and good performers, were still a long way from equaling the capabilities of our great ships, of which I had used up eight in combat and patrol service and was about to be almost destroyed in my ninth. With full war load we could climb to 10,000 feet in eleven minutes. Our ceiling was 19,000 feet and, being a pusher and a biplane, our ship could climb and dive in battle better than anything up to that date. Being a biplane our vehicle could take unmerciful punishment. In formation it had one big advantage that might well be duplicated today in multi-engined planes, especially in rotary-wing craft, having a gun in the base of the rotors. We could supply a very steady, fast-moving gun platform by simply resorting to a circle of the formation, each machine in a vertical bank, following the advance plane's tail, and each gunner having plenty of time to sight, although he did have to calculate and allow for his own forward speed. To attack such a circling formation was sure death. The enemy knew this from sad experience and lay back on his own side of the lines. His only hope was to await a straggler with engine or other trouble, catch him diving for home and jump him. This is how the great Richthofen, who had become expert in this technique, got me and saved four of his pals.

Our trouble was that, under winter conditions, we could only count on three or four serviceable machines out of eight in each flight for three patrols per day. Also I was getting too tense, too jittery. The day before Valentine's Day, Major

Mansfield, squadron commander, said to me, "Hartney, you must relax. I order you to go to St. Omer tomorrow, take the day off and forget things for a few hours. There's plenty of war still to come and plenty more Boche to punish."

But next morning found me at the machine-gun range with my favorite gunner, Jourdan, and some others trying out a new jam-clearing gadget one of the boys had invented. I had detailed two of the ships of my flight for the 2 o'clock mission—a routine affair on our side of the lines at 15,000 feet from the marshes above Ypres, down to Bois-Greniere south of Armentières, the aerial definition of the front of the Second British Army at that time. Mansfield had gone over to Army headquarters at Cassel and I had a hunch something was up, so I postponed my vacation. It led me into a lot of trouble.

Sure enough, about 11 o'clock, Mansfield, with cane, cigarette holder, and bright boots, came with dignified speed onto the field. His first words were a thrill.

"Hartney," he said, "Mottershead has been awarded the Victoria Cross for his show last week."

This was wonderful news for our flight but little good it did Sergeant Mottershead—he was dead. One of the few flying noncommissioned officers in the Royal Flying Corps, I had loaned my eighth plane to Mottershead a few days before. He had been set afire at 10,000 feet, and, although killed on landing, had ridden his blazing plane to the ground and saved his officer observer. Mansfield's next words were of the immediate future.

"You know, Hartney, there's a push coming and the brass hats over at GHQ are shy some photographs of the forest area around Passchendæle to complete their map of the whole enemy sector. I promised we'd get them today. You will take this mission but at least one machine must accompany you as you cross the lines."

No sooner said than done. I was taking Jourdan on account of his reliability as gunner and photographer, and because he wanted to try out a new overall union suit he had imported from the United States and lined with dog fur—a laughingstock in our squadron for a while, now used by practically every military aviator. The only other plane available was Taylor's, with Lieutenant Griffiths at the guns and camera. Griffiths was angry when Jourdan took the camera he had loaned him but had another for use that day—his last day on earth. At 1:15 our two machines were out on the line and Jourdan appeared in his new monkey suit, his camera, three guns and a bountiful supply of loaded gun trays—loaded consecutively one tracer, one ordinary, one incendiary, one armor piercing.

"We've got to be careful with these tracers," said Jourdan. "They came over from England this morning on a ferry job, were hand-made yesterday and cost two shillings each." He was a great boy, cool, courageous, resourceful, and a crack shot. He had quit a job as a clown in Ringling Brothers' Circus in the United States to join the RFC and was never bothered by my acrobacy with the plane because he wore a noose around one ankle to anchor him—a trick he picked up from a fancy horseback rider in the circus.

Promptly at 2 P.M. I gave her the gun and we were off, down the field—my last take-off with the Royal Flying Corps in France. As I rose and circled, gaining altitude, I looked back. Taylor's men were still cranking away on his machine.

I made for the front lines and our rendezvous 12,000 feet over Ypres, hoping Taylor would get there soon with his gunner, Griffiths, before the light waned. It was plain there was lots of air activity that day. Both enemy and friendly antiaircraft fire was popping all over the place. I raced for altitude, while Jourdan tried out his guns and found them "hunky-dory." As always before a fight, I was nervous and, as was my custom, indulged in a sincere prayer for the safety of my gunner, my family, myself, the Allied cause, and the King.

Fifteen minutes later we were over Ypres. Turning northward I could see ahead almost to Holland. Two miles below us the trenches stretched along until they blended into the horizons north and south. Except for the occasional twinkle of an exploding shell, it all seemed quiet down there and I knew that hundreds of thousands of men were watching our every move and probably, at the same time, watching enemy ships that I couldn't discern.

Suddenly, a mile below us, enemy aircraft shells began to burst and Jourdan gave the situation a hasty looking over, then held a gloved thumb and forefinger in a circle. This indicated the circular Allied cocard. It was one of the slow British B.E. 2C gun-spotting "quirks," adjusting artillery and, with a spark-set radio, correcting the fall of our shells. I always felt sorry for those chaps. They led a hard life. With their slow, heavy planes and flying at low altitudes, they couldn't put up much of a fight and were continually exposed to the enemy archies. Antiaircraft artillery was getting better in all the armies. By the end of the war the German archies had shot down 1520 Allied planes. The Allies, on the other hand, accounted for 1029 enemy planes by antiaircraft fire. Of these, the French brought down 500, the British 341, the Italians 129, and the Americans 59.

We could see no enemy planes but to make sure while waiting for Taylor to keep his date with me I tried an old trick. I deliberately lost some altitude, and flew directly over the German lines. I knew if there were no Boche planes in the air the archies would open up on me, but if there were any near they would hold their fire. And sure enough, there was not a peep from the guns. This put me on the alert instantly. I was just turning back to cross over the Courtrai road to our lines when directly in front of me came the flash of sunlight on wings and an enemy crate appeared not over two hundred feet away from me on the port side, slightly above and directly between us and the sun. My sudden pull-up threw Jourdan off his feet, but I got my own fixed gun going as the Boche went into a sharp dive and headed for Roulers. We chased him a few seconds and were rapidly overtaking him, but we were losing altitude and I decided not to jeopardize our photographic mission. So I climbed back to 12,000. Presently friendly archies let loose up north and I galloped over to investigate. I think it was the same flier, perhaps with his eye on the lumbering "quirk." Anyhow, he made another dash for Roulers, and I went back upstairs. And there was Taylor, waiting for me over Ypres.

I signaled him by banking vertically, then wobbling my wings and we both made a beeline for the Forest of "Hooty-Tooty," as the Tommies called Houlthust, fifteen miles away. The usual archie fire greeted us ineffectually as we went over the lines again. Presently I was steadying the ship over the pinpoint of Passchendæle of which our brass hats wanted some pictures and Jourdan was rattling off his plates at great rate. In a few seconds he waved his hand for us to veer slightly, our job very near to successful accomplishment. And again there came to me that peculiar hunch or sixth sense or whatever it is that has so often warned me of danger and saved my life. Jourdan was busy with his camera, his head below decks, when that little voice said to me, "Look for the burglar under the bed." Instantly I craned my neck over the tail. There was Taylor, sailing along serenely two hundred feet back of us and a hundred feet higher. And right over him, like a burst of colored skyrockets, were seven brilliantly painted Albatrosses, single-seaters, Richthofen's famous "Flying Circus," diving right on us—*apparently from our side of the lines!*

What saved us in the next few frantic minutes I cannot imagine. Instantly I clouted the reclining Jourdan over the head in the front cockpit and with my other hand let go the red Very pistol from its fixed position alongside of me, to warn Taylor. At the same moment spat-spat-click-click-spat —bullets from all seven of them began to spatter around us. I fairly danced with all my weight on the rudder bars, slamming down first my right wing, then the left, and skidding that machine as I never had skidded one before. So fast did I slip once that Taylor seemed to be rising away from me, but then he did the same thing and went shooting down past me, left wing down, and missing me by inches.

The Germans were swarming all over us.

And now an old trick came to my rescue. After gaining speed with a slight forward dive, I suddenly pulled back on the joy stick and nosed up until I had just about hit the stalling point. Then I jumped on my right rudder and, in a half spin, I swung about as on a dime and went into an almost vertical pique for the west. And here the Germans showed the ingrained stupidity that so frequently defeats them. The whole enemy squadron, trying to do the silly military stunt of fighting and maintaining their rigid formation at the same time, went right over me instead of plunging onto us with all guns blazing. They flat-circled slowly around and came back for another dive at us. Again I fooled them with the reversement, in exactly the same way. They sailed by overhead again and temporarily lost us. In the split second lull I looked for Taylor. There he was right on our tail where he should have been. All the time we were getting nearer our lines but now the Boche were coming back at us, so I gave Taylor the signal for the old circle maneuver.

Around and around we went, both of us in an absolutely vertical bank like motorcycle riders in the "Globe of Death" at the county fair, Jourdan and Griffiths with two machine guns each poised skyward. Fortunately the gentle fifteen-mile breeze was, for the first time in a month, with us and I knew if we could keep this up we would get some of those babies. Already I could catch away below to the southwest the welcoming glint of good old Zillebeke Lake, but it was still a long way off. On each circle I would bite off a little more westward distance and Taylor did the same. He was magnificent. The pigheaded enemy, meantime, continued his aerial goose-stepping, in formation, but was doing a good job of keeping above us—one of the greatest assets in an air fight.

Suddenly, as if on signal, the right rear enemy ship left the formation and took a swoop at us. His tracer bullets were playing around us for fully two seconds before Jourdan let him have both guns, right in the face. The poor brave kid just kept on going, for all the world like a mortally wounded bird plummeting to death near a river blind. It was his last fight. The other six were parading back over us.

And now I made the greatest and costliest mistake of my flying career. I forgot to watch for reinforcements. I had heard of Richthofen's racket—lurking near a fight to pick off an unwary adversary occupied with other matters. In fact, I had tried it once or twice myself. But it never occurred to me that he would play this game with a whole fleet of planes in support.

We had gained probably seven miles toward our lines and we were still circling beautifully when two of the enemy ships pulled up slowly, gracefully, deliberately, and dived for us. It was their pilots' last earthly act. I am afraid now, looking back on it, that one of them must have scored a hit at the beginning of his dive on Taylor, but he never lived to know it. With Jourdan and Griffiths both pouring bullets into the two Boches at 2000 shots a minute in short, snappy bursts, they were soon done for, one bursting into flames and falling and the other crashed to Eternity out of control in a long but slow spinning dive. I never saw the other four again. They disappeared. So I decided to return to camp. Later our formation got official credit for two of the three we claimed. They were my fourth and fifth since entering the RFC—I am positive we got three in this scrap.

The way home, however, was not so simple as that. We were still circling and my nose was pointed toward Hunland when that precious indirect vision in the corner of my eye caught a flash under Taylor's machine as he circled west, I eastward. Something was falling—part of his propeller. His ship was beginning to falter. There, right above him, was a deadly trail of smoking tracer bullets streaking at him and through his ship from an eighth German plane. Surprise of surprises! Following back the spitting streaks of fire my astonished eyes encountered the Red Knight of Germany, Baron Richthofen himself. I kicked myself then, and I still do, for letting him take us unaware. After my training and experience there was absolutely no excuse for it. But there he was, one of Germany's few great pilots, one of those rare Teutonic individualists, a fine sportsman, who was finally to meet his doom at the hands of another Canadian flier, Roy Brown, born only twelve miles from my own birthplace.

Seeing that Taylor was in trouble, I pulled my spiral tighter, "chandeled" upward and got above Richthofen. Stalling, almost whip-stalling, I ducked down for him but with controls flabby, I did not get response. I pulled my trigger but all my tracers went over the Baron's back and I followed them with my ship. Had the plane not been temporarily out of control, my aileron or rudder would have responded, I could have brought my gun to bear on Richthofen and he would have died then and there.

I was again pulling upward to come back at him and was in a stalling position when *wham!*—*crash!* For a moment I actually thought I had hit another machine. Immediately a terrific, almost unbelievable vibration took possession of my ship, like a train off the track bumping over the ties. I tried to pull my throttle back slowly to dampen it out. It seemed to get worse. My switch would not cut the ignition. Without at first looking I reached down to the floor for the new and unfamiliar three-way petrol valve gadget and then, as cool as I could be looking down at the weaving floor, I deliberately turned the gas to "off." Jourdan was leaning over and out of his cockpit trying to help me but there was nothing he could do. Taylor was gone, Richthofen, the "Rittmeister," was gone, perhaps after Taylor. There was not a friend or foe in sight. And our ship was slowly, quietly spinning earthward. I thought, So this is the way it is when they get you.

Slowly I leveled off at about 6000 feet because pulling out of a spin or dive too quickly has killed many a flier. With the engine off there was not a sound. I could talk to Jourdan as if in a drawing room.

"Jock, old boy," I said. "This crate is about to fall apart."

"My God, yes, old topper," he nodded. "Look at those flying wires." I looked. Many of our RAF streamlined wires were broken and on both sides were flapping out like flags in a stiff breeze behind us between the biplanes.

"Look at your prop!" yelled Jourdan.

Glancing back quickly I saw the big laminated walnut four-bladed propeller standing stock still. And one blade was broken off short near the hub.

It looked like the stump of a severed arm. That explained the vibration. If I had not stopped the engine that now unbalanced propeller would have torn the machine apart.

Zillebeke Lake was still several miles south and somewhat west of us. Ahead of us the trenches, marshes, and shell holes seemed entirely out of reach. And we were losing altitude at an alarming rate. To be exact, we were now five miles north of Ypres, heading straight west toward Poperinge, one mile up.

"I'll stretch my glide as far as I can. We'll probably crash in a shell hole. But we're down on our side, anyway, Jock, old thing. Just watch me."

Jourdan actually grinned.

"Don't crash her too hard," he said. "I've got some good pictures here." That was Jourdan and that's my definition of a gentleman, a man who can act like that at such a moment. We had the satisfaction of knowing later that his precious pictures were successful in completing the Army map and we had made good on our mission.

Even my speedometer was shattered and I had to rely entirely on the feel of my controls as, every now and then, she would get too flat and threaten to stall and "fall off on a wing." I looked at Jourdan. He was the calmest person in the world—and here we were on the verge of meeting our Maker. He was standing up in the wobbling plane, deliberately stuffing his precious plates for the brass hats in a special pocket he had fixed in his monkey suit. Then he sat down, casually, to await events, saying:

"She's all yours, Harold. Do your stuff."

The shell holes were becoming fewer and fewer. Praise be, we were getting back into our own territory. We were down to 500 feet and going nowhere in particular except earthward. How many pairs of eyes do you suppose were watching us?

"There's a field down there ahead to the right," shouted Jourdan.

I saw it. It looked flat and inviting. But my flying senses were still with me and I knew we would have to overshoot it, turn and come back into the wind. Already I was banking and expecting every second that the whole works would let go. And that's exactly what happened. The old plane took the bit in her teeth. The entire ship seemed to go out of control. I pulled everything in sight but nothing happened. One wing was down and absolutely refused to come up. And with a slithering crash we landed in a nice, muddy Belgian field, containing several hundred fifteen-foot hop poles, a familiar farming sight in that district.

There was a terrific smash. Then—oblivion.

The next thing I knew I was yelling:

"Jock, Jock, where are you? Are you all right? Are your pictures safe?"

No answer. My face was half in water, half in sticky mud. Later I learned that Jourdan had been thrown out of the plane and was lying unconscious on the ground.

Then I heard the sweetest sound in the world—the cheery slang of an Australian soldier. We were surrounded by them —God bless 'em! One seemed to dominate the others.

"There's a guy in there," he announced, and started to pull our plane apart by hand. "There he is, right under the motor. Grab hold of the tail."

This was the worst thing he could have said. Here I was with my face in the mud, halfway through the instrument board, and a 775 pound motor resting on my kidneys. The tail of the ship was sticking up in the air. It was this Aussie's idea that if they could tilt the tail away from me it might lift the motor a bit and relieve the pressure on my back. Good idea but it didn't work. They tilted it back and then, wishing to get a better grip on it, they let go for a moment. I'll never forget it. That beautiful engine, pride of England's engineering brains and made with the world's finest metals and precision workmanship, came back on my back with a wallop which caused me to forget all the woes of this troublesome world.

How true in my case was the ditty we had often sung at RFC mess parties:

"The young aviator went stunting,
And as 'neath the wreckage he lay—he lay,
To the mechanics assembled around him,
These last parting words did he say—did say.

Chorus
Take the cylinders out of my kidneys,
The connecting rod out of my brain—my brain
From the small of my back take the crankshaft,
And assemble the engine again."

I woke up on what I thought was a stretcher—it was a section of duckboard—laid as walks in wet fields, trenches, camps—one of the most necessary requisites of war in "sunny France." Presently, I was lying on the ground and someone was sticking a needle in my arm. I didn't care. I began to gripe about Taylor. His gunner, Griffiths, had been shot through the brain by Richthofen. And Taylor, himself, with his propeller shot up by the doughty Baron, had crashed about ten miles from me, inside of our lines. It was the fourth time I had been shot out of the air and later I was officially credited with bringing down a total of five enemy ships while with the RFC out of at least eleven that I actually destroyed. I was what the French called an ace, but a very sick ace.

For this day's work Richthofen was credited with bringing down one machine. He claimed two and should have had credit for them. He gave a good description of our scrap in the book he wrote before he died. It is my belief that his pal, Goering, was with him that day, Hermann Wilhelm Goering, now Field Marshal of Germany and leading brains of the Nazi setup. He was an outstanding flier during the World War and a member of Richthofen's "Circus." Floyd

Gibbons wrote an account of our battle in his book, *The Red Knight of Germany*. (4:45 P.M. February 14, 1917.)

Jourdan and Taylor were terribly crippled. With no bones broken, my muscles were badly smashed and my whole nervous system shattered. We had brought down three of the little Boche Albatrosses before they got us, but none of us had any feeling of elation. For the moment we were fed up with the war. In a sort of coma, I did get a kick next morning when an orderly came to my bed and showed me a message, THE WAR OFFICE REGRETS TO REPORT THAT CAPTAIN HARTNEY IS MISSING IN ACTION! And this was the message my wife got in England. Mentally she was a widow for twelve hours, with a nine-month-old daughter. She says it was terrible.

If my writing just now is a little scrambled, it is because my thoughts, memories, and experiences at that time were in a similar condition. Jourdan and I were carried by the Australians on duckboard stretchers to a dressing station, then off to a casualty clearing station (No. 46 CCS) between Ypres and Poperinge. Jourdan couldn't move for two weeks. Our beds were side by side. A Canadian padre, W. J. Robinson, was a prince to us. They gave me an antitetanus injection just after I hit. It made me itch all over and nearly go crazy scratching, when every moment was agonizing pain. Two weeks in that clearing station. A lonely boiled egg one morning. We must have more chickens in the next war and more eggs. Every member of the AEF will back me up on this. Otherwise I was on a steady diet of Glaxo, a baby food —phooy! A lonely stretcher trek. Trains. A boat. And presently Jourdan and I were back in London, in a beautifully run hospital for Canadian officers in Hyde Park, operated by the Canadian Daughters of the Empire.

Rest at last for a tired spirit in a crushed, weary body. Time will never erase from my mind the memory of comfort and security, friendliness and care received from those wonderful nurses and doctors. I recovered more slowly than Jourdan. A message came through from Buckingham Palace a few weeks after we arrived inviting Jourdan and me to have tea with King George the Fifth. I was so excited that I had to go back to bed and never was able to go. Jourdan went and had a grand time. According to the nurses' story, he got very friendly with the King and slapped him on the back—and the King loved it.

Something was wrong with my bodily machinery. I healed up with a decided leaning to one side—a sailor would call it a "list to starboard." The doctors could not do anything about it. So I privately slipped away—with Irene and June—up to Droitwich to take the salt baths and be pummeled by an old German masseur. Imagine! In two weeks the old vertebra had straightened out and the only remnant I had left of my dive into the hop field was a slightly bent nose which mars my manly beauty to this day. They changed the report from "missing" to "wounded" in action.

When I returned to London for further recuperation I was still pretty weak and just lay around doing nothing for a few days. It was on one of these days that I received word that my brother Jim was leaving for France as an observer. He had followed in my footsteps, up to a certain point. As an electrical engineer and a graduate of the School of Practical Science of the University of Toronto, he had been doing some important diesel engine work in Seattle when the war fever hit him. He enlisted in Winnipeg and went overseas with some replacements for my old 28th Battalion. In England he had been transferred to the Royal Flying Corps, received his commission and was well on his way to becoming a regular war flier.

One day they called for volunteers to go over to France as observers and gunners. Jim stepped forward. I was dead against this and told him so, but it made no difference.

Irene and I went to Charing Cross Station to see him off. We were delayed and arrived just as the train pulled out but we saw him in the distance and waved good-bye. I was concerned about Jim's safety in those slow observation planes. I had seen the ease with which the enemy picked them off. And sure enough, ten days later a telegram arrived at Irene's apartment: THE WAR OFFICE REGRETS TO REPORT THAT LIEUT. JAMES C. HARTNEY HAS BEEN KILLED IN ACTION. He was by far the brightest of the Hartneys and might have had a brilliant career. A letter from one of his buddies told us all about it. As an observer in one of the slow-moving old two-seater quirks, Jim's and another plane were attacked. Hemming them in on all sides, the enemy forced the two British planes to collide and they fell 4000 feet.

In 1923 I visited the beautifully kept little British cemetery at Choque. There were the graves of Jim and his pilot, side by side. And on the other side of Jim was the grave of the officer who had written us about him. He had been killed the very next day, before we had received his letter.

We have named our youngest boy after Jim and is he proud of it?

My diary of this period brings back vivid memories:

"Great thrill! An announcement in the *London Times* that I had received the highest decoration for valour given by Italian Government—a silver medal with blue ribbon. Can't understand getting such a thing from the Italians but tickled pink about it."

"Sent to Dartford training school to instruct students under my brave old pal, Capt. Reginald Maxwell, from the 20th Squadron. It is the life of Reilly after the front."

"Instructed with McCudden, old sergeant of the 20th, in advance combat work." (Later he won the Victorian Cross—greatest of all war decorations. Little good it did him. Shortly afterward, he was killed ferrying a new S.E. 5 scout across the

Channel, on July 9, 1918. At the time he was England's highest senior ace.)

"The first Vickers 'Bullet,' a new fighter, and the first 'D.H. 5' with a backward stagger, dropped in here today. I took the latter out for a test and I believe I was the first to fly this machine on its back. I also rolled it, right and left, like nobody's business. It had single flying wires and never had been rolled before. Responds slowly, gracefully, wonderfully—a dream ship."

"Arrived at Lee-on-Solent for advanced instructions in single seater scout work at Gosport School of Special Flying, exclusively for aviators with front line experience. Used the snappy little Avro. Witnessed some of the finest flying I have ever seen by Major Smith Barry, Bell Irving, Parker, and other famous pilots." (This school gained an international reputation and its methods were later adopted in Europe and America.)

When I arrived back in London, from Gosport, at the end of my instruction period, a surprising order was handed to me. CAPTAIN HARTNEY WILL REPORT TO COMMANDING OFFICER GOSPORT TO BE ASSIGNED TO COMMAND 'E' FLIGHT THERE. I had just left Gosport! I was thrilled and proud to be trusted with the command of a fine new flight right under the very eyes of the War Office—in its pet squadron. I returned to Gosport at once.

And now came a day that was one of the great turning points in my life—September 21, 1917. Almost immediately after reporting back to Gosport an order arrived from the War Office: CAPTAIN HARTNEY WILL REPORT TO COLONEL ROSCOE AT TORONTO, CANADA, TO COMMAND 27TH AMERICAN AERO SQUADRON WITH RANK FROM THIS DATE OF MAJOR, SIGNAL CORPS, UNITED STATES ARMY.

It was a bolt from the blue and nearly bowled me over. Along with other pilots, I had signed a card at the front in France saying I would be willing to go to America to teach some of their fliers and had discussed it later in England.

But even so it was a thrilling surprise when it arrived and the rank of major and my definite change to the United States Army were entirely unexpected. No longer would the Germans bomb my wife and baby—they were doing it almost every day now. I could help the Yanks do the big job in store for them. I would become a citizen of the great American Republic. And a major in the United States Army! I could come back to France with a grand outfit of fliers whom I had trained myself, I, the Saskatoon barrister and cornetist in the town band. My brain was in a whirl.

Three days later we were again on a ship running the submarine blockade, on the way home. Big doings ahead!

CHAPTER 8

Birth of the 27th Aero Squadron, U.S.A.

YES, at long last America was in the war and having a hell of a time preparing to do her part. You cannot turn a great, easygoing peaceful democracy into a powerful war machine overnight. But when 130,000,000 rich, vigorous people unite in one thought and work for two years to put an efficient army into the field—oh, boy! Within six months after the Armistice the United States would have had in France the largest and best army the world ever saw. As it was, with two million men over there and another two million in the service here, we rendered considerable help in bringing the war to a conclusion which would have brought peace to Europe for a long time if it had not been for the greed and thoughtlessness of the British, French, and Italian politicians.

In our next war we shall have it all to go through again— not with the innocent enthusiasm we showed in 1917 and 1918 but more soberly, with more wisdom and experience, and with some of the same problems greatly multiplied. The United States and Canada are infested with German, Italian, Russian, and Japanese spies, information gatherers and propagandists, some of them holding important positions. And there are, of course, many inquisitive men, and ladies, from dear old England and France. International relations are like that. Americans are a friendly people, not prone to anger easily. They treat spies as honored guests who, unfortunately, have slightly overstepped the rules of hospitality. But if, as is very likely, the situation in the present war reaches a point where we take spies and traitors at their true worth—well, America is the land of lynching, the vigilantes, and quick justice. There is little to fear from that direction. But we should make a real start on this matter before the war breaks upon us. Why wait?

Will America have two years to prepare? She will need it. It all depends upon the protection she can get from England, as she did before, and whether she can delay her entry into the war, as before, until the last minute.

Anyhow, I reported to Colonel Roscoe at Toronto on October 22, 1917, paid my respects to Brigadier General C. G. Hoare, the British officer assigned to Toronto for liaison with the Americans, then went to a tailor and ordered my American major's uniform, gold oak leaves and all. I wanted to make sure about my American citizenship. I got Colonel Roscoe and General Hoare together and between us we composed a telegram to Washington. Immediately the answer came back, in substance, "Everything O.K. All clear ahead. You are now a citizen of the United States." My head swelled several sizes. I had sworn a new allegiance without losing my affection for the old. I have never regretted it and I am a great believer in co-operation between the American and British people. I felt like Lochinvar. I would lead the forces of this democracy out onto the battlefield and help them do great things.

I am very proud of the work of two other officers who transferred from the Royal Flying Corps to the United States Air Service. Association with these men, Colonel Oliver Filley and Colonel Harold Fowler, has been a source of pride and inspiration to me. The former's experience with the British proved invaluable to the American forces and, at the time of the Armistice, he was in charge of the assembly of the Ameri-

can-made Handley-Page bombing group. Had the war lasted
a few months longer we would have had these American-
made ships in large numbers. Colonel Harold Fowler became
head of the American Air Service troops working with the
British on the northern front all during the time when the
1st Pursuit Group was in action. Like all detached groups, their
work was overlooked, but a history of their magnificent accomplishments, including the work of Elliott Springs, Henry
Clay, and Bill Tipton, must some day be written because it
does credit to the best air forces in any army and brings out
certain points that I have been unable to show in our experience but which will prove extremely useful in our next emergency.

Then I went out to look over my new command—the men
over whom I would have the power of life and death—mostly
the latter. The 27th Aero Squadron of the U. S. Regular
Army had been chartered and organized on June 23, 1917,
after a funny mixup due to the rustle and bustle of a big
democracy girding itself for war. It had been organized as
the 21st squadron on June 15 but it was discovered that
another 21st had also been authorized on the same date and
was in the process of organization in San Diego, California.
Therefore, our charter was rewritten and dated the 23d. Previously the squadron was known as Company K of the 3d
Provisional Aero Squadron, organized May 8, 1917.

As Company K these men had been through a trying time
in Texas, at Kelly Field, No. 2, clearing the ground of cactus
to make way for their bedding, getting accustomed to the
simple food of Army people and fighting every manner of
snake and reptile for which Texas is known throughout the
world. They told me there was very little military spirit or
control until the outfit was officially designated as the 27th
and an officer and a noncom, Major Davis and Sergeant
Young, began to beat some military sense into them.

On August 16 the squadron left for Canada under a new commander, First Lieutenant Fred R. Harvey, arriving on the 19th at 2 A.M. at Leaside Siding where the 17th and 22d American Aero Squadrons were already ensconced. Harvey for many years after the war devoted his fortune to furthering American aeronautics. He was killed with his wife in the autumn of 1935 flying his own private plane, crashing into a mountain in the aircraft graveyard of the Alleghenies. Although the 27th thought they were veterans after weeks of infantry drill in Texas a tense and irksome period under British Army sergeants reduced them to raw recruits, then elevated them to really "hot potatoes" at "squads east and west" and a couple of months later the squadron was mentioned in Washington dispatches as being the best and most efficient in the Aviation Section of the Army. On September 5 the squadron was broken up and groups were sent to various stations in Canada to learn details of the trades necessary for a flying squadron. The Americans got on splendidly with the Canadian population and many of the friendships made then still endure. On October 22, 1917, the squadron was reunited and I entered its life—with a brass band.

I shall never forget the first meeting with my new command. I felt like a new mother and I had a sudden wave of intense pride as I looked into the sea of earnest, brave, intelligent faces of those American boys. Strangely enough, in big moments in one's life, it is the small details that stand out in the memory afterward. In the enlisted section there was one man who stood out as I faced those two hundred men on the parade ground. He was tall, bald, skinny, cadaverous, and he looked almost frozen to death in his cotton khaki outfit. His name was Dudley. He will be remembered by every officer and enlisted man (as privates were called) in that outfit and he and I shared many exciting war incidents later.

But not everything was "ham and gravy." Although my new American squadron was one of the finest groups of men ever gathered together anywhere, and had become quite expert at British infantry drill—which they had to unlearn later —they had no more idea of what a balanced aviation squadron was than little children. It was an awful shock after the calm, efficient, highly organized atmosphere of unity in the British flying service. And the men were not comfortable. Clad only in cotton pants and shirts, with no blouses or overcoats, they were suffering severely from the cold in the sharp Canadian autumn. I taught them the value of newspapers under you when you're sleeping, but, oh, there was so much else to do. The officers were miserable. They were called "cadets" but they wore white hat bands and enjoyed neither the privileges of commissioned officers nor the independence of the privates. After hours they were having the time of their lives socially but neither they nor I could figure out just what they were in a military sense.

But thank heaven, I had a good adjutant, Jim Pierce, a very successful Wall Street broker, who regarded each cadet and enlisted man as his own child and saw to it that their lot was made easier in every possible way.

We left Leaside on October 26 bound back for Texas and I was astonished to note that on the troop train every officer and enlisted man had a berth to himself. In France such luxuries were unknown and enlisted men herded into the famous *40 hommes-8 chevaux* freight cars had to take turns lying down on the floor and officers riding six to a compartment in the first-class carriages had to sit in their seats twenty-four hours a day with no chance to stretch out even on the floor.

In my years in the Canadian and British armies I had never learned American drill regulations and the boys—the most orderly crowd I ever met—had been confused by their

Canadian training after their months of American drill. But
Ed Clune, my highly efficient first gunnery officer, saved my
bacon, especially in St. Louis, where we debarked for an ex-
ercise march. There, as well as later, he marched behind
me and prompted me on the proper commands to shout to
get the proper results.

I thought it part of my duty to inform both officers and
men of actual conditions they would meet when they arrived
at the front in France and spent hours en route telling them
of my experiences and observations. Did they believe me? No!
My narratives, warnings, and theories were very much too
tame for them. I found that our camp and almost every other
military concentration spot in the United States was on the
visiting list of numerous gentlemen, practically all dodging
front line service, who were spreading an amazing flood of mis-
information among America's new soldiers. A few had been in
action briefly, and had built themselves up into heroes of
astounding accomplishments. Most of them, however, had
never been near the front and some had never even been in
France. But all of them posed as the last word in war experts
with brilliant records when facing the foe.

So far as the Army is concerned the remedy for this in future
wars is very simple. Make everybody who desires to come in
contact with the troops as a lecturer or other type of expert
submit his complete record, with verification, to the proper
group in the War Department, be given a certificate setting
forth his proven qualifications and submit it to the camp or
unit commander before he is allowed to open his trap before
the men. The number of fakers retailing false information and
the number of strange people hanging around the camps
seeking information was surprising and should be discouraged
vigorously.

In Texas we went into heavy flying training coupled with
a lot of hard work getting the camp ready at Hicks Field,

later called Talliafero, about ten miles east of Fort Worth. I think we would have been there yet if it hadn't been for Russell Pruden, our supply officer, one of the most efficient officers I have ever seen. The more I saw of them the prouder I was of the quality of the officers and enlisted men in our squadron.

The airplane situation at Hicks Field was an unholy mess. A number of Royal Flying Corps officers had come down to Texas to help in training our men. At Hicks we were one hundred per cent American but once in a while Colonel Roscoe, commander of the whole area, would send a British officer over to look us over, take a couple of flights with students and coach a bit. My experiences on the front and later at Gosport were invaluable to me—and quickly led me into difficulties.

I organized the 27th Squadron into three flights and immediately a lot of criticism broke out. Even Colonel Roscoe joined in the general comment, "Why make a British unit of this?" But I felt I was right and persevered. Napoleon said you cannot control more than three lieutenants and that must have come from experience. The longer we went on with our three-flight system the less the opposition became and presently it was officially adopted for all American squadrons. Today it is universal practice and the early objections to it seem inconceivable. It is the setup for the present hostilities—three flights to a squadron. A flying leader cannot control properly more than six airplanes in combat.

Other early American ideas of war flying were contrary to what we had learned in the RFC. I shall never forget the look on the face of Lieutenant Fred Norton of Columbus, Ohio, when we went out in the cold gray dawn to take up the first Canadian Jenny and I jumped into the front seat.

Norton was astounded. Never before had he seen an instructor use the front seat. At the American fields instructors were using the rear seat. It was infinitely safer in the accordion-like foldup as the engine plunged in after a fall off the wing and the front man was invariably killed. But this back-seat driving was worse than a correspondence course so far as teaching flying was concerned and it was distinctly not conducive to respect for superiors. We had developed the front seat idea at Gosport. In addition to the greater knowledge an instructor can give from the front seat, it is absolutely necessary to refrain from showing fright before your student, no matter what dizzy things the student does in his ignorance.

So I instructed Norton in a little trick of communication I had learned at Gosport. I handed him a piece of ordinary rubber hose, on my end stuck a medium-sized kitchen funnel and put a smaller one on his end. It was our speaking tube and it worked perfectly, with limitations, in spite of the roar of the motor, when I talked into it and he held it to his ear with one hand. Nowadays, with complete communication between teacher and pupil, our primitive scheme will seem amusing but the lack of just that device caused many bereavements in this country and cost Uncle Sam the lives of a large number of potentially valuable fliers.

In reality these boys didn't know anything at all about flying. They had simply been dragged through the air on joy rides by motors that didn't quit and had tried no maneuvers except the simplest banks on turns. A thousand hours of such flying are not as useful as one as emergency landing. Emergency situations are what create successful war aviators—forced landings, outside landings, aerial combat, acrobacy of all types, and, most important of all, the approach for a landing without the engine. And, truth to tell, the latter is the hardest of all to master. Inability to come in after the engine has ceased to function has killed more of my friends than any other single cause, mostly on the take-off, but sometimes unexpectedly en route to an objective. A high-ranking infantry officer transferred to the Air Service in Texas quickly realized this danger. He issued a classic order: "Effective this date, there will be no more forced landings."

It was necessary to start all over again with these boys and teach them to fly. We did it in Texas. But when hundreds of other home-trained aviators reached France, with hundreds of hours of straight flying behind them, they had to start again at the bottom of the ladder.

When a couple of us who knew from front-line experience what we were doing started to teach the boys actual war flying we were subjected to terrific criticism. They said we were "stunting," "showing off." We were called on the carpet and reprimanded.

Presently other squadrons began to copy us—to teach acrobacy with instructors who had had no experience whatever in it. The result was awful. Those Texas fields got the reputation of being "man killing outfits," "aviators' graveyards." The deaths among students and instructors were appalling. One of the things of which I am proudest is that in the 27th we lost only one life, a student, Captain Alden Davison, in flying during our entire training period before going into battle. He was as sincere and daring a pilot as ever grasped a joy stick. With all of the flat plains of Texas for a straight ahead landing when his engine conked in December 1917, he turned back, spun in and was crushed to death. I'll stack that record of ours against any other squadron in the United States service and I'll stack the ability of our fliers against any similar group anywhere.

Irene and June were living in a little farmhouse about five miles from camp and often I arrived home in a plane which I landed right alongside of the house on the flat Texas terrain. Automobiles were still scarce and expensive but I managed to get hold of a good, modern Model T Ford which, due to increasing demand, I was able to sell at a profit a few months later when we broke camp to go out and save that wonderful thing that needs saving so often and so critically—democracy.

One night Irene and I attended a social function at the Fort Worth Country Club. And there, in the uniform of the Royal Flying Corps, "maternity" jacket and stars, and banging smithereens out of the drums and cymbals was a chap I had seen in exactly similar activities at the airdrome at Bailleul, France—Vernon Castle. He was one of our three hundred British officers and mechanics stationed at Benbrook Field to help our mad rush to turn out pilots.

In Canada these Britishers had inquired about the Texas climate. They were told it was semitropical so the order went out: "India equipment." They arrived in Texas in khaki shorts, pith helmets, and no blouses or coats—in a blinding snowstorm. For two weeks they nearly died until their winter equipment arrived.

Our association with Vernon Castle and his charming wife Irene will always be a happy memory. He was as fine a pilot as he was a special ballroom dancer. In fact, I shall always be convinced that there is something kindred in the rhythms of flying and dancing. The best pilots were always mad about music and if a man could play the piano and was at the same time a good horseman—rhythm and balance—I could not only guarantee to send him solo in about two hours but I could almost certainly be sure that he would have a necessary spirit and fiber to be a "pukka" war bird on the front. We were knocked out completely when Vernon was killed while instructing a student from the front seat.

Orders came through for me to proceed to San Antonio to take a flying test for my JMA (Junior Military Aviator) license. This was an obsolete relic of the old Signal Corps organization but it enabled the holder to draw more flying pay so I was happy to get the chance. However, even for one who had been an instructor and flight commander at Gosport, accustomed to the last word in high powered service machines and to all kinds of training planes, it was rather a risky performance. From planes with a differential of 80 miles between top speed and landing speed to one such as they gave me at San Antonio, having a margin of five—its top speed was 75—and its landing speed about 70—was too quick a transition. And I can tell you that if I had not been thoroughly schooled in flying technique this test would have been my last human activity.

The hardwood longeroned American Jenny with the wheel control was a strange and fearful contraption to me after the light stick control in the lighter, higher powered British ships and, indeed, very different from the Canadian planes we had been flying at Leaside and Hicks. I was given no chance to try out the ship to get the feel of it or even to sit in it for a few moments to study its peculiarities and strange instrument arrangement before leaving the ground—a trick I had learned long before, and very vital when taking off in an unfamiliar crate. This is a splendid tip today to any pilot about to try out a new machine.

At the inspector's word I grasped the top of the wheel so it would act more or less like a stick control and was down the field and off. I was in the air and was about to make my climb to the left when "wham! wham! sputter—pop!" The old motor began to develop the jitters and threatened to stop entirely. All my Gosport training came to the rescue or this tale would have ended at that moment. Acting like a clumsy flying brick, the inefficient, oak-longeroned Jenny with its worn-out engine began to buck like a Texas steer, with its head down and its tail up. If I had tried to turn back I would have been killed instantly. Instead I aimed for a small unoccupied space over to the left and, by a miracle, sat down on it just as the poor old motor gave up the ghost. I was greeted like a hero but nobody knew how scared I had been. Anyhow, I got my license and all was well.

Young, independent businessmen, doctors, lawyers, free-thinking clerks, mechanics, bus drivers, policemen, all sorts of Americans and all highly individualistic from birth. This was the material we were trying to train into the obedient, almost mechanical, mentally regimented things called soldiers. That they made such rapid progress and did such a grand job was due entirely to their own high intelligence coupled with good sportsmanship.

I knew something about aviators which was not known to the vast majority of professional American Army men. It was this—in a sky battle, after the "dogfight" starts—and we will always have "dogfights"—teamwork is seldom more than ten per cent of the problem; individual initiative is at least ninety per cent. The Army system inevitably submerges the individual for the sake of the machine—mass action. But rob a flier of his individualism and you remove his entire value. In such a case he is no good because he has been taught to depend upon others and when they fail him he has nothing to fall back upon.

Hundreds of times I have seen professional officers shocked by the apparent informality of flying men and attempt to "put the fear of God into them," meaning to give them that rigid military discipline so necessary in the infantry and some of the other mass-thinking branches. Whenever an officer with this attitude took command of a squadron and tried to put into effect the strict observance of military forms in which he had been trained, his fliers immediately began to fall off in the quality of their morale and performance. I could name names, many of them. This fatal mistake should be carefully avoided in the training of the thousands of new fliers recently authorized by the government. Rob an aviator of the rugged individualism which led him into the flying service and you have zero. Altogether our squadron trained more than a hundred cadets at Hicks Field, including many later members of the 147th Squadron.

And now about that famous Liberty motor of ours. It was a great technical success—after the war—because in France, with horse transports being submarined at sea daily during the war, we were short of mules and horses and we were able to trade it with the French in considerable numbers for good, honest farm horses. Although infinitely too heavy, installed four pounds per horsepower, it became a fairly practical engine by 1921 after 286 alterations had been made in it and it had been "beefed up" or corrected in many parts. But the terrible expenditure of time—in the midst of the war—in trying to design and redesign a brand new type of motor which would serve for fast scout machines, fighters and long-distance bombers and the terrific cost of creating, destroying and re-creating jigs, dies, tools, and machinery proved entirely futile in bringing about the boast that we would "darken the skies with airplanes." The Liberty motor was a glorious postwar achievement, but next time let us divert our production potentialities on a proper prototype model even if it be designed by the enemy—so long as it delivers power and standup at the time we need it.

The Liberty motor excitement was all part of the seething mass of indecision and lack of experience, knowledge and organization incidental to a great peaceful nation, with all the good intentions in the world, trying to spring to arms over night. This particular phase of the aviation problem will be much worse in America's next war.

If I ever retire from business and aviation activities it will be to settle down in Texas. Before coming to Hicks Field I had thought of Texas as a great, dull, dusty plain—peopled with a few cowboys and moth-eaten Indians. I found it one of the most delightful places on earth, with people simply bubbling over with geniality and real sincere hospitality. Fort Worth, San Antonio, Dallas—all bright jewels in a state blessed with vast undeveloped commercial and industrial possibilities.

There was practically no machinery for getting the cadets their lieutenants' commissions after they had passed their stiff examinations and tests. Knowing that nothing ruins enthusiasm and morale more thoroughly than unnecessary delays in merited promotion, we moved heaven and earth and the War Department and most of our boys were full-fledged commissioned officers before embarkation, while men of equal training in other squadrons remained cadets until long after reaching France.

One of the outstanding men at Hicks was Major Geoffrey Bonnell. Second in command of the whole field, he had transferred from the Royal Flying Corps, as I had, and was now in the United States Army, in command of the 147th Squadron. I had never met him in France but I had heard of him because many people gave him credit for bringing down Boelcke, an early German ace. I'll talk more about him later in my tales of the 147th. I only mention him here because he was such a vigorous and successful cutter of red tape and because he and I had a race on to see whose squadron would get out of camp first on the way to France. He won.

Great excitement and some confusion broke out in our squadron when we received orders to leave Texas to go to Garden City, Long Island, New York. We arrived there January 26, 1918. And here a terrific morale-buster was let loose on us. It seems inconceivable now that a pimply faced little private in the Medical Corps, a mere orderly who up to a few days previously had been working as sanitation engineer in charge of garbage collection for a small Long Island town and had joined the Medical Corps to avoid the draft, could possibly raise such hell with an outfit of commissioned officers and trained men. This young man, when one of our boys developed a slight sore throat, issued an amazing order: "Put them all in quarantine. I'll see that orders come through from headquarters. Meanwhile not a man is to leave camp and wet blankets will be hung between every two men in the barracks."

This deprived our men of the last chance of seeing their relatives before sailing for an adventure from which many of them never returned. It was ridiculous.

In vain I appealed to the Signal Corps major in charge, only to be greeted by loud laughter. "I see you're young at this game," he said. "Don't you know the Medical Corps outranks everybody and can put you in the clink if it wishes?"

Sure enough, day after day, transfers began coming through sending my best enlisted mechanics and other vital experts to other units, many of them on home defense. In this, great help was given by the garbage-collecting youth. In vain we applied for a qualified doctor. A slight common cold was diagnosed as impending pneumonia and, bang! the patient was shipped to another outfit and I would lose an experienced welder. Stomach aches were declared to be appendicitis and headaches became coronary thrombosis.

By the time we sailed I had lost sixty-one expert men from my outfit. My fine, trained, trade-tested mechanics were replaced by green recruits with no experience whatever. Screwball stuff, this, but it is one of the prices we pay for democracy. I have often wondered if this was cleverly planned sabotage.

CHAPTER 9

Back to La Belle France

EVEN TO ME, an old veteran, there was a real thrill in our secret embarkation from Hoboken with other troops and fliers on that greatest and most useful war prize—the good old *Leviathan,* formerly the *Vaterland.* We sailed February 26, 1918, in the company of two other transports and several destroyers and here a strange and bothersome character entered our lives.

Soldiers are generally an innocent and unsuspecting species. When this bozo appeared among us we took him at face value. Vigorous of voice and manner, entertaining and hail-fellow-well-met, he was a soldier of fortune who had long been an adventurer all over the Allied armies, everywhere except near the front lines. He had talked and written his way into a major's rank, largely by telling gullible congressional committees about his personal exploits in air battles he had never even seen and bamboozling the Secretary of War in various ways, bordering on quasi-blackmail.

No sooner had we left the dock than our hero announced to the various squadron commanders, including Bourne, Angstrom, and myself, that by virtue of verbal orders from the commanding officer of the Eastern Department he was in command of all air service troops aboard that transport. This meant the 27th, 139th, and the 148th Aero Squadrons with many unattached airmen. This was good news to me. I needed a rest. So tired was I that once, as Fred Ordway talked to me, I dozed off to sleep in his face—my prized ability to relax became an embarrassing asset. I wanted time to get better acquainted with my officers and cadets and to hold a number of combat conferences and other meetings which I had planned. The phony major immediately began to work the very life out of our troops, rushing them to their submarine watch stations, drilling them on deck, exhausting them with calisthenics, and generally acting like a little Napoleon. Finally I received so many complaints through my noncoms that I determined to interview the commanding officer of troops on board about him. I chanced to meet him on the deck.

"You fliers are the funniest people," he said. "I just can't understand that officer who is in charge of you all."

This was my golden opportunity.

"I was just about to speak to you about him myself, Colonel," I replied. "Have you seen orders directing him to command the air troops on this ship? He's notified us only verbally. You know, he received his commission only a couple of days before we sailed. We know nothing about him but he certainly is taking off quickly and in a big way."

The colonel ducked back into his quarters and I can imagine what transpired when he failed to find the orders "from the Commanding General Eastern Department." For the rest of that voyage the doughty major was confined to his quarters with a slight cold and we had a temporary respite from his tin-soldier stuff.

Shortly after we docked at Liverpool on March 5, 1918, he put over another set of "verbal orders" on the officials over there and our 27th Squadron received orders intended for the 148th, of which he had assumed command.

We were ordered to camp at Winchester for six days and then to Issoudun, France, while the 148th was sent to Winchester and then to a Royal Air Force school in England.

These were exactly the reverse of the intended orders but he wangled it through "verbally," believing it meant a soft, cushy job in England, far from the annoying sights and sounds of the front lines. We caught on to this but our boys voted unanimously to go to France instead of an English training camp, so we apparently "fell" for his little game. Later, in France, he caused the death of ten American soldiers and, fifty miles from the lines, deliberately shot his pistol at the door of his car and pretended he had been gassed. Finally he was rushed home to get him out of the AEF and once safe in the U.S.A. he spent his time giving phony testimony to congressional committees and did the United States Army an incalculable amount of harm. How can we protect ourselves from such fakers in future? We can't!

He caused a lot of trouble at Winchester, where we mixed for the first time with troops of the regular U. S. Army, sojourning there in the rest camp—I never saw anybody get an hour of real rest in a rest camp—awaiting embarkation to France. In this camp there were the usual stuffed shirts you find in all groups of men. As a field officer I was supposed to wear spurs but I knew, from wisecracks I had heard, that my cadets were dubious of the value of spurs on a flying major, so occasionally I deliberately left them off in the belief that a whip socket is out of place on an automobile and that spurs on an aviator tend to hold the service up to ridicule. Having never ridden a horse since the start of the war and never intending to, I left the spurs off on a squadron march from one set of barracks in the camp to another. That night I was called to the office of the CO of the camp. When I reported to his headquarters I was greeted by one of his subordinates. "Major Hartney," he bellowed, "you paraded your company this morning improperly dressed."

This "gentleman by act of Congress" had the sneakiest

looking eyes I ever saw. As a brother major, however, I decided to greet him informally.

"Listen, old topper," I said. "I purposely left off my spurs this morning for a reason I shall be glad to tell you privately but if I am guilty of a violation I must take the consequences."

My attitude of friendliness was immediately construed as weakness. He bellowed again.

"I said you paraded this morning not in accordance with Army Regulations."

Never in my life have I been so mad. I really considered jumping over the desk and taking a sock at him. With my men actually suffering from lack of clothing and food, with a war on and all of us going into deadly combat in a few weeks, this guy who probably would hang on with a vice-like grip to his soft, safe job far from the lines for the duration of the war, got my goat in a big serious way. I went to town with him.

"Will you kindly go to hell," I said. "You don't even know there's a war on. The hell with you and all like you."

Turning to a captain who had come in to find out what all the yelling was about, I said:

"Will you kindly present my compliments to the commanding officer and tell him I am in my quarters if he wishes to see me."

The major uttered not a word and I never again heard of the matter. Another little incident sticks out in my memory of Winchester.

You may remember I mentioned noticing a tall, cadaverous bald man, named Dudley, on my first inspection of the squadron in Toronto. Well, Dudley had become my orderly, striker, dogrobber, batman, or whatever the proper title was for the helper who looked after my uniforms and general comfort. He was the acme of faithfulness and certainly made the whole war easier for me. Every enlisted man and officer in the 27th Squadron will remember him pleasantly. He became my devoted and worshiping slave. He was a heaven-sent miracle worker.

England was suffering from lack of food in those days, much more so than the people on the Continent, and Dudley was worried about my health and strength. The truth is that our men were not getting the nourishment they needed. One day we were marching down a winding narrow lane to inspect the beautiful Winchester Cathedral. I was on the foot path at the side of the column. Lieutenants Norton and Clapp were alongside of me. The men were marching "at ease" on the flint English lane. Dudley was about twenty paces to the rear, marching by himself, taking in the sights. We passed a beautiful little house in front of which a scraggly, lonely hen was trying to scratch a bit of food out of the hedge.

Presently I heard Dudley's voice in my ear and his southern drawl was leading me into temptation.

"Did you see that chicken back there, sir? Ah know yo all ain't had nothin' good to eat since we left Long Island. You jest give me the word and that bird'll be sizzlin' in yo' quarters befo' you gets back."

Not far from Winchester was Gosport, the famous yacht-building town where I had organized E flight—Avro flying trainers—at the School of Special Flying. I wanted some of my boys to go over there, for two purposes. One was to give them a glimpse of a real maneuverable airplane. Up to this time the only ships my pilots had seen were the Curtiss or Canadian Jennies—heavy 90-horsepower Curtiss 8-cylinder water-cooled and an occasional oak-longeroned heavier Jenny. These planes were all, in my opinion, aerial trucks. They could fly straight and nose-dive but had none of the vitally necessary ability to maneuver like a polo pony, or, a better

simile, a swallow in flight. To face the enemy in them would
have been sheer suicide.

My second reason for wanting the gang to go to Gosport
was to meet a group of young English public school lads
who had gone there to train under my successor in E flight.

The English public school is probably the finest in the
world. The quality of the boys it turns out was a revelation
to me, after knowing the slap-dash education and the thin
veneer of culture daubed on one going through the public
schools of Canada and the United States. The English public
school builds character and moral fiber. Perhaps this is because it has to deal only with boys of one nationality, one
tradition. I'll grant that the French and German schools may
be better in technical, matter-of-fact, materialistic training
but when it comes to culture of the intangible (and most
important) phases of the inner self these unique English
schools lead the world. They breed patriotism, devotion, self-
sacrifice—those attributes prerequisite in a fighting pilot up
there all alone with failing motor, fear, anxiety, vacillation,
and a hundred other emotions beckoning him home when
he gets into a dogfight far over the lines two or three miles up.

I never had to wonder how an English public schoolboy
was going to act in a battle in the air. I knew in advance and
not one ever let me down. Doggedness, determination, loyalty,
fearlessness, gallantry, and good sportsmanship—many of
those things which count for practically nothing in business
but are priceless when men's souls are in stress—are bred in
the bone of the English public schoolboy. No wonder the
British are invincible. You cannot beat character even with
the most modern of war inventions, as the world is going
to learn again in the near future.

I wanted these fine young tyros of mine to meet these boys,
mingle with them and get the feel of that team work, fair play,

and gentlemanliness which are so vital to an honest-to-good-ness war pilot.

An unexpected trip to London by a majority of the boys cut in on these plans but those who did go with me were greatly impressed both by the Camels and the public school-boys themselves.

Instead of lumbering and staggering off the ground, like going up a steep sidewalk, those new Sopwith planes bounded into the air like gazelles. The eyes of our men popped and they stood in wonderment as the Camels, instead of circling in wide paths consuming a minute or two, turned the full 360 degrees instantly, almost "on a dime."

"Shucks, I just can't fly," said W. B. Wanamaker—now a federal court judge in Ohio. And it was true, although "Wanny" had flown those old Jennies back home for several hundred hours. Later he became one of our very best pilots but had the misfortune to be brought down and taken prisoner on July 2, 1918, by Udet, today Hitler's chief of production in the German Luftwaffe (air force).

The English public school pilots did not let me down, either. They increased the confidence of my lads in their CO by taking us into my old flight office and illustrating the American system I had installed for keeping track of the flying time, progress and personnel, stimulating and affording incentive without semblance of regimentation.

On March 11, 1918, we hiked with full packs the fourteen miles to Romsey and left there for Le Havre, France, on the 17th, in the night.

After we landed at Le Havre, climbed the long, hard hill and got into camp we thought we would be there for many days and everybody began to relax. I discovered a buddy, an RFC major who, like me, had transferred to the American air service, and that night we went out to see the sights of the town. I felt a little giddy, anyhow. My squadron, the 27th, was actually in France, whereas Washington and London had decreed that we should receive super-training in England and later go up with the 54th Royal Flying Corps squadron on the northern front. But the synthetic major, with his verbal orders, changed all that and here we were in Le Havre, not knowing where we were going and with the finest bunch of boys in the world pretty well prepared for front line work.

This British major I met was the type who should never touch liquor. But in moments of relaxation he practically bathed in it. For some strange reason he had a terrific yen against MPs. I don't like them myself. And I don't think MPs like themselves. MPs are Military Police. They were a necessary evil in all armies. They were simply soldiers who had sought to evade front line service by enlisting in that strange branch or others who had, because of physical deformities or other reasons, been taken from the ranks and placed in the Military Police. Their unpleasant job was to try to keep peacetime decorum among several million officers and enlisted men engaged in a foreign country in the greatest adventure of their lives.

The U. S. Army was particularly unfortunate—or unwise—in this respect. Not only was every American or French town where American troops gathered overrun with young thugs whose authority was greater than that of any major general's but a horde of professional detectives was imported to France to spy on officers and men in their moments away from the front. This got under the skins of countless sincere Yankee warriors and changed their whole attitude toward the war. The disgraceful situation that was allowed to exist at 10 Rue St. Anne, Paris, with "Hard Boiled" Smith and others of his ilk to beat the stuffing out of American officers and doughboys who had overstayed their leaves or who had imbibed a little too much of the wines of la belle France, is one reason why the U. S. Army in France was not the patriotic, enthusiastic horde of Sir Galahads it was supposed to be. It is the reason why some of its highest officers today are anathema to veterans of the American Expeditionary Force instead of being the honored leaders they might have been. Coupled with this, of course, was the fighting man's contempt for all members of the service who had selected jobs in which they would always be safe from enemy bullets and bayonets.

Anyhow, my British flying major, now an American officer, didn't like MPs. And Le Havre was infested with British Tommies with MP on their sleeves. The more drinks he had the more he insulted them. Like true Britishers, with their caste system, they took it grinning, whereas the American MPs would have slugged him over the head with their police night sticks and thrown him into the hoosegow perhaps to be demoted and sent home in disgrace.

The more he drank the worse he got. Presently the whole situation got too thick for me and I steered him to a hotel run by a very understanding French gentleman who undertook to chart a sensible course for him—with the help of two alluring French demoiselles. Their final drinks cost me five francs each.

Having had more of the juice of the wonderful French grape than was my wont—I was always a teetotaler when I was on military service—I retired for some much needed sleep. At 4:30 A.M. I awoke with a strange hunch tugging at my sensibilities. I was dreaming of my troops and they were in some kind of a jam. As I opened my eyes I found standing by my bed one of the girls with whom the major had been when I last saw him. Although she was not supposed to speak English and I had suffered trying to make her understand my army French, she addressed me in perfectly good American.

"That bum you turned us over to won't give us any dough, so you're elected."

I reached out and hastily explored my pockets. Not a thin dime, only some United Cigar Store coupons and I knew that by now she was too wise to fall for those. By this time my brain was beginning to function and the hunch I had dreamed was getting stronger. So I said:

"Pardonnez-moi, mademoiselle. Si vous will go across the chamber for un petit moment I will put on mes vestments and soigner the situation toute de suite."

Blushingly the old blister turned her back. I arose, put on my trousers and blouse, calmly walked behind a screen in front of the window, dropped out of the window, ten feet to the ground, and started to run toward our camp. Under the circumstances Napoleon could have done no better.

Our camp was several miles from town and a singlehanded marathon at that hour and in my weary condition was no part of my plans. But to my rescue along came a snappy little Crossley station wagon—like those tenders we saw in England when we first arrived, driven by a bright "Ack Emma"— British slang for air mechanic. I stopped the driver and told him tales of the old 20th Squadron, RFC. He was really a splendid egg and we found we had had many friends in common in the now famous 20th. So my dismal trek to camp became a simple problem.

But once arrived there I ran into the damnedest situation that ever confronted any officer in any army in the world.

I expected to see a big expanse of barracks and tents and a parade ground bathed in peaceful moonlight and I was all set to sneak off to my bunk for a couple of hours of slumber. But what did my horrified eyes behold? Six hundred stalwart American soldiers, with packs on their backs, rifles at "order," standing at attention, waiting for orders.

Out of this mass one figure rushed over to me. It was the sergeant major, Miller, of the 27th. Breathless, he said:

"Where are all the officers? We have orders to move."

It was a solar plexus blow. Both squadrons—27th, 147th—and the two hundred casuals lined up ready to go and every commissioned officer except myself asleep in some hotel down town. No wonder I had had such a strong hunch. Some instinct came to my rescue; probably it was my years of military training. Anyhow, I called for the sergeant major from each unit to advance to my presence.

"Each of you men will act as commanding officer of his squadron or detachment until your own officers arrive from the conference they are having at headquarters."

"Yes, sir," said each of them, saluting snappily, but each with a dirty twinkle in his eyes.

At that moment an orderly came up and handed me a paper.

"You will move forthwith to entrainment, etc. Compliments of His Majesty's Brigade Major Dudley." Compliments, hell! Here I was on the worst spot of my life. I had to get out of it. So I proceeded to commit a boner which is still a classic in the United States Army.

Marching over to the head of the men I suddenly reverted to the training I had had in England and Canada. In my best diction, slowly, loudly, I bellowed a command never intended for American troops.

"Squadrons, form fours—right."

Luckily those boys had had their first drilling in Canada.

Actually, I believe, a look of sympathy came into six hundred faces. They say soldiers are automatons. Not the American soldier. Not batting an eye but with an attitude I could actually feel of, "O.K., boy, we're with you," they formed fours instead of American squads of eight, almost as snappily as they had done at Camp Borden, at Toronto, without even counting off. It was a military miracle.

"Carry on, Sergeant Major." I uttered the phrase which has, at least once in his life, saved the career of every British and American officer. "Carry on as if I were not here." Nor was I there. In my thoughts I was back in that hotel with Major X snoring his head off and with other officers all about town.

I told the sergeant major to have two good men from each squadron report to me at once. In a trice they were there. "March your command onto the train," I told the sergeant major. To the eight men, I said, "I appoint each of you my personal representative. You will take four motorcycles and sidecars and ride slowly around this town and find your officers. Tell them that we are entraining at once on Track No. 2, RTO Station No. 3."

In forty-five minutes our string of *Huit Chevaux's* pulled out. Every enlisted man and every officer of every squadron was aboard. But I shall never get over that incident. It gives me goose pimples to this day.

En route to Issoudun, the train wheezed to a stop by a peasant's field for many minutes. Someone made a deal with the old man and suddenly the train was flooded with wine. I have seen some commanding officers act very stupidly in similar circumstances, but we controlled the situation by confiscating what we could find of the wine in a cursory search and the rest did nobody any harm.

Presently, after a six-day stop at Tours, we arrived at the now famous training center for American fliers, Issoudun, a small town by the River Loire south and west of Paris. Two of our squadrons had been trained by officers who had learned flying with the British, my 27th, and the 147th trained and commanded by Major Geoffrey Bonnell. We were soon referred to as "British trained." As a matter of fact we were both entirely American trained but the methods of teaching had been somewhat different. The normal system in most squadrons was to make the students pile up as many hours of straight, plain flying as possible. Bonnell's and mine had been to insist that they never indulge in straight flying after having once learned it, but to concentrate on practice forced landings and maneuvers of all kinds. I am still thoroughly sold on this method for training war pilots and commercial fliers. That is one reason why I like glider flying. Our fliers were practically ready for the front. The others hadn't reached first base yet.

Arriving at Issoudun, we thought we would be on the front in a few days. It was an empty dream. In the first place, there were no planes for us to take away. In the second place, the staff believed we, like those units which had preceded us, had done nothing but straight flying and insisted that we should learn all over again—on French planes. These ships, mostly Nieuports with different wing areas and equipped with French rotary motors of varying speeds and averaging three hours gas capacity at cruising speed, were lighter than our training ships at home and much more handy and maneuverable but much more dangerous to fly. Their controls acted instantaneously and they had the graceful, darting flight of the swallow. The engine, however, was difficult to manage and eventually snuffed out several valuable lives at the field in other squadrons. It was not entirely the fault of the engine; part of the blame was due to our own manufacturers at home. Being a rotary engine with a block-tube type carburetor which really wasn't a metering jet at all, nothing but a connection which demanded constant manipulation and adjustments, this machine had an apparently incurable habit of quitting cold at the slightest provocation, especially in that most dangerous of moments just after the take-off when the altitude of any fixed wing aircraft is bad and the motor is pulling full out. This happened invariably unless the pilot knew exactly how to manipulate the menets or throttles. On these planes the menets were all where they should have been, on the right hand side. At home the indecision and lack of co-ordination in our factories, or, rather, in the powers that exerted wartime supervision over their orders and specifications, brought planes through with throttles wherever it pleased the designers to place them, usually on the left side. The right-hand position on the French Nieuport and Morane planes confused several gallant boys on their first flights in France; the engine quit; they turned back into the field and spun to Eternity.

Major Bonnell was greatly irked by the fact that all the pilots in the 27th and 147th, intensively tutored in forced landings and all the tricks of acrobacy should be forced back to "flying kindergarten." He had built a magnificent morale in his squadron and his boys were full of eagerness to get up to the front. One night at taps about five days after we arrived at Issoudun he came to my quarters. His face was flushed and he was sincerely excited.

"Major Hartney, you're surely not going to stand for this nonsense here, are you? My men are going stale; they're going to mutiny on me unless they get going."

"Yes," I replied. "It looks as if we're stuck right here for the duration of the war. But what can we do? You're not in the RFC now. This is a democracy and no complaints or suggestions will be welcomed."

"Right," he said. "But it's up to us to take the lead because we've had experience and know the seriousness of this thing. Now listen here, Petit (he always called me *Le petit commandant*), you and I are not going to rot on this vine. We're going to get ships somewhere."

"We can fly that whole bunch of miscellaneous condemned jobs over in the mystery hangar," I put in meekly.

"What do you mean?" asked Bo.

"Just what I say. We can put all those ships condemned because they didn't fly properly, into first-class shape in three days."

Bonnell jumped to his feet.

"Do you mean that, Hartney?" a twinkle of hope in his eyes.

"With that gang of ours out there we can do it, positively," I replied. "Those ships are dangerous, as is, but line them up scientifically, as Sergeant Albaugh of the 27th and his boys can, and providing the pilots know how to operate the rotary motors, we'll have the finest bunch of new ships flying in a day or so that you ever saw. Whittle down the struts to fit their sockets, straighten out the wings or give them the proper camber by taking up on cables and inaccurately cut tie rods—it's all a matter of engineering. There's nothing basically wrong with those ships."

Bonnell was walking up and down excitedly. He stopped in front of me.

"You're positive, are you, that we can put those planes in shape? You'll gamble your career, your reputation, the respect and lives of your men and mine on it?"

"Absolutely," I said firmly.

I was never so sure of anything in my life. I had spent a lot of time inspecting those condemned planes.

"All right," said Bonnell. "How many ships are there that we can fix and what are they?"

"There are six 23-metre jobs, twenty 18-metre and ten of these heavy 'bee place.' There's a portable engine test block, too. You watch the boys burn up those spare rotaries but it will be worth it. They'll soon learn how to and how not to play 'Nearer, My God, to Thee' on those throttles."

"Very well," Bonnell announced. "I'll make this deal with Colonel Mike Kilner: give us one week, if we can put fifty per cent of those planes in shape to satisfy the engineering officer and have every one of our men do some solo work in them, he will approve orders sending us along out of here."

"O.K. by me," I said.

"And it's five hundred francs for you," said Bonnell, "if we win. And if the reverse happens, I'll beat you to a pulp and go home voluntarily in disgrace. I could never face my men again."

He was—and is—like that.

Reveille, breakfast, at seven next morning. Then a parade of Bonnell's men and mine, led by Sergeant Albaugh, to the laced-up canvas Bessoneau hangar. Off with the lacing—a glimpse inside—a jumble of ships—little 27s, even a brand-new ship added to the list the day before—all looking trim and perfect, but each, so they said, harboring a death bug.

I should have notified all officers and men on the field what we were going to do. As it was, they were consumed with curiosity. And by nine o'clock they were dizzy with surprise, for out in the sunlight, looking as if ready to take off, were thirty-eight of the sweetest-looking airplanes in the world, new and glistening. At one end was the very latest type Morane Parasol—a little dream ship, like a graceful butterfly, with a 165-horsepower rotary Monosoupape (single valve) rotary engine, that barked like a continuous succession of backfires.

From the death house we dragged them out for rejuvenation and a new life in the sky. Our men attacked them like a swarm of ants. Every plane crew had its blue print and knew just what to do. Tools! A shortage of tools! But leave it to soldiers to forage and find what they need. Officers and men forgot all about lunch and by two o'clock five of those ships were perfect and had had their first trips in the air. When we quit at dark ten more were ready for their test flights the next morning. Over near the hangar each pilot did a ten-minute tour of duty abusing a rotary engine on the test block and getting himself thoroughly drenched with castor oil.

It was exciting stuff, especially for me. Fresh from a terrible siege on drab Jennies at home, it was like going from the lumbering trucks of prewar days to the lightest and liveliest motor cars of 1940. Never have I experienced such a contrast in flying. You guided one of these ships as if it were part of you. They responded almost in exact accordance with your thoughts, instantly, and not like the heavy Jennies in which you would put the stick over and then wait for the wing to get good and ready to come up in response. There was none of that painful old lag. Those French planes, wonderfully maneuverable, the fast ones capable of 128 miles an hour but with a slow landing speed of 40, and carrying 25 gallons of gasoline for three to six hours of flying, were just about the equal of the Sopwith Camels some of the boys had seen at Gosport. And naturally, the men who had gone to Gosport with me were anxious to give those who hadn't gone a thrill by showing them what they could do with real war planes.

If it is true, as someone had said, that I was born with twice the nine lives of a cat, I was now about to put on a stunt that must have cost me life number eleven and would certainly have blotted out anybody not so bounteously endowed with durability.

Perhaps Issoudun wanted to get rid of us. Perhaps we were too cocky, or something. Anyhow, when I announced I would fly the little Morane Parasol, the ship with the ball-bearing controls, which most of those at the field considered too dangerous even to look at, much less pilot through the air, it was the final "kick in the pants" for the conservative element of the field personnel.

Familiar with the big Monosoupape motor and having qualified as an expert on the Gosport Camels, I roared across the field on my take-off, gathering speed with every inch. I intended to do every trick in the pack—upside down flying, barrel rolls, tail slides, everything—the only way to lead a flying outfit. Going 50 miles an hour the big motor was just about to lift the ship into the air when *wham!*—a tire blew out. The dainty little mechanical bird slewed around and flopped gracefully over on its back. And in full view of six hundred officers and men, the Petit had to unfasten the peculiar French shoulder-type safety belt, drop upside down to the ground and shamefacedly get himself out of the mess.

Someone got a new tire from Paris two days later. A French pilot took up the machine and, in a simple tight spiral the frail wings let go and the fuselage and pilot plummeted to earth and oblivion.

But the CO of the field made good on his promise. Within six days we had thirty-eight ships repaired and flying and along came orders to the COs of the 27th and 147th, "You will proceed to entrainment, etc."

CHAPTER 10

American Flyers Edge
Toward Danger

ALL OF THIS business in France—the anecdotes, personal experiences and the growing pains of a fighting squadron—are essential to show the normal transition of a crowd of high-spirited American boys from independent democratic businessmen and students into a well-knit, disciplined unit of technically educated Boche-killers, so superior to their enemy that they could not be mentioned in the same breath. The Germans produced a few good fighting pilots—one superb one, Richthofen—against whom we Americans had a dozen of equal worth in the few months we were in the war—Rickenbacker, Lufbery, Luke, Springs, O'Neil, Vasconcells, Cook, Grant, Hall, Chambers, Sewall, Curtiss, Porter, Hudson, Campbell, Meissner, White, McLanahan, Simonds. Please notice the ancestry back of those names. I hesitate to name only these few lest others equally good feel justly that I have overlooked them.

The average American war flier, although not the equal of the British in unbridled daring—the American was on the average older—was vastly superior to the average German who, in turn, was surpassed by the average French pilot. Perhaps the explanation lies in these facts: The British are one race and their aviator-type youths are bred in one tradition with a peculiar singleness of loyalty, sportsmanship, courage, independence, and doggedness. The French, like the Italians, are more brilliant in spots but after ten centuries of almost constant warfare and economic struggle their blood has been stabilized and it is only the exceptional individual who, through the hotness of his Latin blood and the keen scientific brain to which he is heir, can rise above a mass mind perplexed by politics, labor disputes, political confusion and the inevitable social and mental hodgepodge which has been the aftermath of the French revolution. Such men, for example, as Guynemer, Fonck, Nungesser, Pinsard, Dorme, Madon, Viallet, Guerin, Heurteaux, Pegoud, Garros, or their neighbors, the Belgians, Thiefry and Meulemeester, or the Italians, Baracca, Scaroni, and Ercola.

A valuable psychological study would be a comparison of all these men, the German aces and the following British: Ball, Bishop, Barker, Mannix, Collison, McCudden, McKeever, and McLeod.

The Germans were up against a terrific psychological handicap. Never having known democracy—the liberty of the individual—it was only the Teutonic superman who could overcome the burden of hundreds of years of blind following of leaders and amount to anything in the air, where, unique among all human situations, individuality comes into its supreme importance. The Americans are totally individualistic. They are just emerging from three centuries of hewing down trees and fighting the wilderness and its savage inhabitants to create a living space. This accounts for the lawlessness in the United States during Prohibition and in the vigorous things the American public does at the polls on Election Day. It accounts, above all in this story, for the fact that the American air force, numerically weaker, only half-trained and with many of them using borrowed planes of dubious quality, brought down in a few months 753 German airplanes and balloons and lost only 227 pilots in death,

1. Harold E. Hartney. U.S. ARMY

2. Maurice Farman "Longhorn." USAF

3. F.E. 2b. USAF

4. Morane-Saulnier "Parasol." USAS

5. Nieuport 27. USAAF

6. Captain Eddie Rickenbacker of the 94th Aero Squadron. USAF

7. Lieutenant Frank Luke, Jr. of the 27th Aero Squadron.
National Archives

8. Enemy Balloon. *National Archives*

ptain Douglas Campbell of the 94th
e his Nieuport 28. U.S. ARMY

10. Major Raoul Lufbery, U.S. Air Service,
94th Aero Squadron. U.S. ARMY

11. Major Reed Chambers of the 94th beside his red, white, and blue
Spad. USAAF

12. Another colorful Spad of the 94th "Hat-in-the-Ring" Squadron. USAF

13. Captain James Norman Hall, also
of the 94th, formerly of the Lafayette
Flying Corps. U.S. ARMY

14. First World War and latter day members of the 94th Pursuit Squadron. USAS

15. Brigadier General Billy Mitchell in the front cockpit of a two-seater Spad XVI. *National Archives*

16. Lieutenant Billy Bishop beside his Nieuport 17. Like Hartney, Bishop was a Canadian and second ranking Ace of the RFC and RAF with 72 victories. RCAF

17. Major James T. McCudden, RFC, in his S.E. 5. *National Archives*

289 planes and 48 balloons in the process. In training 12,499 aviators we lost 500 in training accidents. We do not know what the German training casualties were.

Man for man the German flier was no match for the American. This is one reason why I take with a great big grain of salt the present German boasts about the invincibility of their terrifying air power. No machine is bigger than the man behind it.

And while I am on this subject of national differences I might mention that the most natural mental companions on this earth today are the Americans, the Canadians, the Australians, and the New Zealanders—all products of the newest in civilizations. We found that out in France.

It may have been on account of our nuisance value that Colonel Kilner was so glad to throw us out of Issoudun toward the front, or it may have been because they had a vital need of new aviators and equipment up there to stem the German hordes. The awful break had occurred at just that time up north in the British lines and my old pals in the Royal Flying Corps, pilots and mechanics alike, were obliged for the first time to take to their rifles in retreat and leave behind whole squadrons of airplanes, trucks, and equipment.

On April 20, 1918, Bonnell and I rushed up to 45 Avenue Montagne, in Paris, with a small detachment of men. Here was the headquarters of the American Air Service, and, like all other units in the United States Army, it was run by individualists. Already two American squadrons had gone to the front, the 94th and the 95th, the nucleus of the 1st American Pursuit Group. And on a cloudy Sunday morning, April 14, Lieutenant Douglas Campbell of the 94th had brought down a Boche in flames and had thus achieved the first victory of the war for an all-American pilot. A few minutes later Lieutenant Alan Winslow of the 94th had forced another German plane down out of control and it crashed near the first one a short distance from the Toul airdrome. Poor old Raoul Lufbery had transferred from that great flying outfit, the Lafayette Escadrille, to the U. S. Army and had been given command of the 94th.

No such thing as a "squadron initial equipment" manual had ever been printed—nor even thought of.

"You'll have to make out your own requirements," said the supply officer. "Take what you can get."

In my memory I can still see the list of cameras, telescopes, trunks, and other items that Bonnell made out. It was, as the French would say, *magnifique*. And, miracle of miracles, we actually got most of it when we arrived at the front.

While we were in Paris a great blow fell on me. Pat Ingersoll and Jim Marquardt, two of my most promising flying officers, were killed back at Issoudun in two separate crashes. They were buried in Field No. 13 before I ever heard of it. While pilots had been dying like flies in training camps around us these had been the only deaths in our entire squadron since we had started training in Texas, except that of Captain Alden Davison at Hicks, in spite of (or because of) my policy of teaching the boys really to fly, with acrobacy, simulated forced landings, trick turns and other non-straight-flying maneuvers. Lieutenant Ingersoll's parents had come down to New York to say good-bye. His father, W. Ingersoll, from Rockford, Illinois, had taken my hand and said, "My boy's in your care, son. God bless you." I have always regretted not being there on the last days of these fine boys. And how do you suppose they died? You've guessed it. Turned back to the field when their motors quit on the take-off. Only five days before, Ingersoll had said to me, as most student fliers say to this day, "I know it's fatal to turn back. But they all do it—and I'll do the same thing when my time comes." It's a strange and lethal impulse.

Rushing back to the mud of Issoudun, another shock

awaited me. My adjutant, Jim Pierce, the world's best, had been transferred to the Personnel Department at Tours. Lieutenant Seward of the 139th went west about the same time and although not a member of the 27th, we mourned his loss because we had always looked upon him as one of the gang. Bonnell and I found our outfits pawing the ground like impatient dogs on the leash. Without any planes but with a fine quota of ground officers, including Pruden, the best scrapper with higher ups that ever lived, we left that place on May 6, 1918, the envy and, at the same time, the disdain of everyone in camp. "Those two squadrons went through this mudhole like a Kansas cyclone," they said.

And now, thrill of thrills, your reporter with his gang of magnificent young ground officers, his twenty-eight flying officers including three picked flight commanders, and two hundred loyal, well-trained, trade-tested and balanced enlisted men entered the Zone of Advance along with the 147th Squadron. "It won't be long now," drawled "Cap" Elliott of Missouri as we debarked from the little French squeak-box train. Our boys were in fine fettle. They were primed to the muzzle with that priceless ingredient for a flying unit— morale. Let critics say we were not adequately trained—the record will answer. But let no one say they were not bubbling with enthusiasm, pride, cohesion, and spirit. And why not? These were the first two squadrons to arrive at the front in which most of the officers including leaders had trained together from the beginning, with fundamentals taught by two men of actual front-line experience. The enlisted men were just as intensely interested in the coming sky battles as the pilots who were to squeeze the joy sticks and trip the Bowden wire grips of the machine guns.

Our first stop was some eight miles back of Toul, at Epiez, on the side of a hill. Amanty was the name on the map but a pilot could easily get lost looking for it. It was so tiny it looked nothing like an airdrome. The runway was on the side of a hill and if a landing plane got out of a tyro's control in a gust of wind it just kept rolling down to the bottom. We had no brakes in those days.

Still a goodly distance from the front lines, the boom of the guns could be heard plainly when the wind was right. I knew just what those boys of mine were thinking as they lay in their bunks at night. I had been through it before. One of the real thrills of a young war pilot is to get his first sight of an enemy ship. In the next war this will not be so exciting because the civilian population and the troops in training will see them—and how!—long before the front rank fliers. Our men saw their first German plane early one morning after we had been there a few days. They had heard one the first night but as the searchlights and antiaircraft guns both missed it by about ten miles it had gone off *zom-a-zom-a-zom* after laying eggs on some unfortunates in a camp near us.

This first daylight raider was a photographic single-engined high-flying two-seater Rumpler. I turned away from it to watch the faces of our fledglings. Speechless, they just stood there with eyes glued to that machine, yearning to be up and at it.

It was at Epiez that Lieutenant Plyler achieved one of the most remarkable feats of the war. He swam across the Meuse River and captured two geese that remained with us as mascots until shortly before we returned to the United States. I knew what type planes we were getting but said nothing about it. The boys picked up a rumor that were to receive heavy two-seaters instead of the swift single-chasse planes they hoped for. In the army of a democratic country it is good to let the men bellyache once in a while so I let them go to it. In a land where the soldiers have been regimented almost from birth it is dangerous insubordination. This will be one of our big advantages in the coming hostilities. The men on both sides will have plenty to "grouse" about.

I don't blame the men for being impatient. War is like that. With only the General Staff knowing what is really going on—and at times we suspect they know only a fraction of one per cent of it—it is no wonder that the rest of the Army is subject to deluges of rumors, most of them totally inaccurate. Another reason lies in the independence of thought of democratic soldiers. Given anywhere near equal training, the free-thinking citizen-soldier will always outfight both the professionals and the compulsory military slave of any non-democratic country. Let's look for a moment at the peacetime occupations of the officers of my squadron. We had one theater proprietor, four salesmen, three lawyers, two journalists, five electrical and gasoline engineers, a concert pianist, a banker, a cotton planter, an automobile race driver, a broker, and a mining man. To keep one's head above water in any of those professions requires clear, independent constant thinking—not mere mechanical obedience to orders. It was inevitable that these men fought harder because they knew, from their own intelligences, what they were fighting for—an ideal, rather than an immediate military boss. There were also many college students among our fliers. They are harder to analyze because their minds were immature, but some of them became superb pilots and fighters.

Our men were in a gloom over the expected arrival of inferior planes, when there landed on our funny little field the first of the ships we really were to use. And what a superb machine—a Nieuport 28! Of French design, although in disfavor with their own pilots, it was a fast moving, fast acting gem, with a nine-cylinder 165-horsepower Monosoupape rotary engine with which we were so familiar after flying the Nieuport 27s we had patched up at Issoudun. It had what was known as a selector switch—an ingenious gadget which enabled us to cut out and skip cylinders in such a manner as to hit each and every one only once in three revolutions, thus cutting down engine revolutions but still retaining perfect balance. Previously, on the rotary engines we had tried, they either ran full open or they didn't run at all. It burned almost as much castor oil as gasoline and operated with a terrific roar, much greater than our modern engines. Housing one horsepower for every two pounds of weight, the French had taken up, by the sheer quality of metal, the inevitable shocks of heat and revolutions which nowadays are absorbed by fineness in design. Each cylinder was cut from a solid ingot of nickel steel and, while the finished job had two magnetos, it was entirely lacking in carburetor, temperature gauges, manifold pressure indicators or any of a dozen instruments that now enable a pilot to sense coming mechanical trouble.

The *avion* itself was a biplane, trim but fragile. Its tail was a good deal longer than that of the Sopwith Camel. This was disturbing to me because I always felt the stubby tail was one of the reasons why the Camel could turn almost in its own length compared with the slow, wide turns of the heavy Hun ships.

A particular hazard was the reserve gas tank mounted on the right-hand side inside the cockpit about where the front seat elbow rest is located in a motorcar. This, according to Wanamaker, was put there as a special target for the enemy's incendiary bullets, "to get things over quickly." Two beautifully made fast-firing air-cooled Vickers .30-calibre machine guns were poised on the left side of the cowl just about on a level with the pilot's eyes. Squarely in front of the pilot was the Aldis telescopic sight so aligned that to get an enemy in it, diving away, was sure death for him.

The guns firing through the propeller were coupled up with a new type mechanical gear, which interrupted the shots when the blades of the propeller were in front of the muzzle. A terrible weakness in this otherwise almost perfect plane was the construction of the leading edge of top and bottom wings. Without reinforcing, the fabric came off when pilots pulled out of a steep dive too rapidly. This happened twice, in other squadrons, and the poor boys kept on going, without wings. It happened with Eddie Rickenbacker once in an actual combat and, although his wings did touch the enemy plane, I still am convinced the inherent weakness of the wing contributed to a nation's bit of good luck—that Eddie was spared and came home with all the fabric off the top side of one of the wing panels, after dropping a mile or so in a spin out of control.

Nobody told us about this weakness; nothing was done about it. We had to learn it ourselves. Early in my flying career I had observed that it was the weakest point in all these early airplanes, and I warned the boys about it. In fact, on one annoying occasion, I had to send to the rear a pilot who refused to believe that I knew what I was talking about in this matter and crudely pulled back his stick at the end of a dive. It broke his heart but it saved several valuable lives. Another weak spot was the landing gear—the legs—of this plane. Being made of ordinary sheet aluminum—streamlined tubing, light gauge—instead of hardened aluminum (Duralumin), I knew they would collapse after even a few soft landings.

I jumped into this first of our very own machines and spent a half hour sitting there studying the instruments. "Contact!" And I was off. She climbed even better than the Camels at Gosport. For the first time in all my flying I felt that the plane and I were really one. She maneuvered like a bird in flight, almost in response to my thoughts. Lucky for me I had that Gosport training and knew that Monosoupape motor so well. I was only up 400 feet when, with a burp, the engine quit cold. Instantly, by feel alone, I checked with my hands to make sure the switches and selector were on, lowered the nose very slightly for a gentle glide, then very, very slowly began opening up on the throttle—the gas valve. Soon, like music to my ears, came the smooth roar of the revived motor, so suddenly that it pulled my head back. If, before the motor came back to life, I had tried to turn back to the field I would have been killed. That was especially true in these planes, with very small wing area and built for speed and climb. With no inherent stability they invariably tucked their noses earthward and took a good hundred feet or more to pull out of the resultant spinning nose-dive.

This little ship could zoom, dive, and about-face much better than any of our modern fighting planes and I stayed up in it so long that I was accused of being afraid to land. But I took it in good nature. In the flying service the CO's job is different from that in any other branch. Among other things, flying officers can kid their commander and get away with it.

In spite of their pleading to take a spin in the new ship, I wanted to try out the gunnery equipment before I turned her over to the boys. And here I certainly lost life number twelve. It is the only explanation of why I am on this earth today, living "on velvet." Loading up both belts with ordinary ammunition and tracer, in the usual proportion of three ordinary for one tracer I was soon showing the squadron how this ship could dive vertically at the ground and fire into a target we had quickly placed nearby.

Everything was doing fine—*rat-tat-tat*—*rat-tat-tat* single fire, then *tat-tat-tat-tat* as both guns blazed forth. I was making my third vertical dive at the ground, my eyes riveted on the target. I actually saw something leave the muzzle of one of the guns and come flying at me over the windshield. Before I could dodge, there was a terrific impact on my forehead. I saw a million stars, everything went totally black, and I realized I was losing consciousness. Some stubborn determination took hold of me and kept me from going under. Slowly I pulled out of the dive only a few feet from the ground and groggily made a safe but sloppy landing. Then I discovered that some brilliant ordnance engineer had fixed up a very wonderful compensating gas cylinder for the muzzles of the Vickers machine guns and the vibration, uncommon on the ground but plenty bad in the slipstream of a diving plane, had jarred it loose. With no provision for locking it on, it had followed the line of least resistance and caught me squarely between the eyes.

"Pilot error"—I can hear the excuse as part of the benediction had I gone on into the ground, as many a man has done from failure of some mechanical part or gadget. Of course, we sent word back immediately and about ten planes later these gas cylinders began to come through properly locked down.

Next morning another Nieuport arrived. The ferry pilots flying them over from Orly, on the outskirts of Paris, were cracking them up at the rate of about two out of every three. The French, who never liked them, were practically "giving" them to us for $18,500 each. When one cracked up it was usually a complete washout. But presently our quota was gradually coming through to us.

"Red" Miller, third senior flight commander, flew tests all right but on his first landing there was a slight side wind, the ship veered and he proceeded to climb one of the guy wires on the Bessoneau hangars. Exit an $18,500 plane and almost exit a good flying officer. The next day one of the pilots, very cautious about dirty gasoline—and a very wise cautiousness it was in "that man's war"—strained his fuel through a chamois. Not grounding the nozzle of the hoseline, the inevitable happened. Static set the whole works on fire. Loss: one hangar, all the contents thereof and one perfectly good plane. Another $18,500 shot to hell.

All of this was most irksome to a crowd champing at the bit to get up to the front. Bonnell's outfit, the 147th, however, was not doing any better, or even as well. They were all good pilots there. All had trained thoroughly at Hicks and Issoudun. They knew the Nieuport 27s thoroughly and had "transitioned" to the 28s with little trouble. But they were having all sorts of mishaps and delays. Bonnell was practically frantic to take his boys on a "Cook's Tour" over the front lines. But before he could sneak them over unobserved in a spell of bad weather orders came through for us both to move our units to Toul and join the greatest flying organization America has ever had, the 1st Pursuit Group, and to take our squadrons right into front line work.

Two days of "dud" weather prevented our moving but provided two incidents which still stand out in my mind— one stark tragedy, the other the unconscious comedy of a democracy. A thunderstorm drove us all indoors. While I was telephoning, my ears were almost flattened by a stroke of lightning. And it was that stroke that instantly killed one of our best enlisted men. We buried him with full military honors in a lonely French cemetery near the slopes of Amanty.

The morning of the day we were to leave for the front to be shot down in flames or shoot to death the young fliers of Germany, we were lined up on the parade ground while a young lieutenant of the U. S. Army Dental Corps addressed us with religious seriousness.

"Men," he said, "I am about to address you for the last time. I want you to promise me—in fact, I am putting you on your honor— You will keep your teeth clean. Now, I have here a tooth brush, issue, just the same as you will find in your kit. You are to brush your teeth, night and morning, like this, up and down—not sideways."

And he proceeded to give us an exhibition of how this miracle was accomplished.

After dismissal we were all silent and serious, until:

"I wonder if he thinks we're going to bite the Germans," said a giddy lieutenant, and the awful tension was lifted.

CHAPTER 11

Into the Flames of Glory

IT WAS ON June 1, 1918, that the 27th and 147th Squadrons took the short jump by truck and plane to Toul and roared like conquering heroes into the camp two miles out of town. Here we found the 94th and 95th. Those fine squadrons had begun operating over the front and our boys were all full of spiders and vinegar to get going with them. But before we were out of the trucks the front came to us. Two enemy ships, Rumplers, droned out of nowhere and circled over us so high in the sky that they were barely discernible. Our antiaircraft guns went after them but fell short at least a mile and a half, as the little fleecy white and black puffs of our archies dotted the heavens.

A couple of days later a German ship came scudding over and dropped a beautiful photograph of our airdrome, with a message on it, *"Welcome 27th and 147th. Prepare to meet thy doom."* Clever people, the Chinese! It was the finest air picture I had seen up to that time but I didn't let any of the crowd see it. By this time the 94th had chalked up seventeen victories and suffered only four casualties.

Major Raoul (French for Ralph) Lufbery, commander of the 94th, had been killed on May 19, just a few days before we arrived. Originally an aviation mechanic of Wallingford, Connecticut, Ralph had done outstanding work for the Lafayette Escadrille before America got into the war and is now honored as our third ranking ace, with seventeen German planes officially to his credit. Flying a Nieuport 28, he had engaged an enemy plane in a scrap that everybody knew must have seemed "easy meat" to him. But a fateful bullet entered the little *nourice,* the reserve gasoline tank by his elbow, and in a second his plane was aflame. Lufbery had instructed dozens of students and had always told them, "If your plane catches fire, don't jump. Stick with it and you may have a chance. If you jump there is no chance whatever." But when his own plane caught fire he jumped (or fell) 6000 feet and was impaled on a picket fence near the airdrome. The results were too horrible to discuss. When we arrived the French peasants were still making pilgrimages to his grave. They looked upon the airmen as the saviors of France and shed many tears over Lufbery's passing.

This brings up the vital matter of parachutes. Why our fliers didn't have them during the war I shall never know. Our balloon service had them and, as a result, lost only one man, First Lieutenant C. J. Ross of the 8th Balloon Company, whose parachute was set afire by sparks from his flaming balloon on September 26, 1918, as he was descending after an attack. Thirteen enemy pilots got down safely from planes our group destroyed in the last thirty days of the war. Every flier in our coming war must have efficient parachute equipment. It is now regulation. In the World War it would have saved us scores and scores of our aviators' lives. A parachute gives a flier more nerve and consequently lightens the important task of constantly building morale.

I inherited the little ancient stone house which had been Lufbery's billet and set up housekeeping very comfortably with my trusty orderly, the efficient Dudley. Shortly after we arrived we reported to the group adjutant and in him I found one of the most understanding officers I ever met in any army. He was Captain Philip J. Roosevelt, cousin of the great Teddy, and was later destined to be Operations Officer of the

Air Service of our entire First Army. When the war ended and all key officers were ordered to turn in frank reports concerning their views of that part of the air service which they had most closely observed, Phil obeyed promptly. Frank? His document of criticism was a masterpiece which was quickly suppressed and has never officially seen the light of day.

Officers and men were assigned to comfortable stone barracks. We found the hangars were of steel and very roomy. In addition to our four squadrons, part of the 122d French Escadrille was using the same hangars. This airdrome was the finest we encountered in our entire stay in France. What a relief to promenade on concrete walks after the ankle-deep mud of Epiez and Issoudun!

Walking around the officers' quarters to get acquainted, I encountered a familiar face, that of a lad named Curtiss whom I had known at Lake of Bays, Canada, when he was a very small boy. We became good friends. He had already been baptized in the blaze of German machine guns, had not been taken by surprise in his first combat and later became one of the best fliers in the 95th. The commanding officer of the group was Major Atkinson.

And now the war was supposed to stop for a few hours while Major John F. M. Huffer, commanding officer of the 94th, threw a party. Huffer was born in France of American parents but had never been in the United States. He had succeeded Lufbery as commander of the 94th and the gallantry he had absorbed through living in France all his life demanded that he welcome the two new squadrons with a real blowout. He invited all the American nurses he could find in the neighborhood, two dozen of them. And, in addition, he dispatched a spectacular young New York advertising man, Lieutenant O. J. Gude, Jr., to nearby Nancy with a couple of trucks to gather up all the serious French ladies he could find and a handful of chaperons, including the mayor's wife. It was an international gesture of a very complicating nature.

What a night! A combination American barbecue and gala French fête. At 4 A.M., after countless dances and beaucoups refreshments, we decided to call it a day. Everybody gathered on the field to sing "Lafayette, We Are Here!" And at just that moment the disreputable Germans decided to crash the party. Suddenly the sky was full of Boche bombers and Lieutenant Le Roy Prinz, most beloved officer of the 27th, was trying to lead everybody to the *abris,* or shell shelters. What confusion! The air was literally raining bombs. There were squeals and yells on all sides. But presently it was over. The Huns went home. Nobody was hurt. And the 27th and 147th had had their first baptism of fire— co-educationally. Oh, boy!

Strange as it may seem, little attention was paid at this party to alcoholic beverages. Plenty of American officers and soldiers, including aviators, got drunk in their spare time. But in our particular niche of the air service it was never a problem. The whole group had adopted the same attitude toward liquor that I had adopted long before—it was entirely up to the individual. A flier could indulge or not, according to his choice, but if, on any job, there was the slightest indication of his drinking habits prejudicing his work his ticket to the rear was as good as written. The men knew this and acted accordingly.

There was keen rivalry between the 27th and 147th for the vanquishment of the first Boche plane. We carried on regular patrols over our lines but it was a quiet sector and there were practically no enemy machines around. Long accustomed to the "Cook's Tour" idea of the Royal Flying Corps, which I know is correct, I decided to take my whole gang over en masse one day after we started our flight

patrols, less a small reserve on "alert." It worked perfectly.
I often wonder what the German ground troops thought
of this parade of eighteen ships in a sector where their air
service didn't even seem to be functioning. They must have
thought we were French because we still displayed the
French cocard on our wings and we were flying the very
latest Nieuport 28s, with their roaring motors that barked
worse than a modern 1000-horsepower Cyclone or Hornet.
God help humanity the day they silence airplane motors,
with air power in the hands of baby killers and mongrel
savages.

The Boche fliers were not fooling around our sector because a great light had burst on their General Staff. They
were giving all their attention to matters up on the Chemin
des Dames and farther north around Albert, in a last desperate effort to take Paris. They were just beginning to realize
what an opportunity they had lost earlier in the spring of
1918 by not pushing through when they had defeated the
entire British Second Army, and it was just beginning to
dawn on them that France was being inundated with hordes
of fresh and vigorous American troops.

Our patrols began June 2, 1918, the day after we arrived
at Toul. The first one, with five planes, was executed from
6 to 7:15 A.M. by Lieutenants Grant, McElvain, Hunt,
and Raymond of the 27th, led by Lieutenant Taylor of the
95th. This was followed by a patrol from 8:50 to 11:04
A.M. with five planes manned by Lieutenants Norton, Hudson,
Vasconcells, and Elliott, of our outfit, led by Lieutenant
Buford of the 95th and another from 11:30 A.M. to 1:30
P.M. consisting of our Lieutenants Miller, MacArthur, Rucker,
and Plyler, with Lieutenant Heinrich of the 95th as guide.
These flights, at around 16,000 feet, the first front line work
of our boys after their long months of training, covered the
territory behind our line of balloons from Commercy to Dieu-

lard to Bey. No enemy ships were encountered but the boys got a good look at many miles of No Man's Land. The patrols were repeated with similar results the next day with the addition of Lieutenants Clapp, Schmitt, Wanamaker, and Gunn and myself taking part. This went on day after day until June 6. Then, suddenly, two of our patrols got some action.

The first of these combats took place during the one-hour patrol of Lieutenants MacArthur and Miller, starting at 8:32 A.M. while escorting on a reconnaissance mission a biplane Spad which had arrived at our field the day before and whose French pilot and observer had been our guests overnight. There were no results on either side.

A couple of hours later MacArthur got into another fruitless combat and was quite a veteran by the end of the day. He was accompanied by Lieutenants Roberts and Rucker.

That isn't all that happened on June 6, 1918. Among other things, I lost Lieutenant Le Roy Prinz, the idol of every officer and enlisted man in the squadron. He wasn't killed, wounded, or made prisoner but he left us flat to get into Rickenbacker's squadron, the 94th, to be with a lifelong pal of his who was a pilot in that outfit. Lieutenant Fred Ordway of the 94th took his place with us in exchange. I didn't blame Prinz in the least but just before he left, he pulled a stunt for which I wanted to give him a couple of good swift kicks and nearly did. Rickenbacker was doing a lot of flying these days and almost every morning we would hear his big Monosoupape roar over us, sometimes with three or four others. Prinz had not been assigned a ship yet with us but he wanted to borrow one, fly it into the air and join one of Rick's patrols over the lines—to show Rick how good he was. And in selling this proposition he approached two weakminded people—Lieutenant Wanamaker and myself. Wanamaker explained it to me, thus:

"Major, Prinz wants to go up and join one of Rickenbacker's patrols. He's passed all tests on the Nieuport 28s but he says you won't let him have a machine. I'll lend him mine right now, if you'll approve it." "Please, Major," said Prinz. "I'm not mad at the Germans but I want to get up there and show 'em how it's done."

Here I made one of those decisions which I would reverse if I had it to do over again. I let Prinz go. Within eight minutes he was in the air. Like an old war bird he roared off the field and soared away to the east to try to catch Rickenbacker's outfit which had gone over a few minutes before. In due course Rickenbacker's crowd came back and Wanamaker and I dashed over to find out about Prinz.

"We saw him up there," said one of the boys, "but he wouldn't let us get near him. I 'piqued' on him and he started flying west, nose down and going like hell."

"There he is!" yelled Ack Grant, running up and pointing far off to the west. And sure enough a mighty buzz and Prinz was right over us, circling for a landing with motor full on. For some strange reason he tried to make it downwind, east to west, going great guns, as he dashed over the airdrome, scarcely touching the selector switch or buzzing his joy stick control. Zooming up he circled back and into the field—still downwind. This time patience failed him. Touch the wheels he must. If you have ever seen a schoolboy doing a series of perfect cartwheels, you have a mental picture of that plane from the moment the wheels contacted the ground. It literally went wing over wing until it collapsed, smashed into smithereens as only a Nieuport can fold up. We had an active little ambulance at the field and it was out there by the wreckage before Prinz could extricate himself from the pretty wings draped around him. He was not injured, only shaken up a bit. I could not tell, from the loud torrents of strong words and invectives, which burst simultaneously from Wanamaker and me, which of us was angrier at Prinz. And that gallant, as he was carted off in his stretcher, smiled blandly and said, "Well, Major, I'm not mad at the Germans, anyway."

If Prinz's stunt did any good it was this: it showed you could crash a Nieuport unmercifully and still walk away from it.

Most of our patrols were unfruitful. During the entire next week there was only one combat out of nineteen patrols over the lines. The enemy just didn't deign to give us a tumble. It was during this period that we were ordered to establish a system of "alert" work. Consequently, at stated hours, three or more ships would stand by on the airdrome ready to go at a moment's notice—which the Nieuports could do without warming up the motor. But apparently there was nothing to be "alert" about—no enemy planes. By now, also, I was encouraging each man to have his own plane to give him more assurance, more feeling of responsibility toward it and to help keep it in better shape. But ships were scarce and there were no American pursuit planes. In fact, during the whole war there weren't any. I always considered it better, anyhow, to use Allied planes for pursuit, rather than use up priceless cargo space on steamers for pursuit planes that lasted only twenty hours, on an average, before being shot to pieces or wrecked.

By this time I really believe I knew every flight commander, every leader and every officer in the 27th better than he knew himself. In addition to studying them constantly, I had taken each one of them on in mock combat and was so familiar with the way they handled their planes that I could almost name them without seeing them as they flew overhead. Now and always after, I made a deep study of the reports of every combat, every patrol, and every sortie (flight by an individual) and held quizzes on them. Did the leader fall back into reserve after launching the initial attack? Did so-and-so open fire before he had the muzzles of his guns in the enemy's cockpit? Did the leader display the patience of Job in the preliminaries to the engagement? Did the enemy spot my men before they discovered him? Did anyone dive away? Did you make full use of the sun? Did you watch the wind and drift? Did any guns jam up? Did our men use the surprise effectively? Who was that pulled out of that dive so abruptly? Why did our men break off to fight so soon? These and dozens of other questions followed every activity and the boys were full of pep and excitement. It was like a great, wild game, the sport of sports.

I had promised MacArthur, back at Amanty, when he beat me at pistol shooting, that I would retaliate by personally downing a Boche ship on the front before he did. This promise recurred to me on the beautiful evening of June 25, 1918, at Toul. At 6:30 the sun was still high and there was but a gentle zephyr blowing from north to south. The reports said it prevailed all the way up to 15,000 feet. Kenneth Clapp of Fort Wayne, Indiana, one of my flight commanders, was perched on the far end of the field, with MacArthur and Hill and their pretty camouflaged little ships, waiting for Hill to get going, on the evening "alert."

As I strolled over to them for a chat a strong hunch seized me—sort of an uncontrollable impulse.

"Gonny," said I, to Clapp, "you said you wanted to go over to Rozoy tonight after your alert. Why don't you and Freddie Norton buzz off right now? I'll stand your alert. There won't be anything doing."

Clapp didn't like this one bit.

"Now listen here, Major, you may be my CO but that's my ship. Why don't you get one of your own? I've got fifty more revs. out of that old Mono than any Frenchman could ever get. Albaugh and I drilled holes for that castor oil to circulate through the pistons better and she nearly tears my block off when I buzz the selector, yet keeps cool as a cucumber."

Before he had finished I had "borrowed" his helmet and goggles and had swung myself into the cockpit. And just as I did so an orderly rushed out and gave me a sealed envelope. By this time MacArthur and Hill were astride their steeds. We shouted "Contact" at almost the same second.

Down the field we raced and into the air. Headed northeast, the ground was falling away fast as we surged aloft. In those light planes we had a feeling that no pilot is going to have in the coming war with the heavy modern ships. As I have said, these little fellows responded more to the pilot's thought than to his touch. And sure enough, I had about fifty revolutions more than the others and bounced right ahead of them. They lined up nicely on either side, about two ship lengths back. Then, and only then, I uncrumpled the field orders the orderly had given me.

TO THE OFFICER COMMANDING 27TH SQUADRON ALERT: TWO EA AT 3000 FEET CIRCLING FOR ALTITUDE TEN KILO-METERS NORTH AND EAST OF METZ. YOU WILL DESTROY THEM AT ONCE. ROOSEVELT, OPERATIONS OFFICER, 1ST PURSUIT GROUP.

Surprise! It was up to me now. My superiors and subordinates had me right on the spot. OK! So be it. I wobbled my wings, the signal for attack, but I knew Hill and Mac would understand there was game ahead, but not at that spot or altitude. There was no other method of communicating the good news. In the coming war we will just talk to them by ultrashort wave radio over a secret wave length and discuss the whole matter thoroughly.

The tactics to follow were easy—just climb and climb into the sun. Get above them and when they dash over the line close in in back of them. The Lord gave me the best eyesight with which the human machine can be equipped and as we climbed east and north, I kept straining my eyes for a glimpse of our prey. Nearing the lines I gave the guns a little try-out. They answered sweetly and perfectly. "I wonder where all those bullets go?" I said to myself, as I always did when firing guns in the air. To this day I don't know the answer. There was no sign of the enemy. A false alarm, perhaps.

Just then a couple of puffs of enemy archie below us made me realize I had committed a faux pas. I was too far over the trench lines now and the enemy ships, even against the setting sun, might get the signal. Almost at the same moment my eyes caught a wing flash, at about our level, 10,000 feet, still north of Metz. But I could see no ship. On looking higher, however, there was an Albatross scout, a single seater, undoubtedly protecting the heavier two-seater which I could now make out below and way off in the distance. So up we went. Good old Hill, good old Mac. Right there, moving bank for bank with me, they must have been wondering what it was all about. Eleven thousand—twelve—thirteen—fourteen thousand—and on, up and up. The view was beautiful.

"Take your time," said I to myself. "The Germans are up to something."

For twenty-five minutes we played back and forth, giving the enemy time to gain altitude for his dash over the lines. We were now at 18,000 feet—more than three miles in the air. They were at 18,000 and 16,000 respectively, about eight miles downsun, east and south. Three of our ships to two of theirs, but three men on each side; on their side one on top and two in the big gun bus below.

Proceeding away from them, still climbing for all my Mono was worth, I was glancing back at Hill and MacArthur when the lower enemy ship banked abruptly and, nose slightly down, headed straight for Pont-a-Mousson and Toul—our airdrome. And then the upper ship did the same thing. As they crossed west, we crossed east and six miles north, over the lines and in back of them. The lower ship, slower than the fast scout above, seemed to hesitate as if its driver thought he should return. It would have done him no good.

Then an archie began to play behind us. What on earth's up? Either they are trying to fool the enemy and help us or there's an EA behind us. Too late now to figure that one out. Our ships were just about over Metz and the enemy archie was ominously silent. Another Boche behind us, sure as shootin'! Disregarding the upper EA I wobbled my wings for the attack on the two-seater below. For some reason Hill and MacArthur did not seem to follow me properly. Then suddenly, as if MacArthur had spotted the enemy for the first time, he overtook me. As I opened fire right into the rear cockpit of the Boche ship from above and right into the sun, MacArthur passed me, streaking like lightning. I let go three short bursts which killed the rear gunner instantly but did not stop the ship. Then, true to the teaching I had given my boys all the way from Texas to Toul, I pulled back, up into reserve and let MacArthur have him, which he did to the queen's taste.

Veering sharply and climbing to the left, I looked around for Hill. Where was he? Slightly to the left and above was the alarming answer to that question. In a beautiful, spinning nose-dive, Hill's machine was flicking past me earthward, his wings, green and white with dashes of red and cream, flashing in the glorious summer sunset. Streaks of smoke and fire from tracers and incendiary bullets were going clean through his ship and there above him, under perfect control, was the other EA, diving on him almost vertically, spitting death and cutting my pal to pieces.

At such moments the best of planes seems agonizingly slow and the air hard and sluggish as, straining at the shoulder harness, one tries to maneuver ship and guns into position to do a quick and needed job. But luck was with me. It took little effort. In the crosswires of my Aldis sight I could hold the EA with the greatest of ease as I gradually steepened my dive pouncing on him. He was heavier and seemed to dive faster than I. Hill, spinning down, was whirling like a falling maple seed. What a picture! Almost unbelievable! The EA pulled up slightly. I pulled, too—not the stick but the triggers of my guns. The poor chap in that scout plane was astounded. It was a complete surprise. He started to turn his black-helmeted head toward me but a sudden, shivering upward jerk of his ship's wings and I knew it was all over with him.

Down he went, seemingly still under control. "He's only wounded and is going to hedgehop home. Well, he can't fool me," I said to myself. But his glide grew flatter and flatter. Presently his ship fairly shuddered and then went off on one wing, into a spin, completely out of control. "Watch him, watch him—look behind but watch him," I murmured. Nowhere could I see a trace of Hill or MacArthur. I looked down at the falling German plane and saw him hit the ground. He seemed to be making it all right but his nose must have been steep down, for he cartwheeled and the white belly of his machine rolled over and over and glinted in the rays of the setting sun which had cost him his life.

"We got him, Philip," I said aloud, addressing my thoughts to Phil Roosevelt. "We destroyed them both as per orders. But they got poor old Hill. Maybe I should have done differently and jumped the top one first." My sense of victory—my sixth—and the gunner in the rear cockpit of the other machine—was mingled with remorse and self-blame. Perhaps I didn't look over my tail soon enough to spot the attack on Hill. He wasn't on the job, either.

I started to look for MacArthur. And there, up toward

Metz—I was now over Pont-a-Mousson—I spied another ship in a fleck of sunlight in the reddened sky. I caught a flash of red on the tail. That meant it was a friendly machine. It was Mac. Climbing like mad, and cutting corners, I was soon up with him and together we started home. Three had gone out; two were coming back. For a second I thought of three German families—with none coming back. Such is war.

With a roar, intermittently buzzing our joy stick switches, we arrived over our field. Taxiing to the hangar, the boys were already running out to greet us. "Where's Hill?" "Did you have a scrap?" "Gee! Look at this one!" pointing to a bullet hole through the machine-gun support not more than a foot from my head. "Yeah, but look at these," indicating a dozen holes in MacArthur's machine even nearer to his head.

I was tired, as always after a fight. I wanted to lie down and sleep. Sergeant Irwin Kruger came running up. "You're wanted on the field telephone, sir." It was good old Phil Roosevelt.

"Hill's down on our side and they're shelling him. But he's all right. You got the first one and in a few minutes we'll probably have confirmation from the balloon line on the second. It disappeared over a hill and the ground troops are not absolutely certain. But you got him all right. Good work, Hartney."

And then, with all the gall in the world, Ken Clapp came running up. "Some ship!" he exploded. "I knew you'd do it —you got it all shot up for me."

"The hell with you," I said sleepily. He was kidding. So was I.

From that moment on, not one word that I uttered nor any wish that I expressed was doubted or debated by my men, officers or enlisted. So far as discipline or confidence were concerned, it was the luckiest break I ever had in my life.

In the midst of all this carnage, mud, labor, and anguish, there came to me a brilliant flash of sweetness. On June 26, 1918, just as I had finished a long letter to Irene telling her of our exciting and victorious fight of the day before a cable message was handed to me announcing the birth that day of our second daughter, way back in Saskatoon, on the banks of the Saskatchewan, where Irene was staying with her sister, Isabel ("Ding Dong") and her brother Melville. For a few minutes I closed my eyes and mentally jumped the thousands of miles to that little hospital room where lay my beloved Irene and the mite she had brought into the world for me, and for our other darling daughter June. Then I wrote her another long letter pleading with her to name the baby Irene, after herself. In this, however, I was heavily outvoted, and the child was christened Doris, but has ever since been called by everybody Didi. Her advent gave me a new reason to love life—in the midst of death.

Our unit and our fliers were now suddenly elevated to the standing of the other squadrons in the 1st Pursuit Group. In the eyes of the high French command of which, up to that time, we were a part, our group was too good to be left any longer on a quiet sector with so much doing elsewhere and so much at stake. It was now "in the cards" that we should be shifted to a spot where Huns were plentiful and every patrol a dogfight.

Two days later the officers of all four squadrons were called to Group Headquarters. The Group commander, Major Atkinson, and Phil Roosevelt were there.

"Gentlemen," said Roosevelt, "we are about to be flattered and honored with some action. The German Army, in desperation but with complete organization and consistency, is about to make a stupidly belated drive on Paris. Already some vital units of the civil government in Paris have been evacuated. The German attack will take place some time about the middle of July. The 1st American Pursuit Group has been chosen to join its gallant French and British flying comrades in the coming battle. We will be stationed halfway between the apex on the front lines and Paris and we'll do our job to the best of our ability."

Then followed the usual details of movement. Everything was to be done with the utmost secrecy—at night—except the actual hop of the planes in daylight in a casual manner to avoid suspicion.

Learning just where we were to be stationed, I jumped into one of our little Nieuports and sneaked away for a lone voyage of discovery. By way of the Argonne Forest, then very quiet but later the graveyard of German hopes, and Rheims, I made my way over Château-Thierry, then just a spot on the map, now a name of world-wide fame, and Coulumniers to a little town called Saints. Near it was another small place by the name of Touquin. And it was there, on the wide fields of a local farmer, sixty acres, that the 27th and the rest of the 1st Pursuit Group were to get their first real high pressure test of modern warfare. Landing, I found only one hangar was in place and I wondered how the whole group, with 1600 men, could possibly find accommodations at that spot. A local resident gave me the tip that it might be within reason for one of the squadrons to occupy the Mirabeau Castle nearby, one of the most beautiful and historic castles in France, if M. Mirabeau could be persuaded we would take care of it. With a Machiavellian scheme in my mind, I set off home and after peeping at Paris and the *Folies Bergères* and Montmartre from 10,000 feet in the air I covered the hundred miles back to Toul and went into executive session with my supply officer, Russell Pruden, absolutely the best go-getter in the AEF. In a matter of minutes he was on his way to grab that castle for the 27th.

At this time the Boche were using Pfalz and Albatross scout ships. Their reconnaissance machines were Rumplers and LVGs with a few Halberstadts. The Huns confined most of their activity to artillery regulation although a number of photographic machines came over at extremely high altitudes. They were keeping particular tabs on the movement of rolling stock on the Nancy-Toul and Neufchâteau road. They avoided fights. Their heavier ships were no match for the lively Nieuports and their pilots were fully as inexperienced as ours. It was during this period also that we began to notice a great improvement in the accuracy of the German anti-aircraft gunnery. None of our ships was hit but they were coming darn close. Another discovery was the Flaming Onion. This was an archie missile of most peculiar habits. It burst with about the same sound as a high explosive but let loose a ball of fire which "corkscrewed" through the air in ever widening circles, much like the "Nigger Chaser" of Fourth of July fame. A terrifying beastie to meet in the air!

It was on June 23, 1918, that the 27th celebrated its first birthday. Since its arrival at Toul it had brought down four Boche planes and suffered only one casualty—Lieutenant Plyler on June 13 had the bad luck to become a German prisoner but came through his incarceration for the rest of the war in good shape. He was a gallant lad and we missed him.

Part of the squadron moved from Toul on June 25. I stayed behind with the rest until the next day and that night the Germans decided to give us a good strafing with bombs. It was terrifying, as all bombing raids are, but harmless as usual when tiny bombs are dropped—just a few holes in the airdrome. The next day, the 27th, we left by car and truck. At Touquin we found the airdrome, although small, ideal for the light, quick-rising Nieuports. The officers and men of the group moved into various residential quarters on four sides of the field. Pruden had done his work well. The 27th got the castle. It was a Paradise. Leading eight of my officers on a tour of the estate we came upon a simple wooden cross. It was the grave of a British infantry colonel who had sacrificed his life in this war four years previously, in the First Hundred Thousand, when some of my boys were still in knee pants. It gave us a sober and reverent pause. Near the grave I took a picture of my eight fliers. Within four days six of them had been killed, wounded, or taken prisoner.

Carefully, we put cheesecloth on the stairs of the 900-year-old château to protect them from our muddy boots. Each officer had a room about an acre square and one of them actually had white bedsheets. Some war! The next morning our first orders arrived:

GET INTO THE AIR AND LOOK AROUND. GET TO KNOW EVERY FOOT OF GROUND FOR THIRTY MILES ON EVERY SIDE OF THE AIRDROME. YOU'LL RUN INTO EARLY MORNING GROUND HAZE BUT YOU MUST BE ABLE TO GET BACK EVEN IF YOU HAVE TO SKIM THE TREETOPS.

Officers and men were on their toes. Every plane was in perfect condition. We found, much to the surprise of the French factory representatives, that we could get thirty hours' life out of their engines between overhauls against their best —twelve hours. Sergeant Albaugh, an expert on lubrication and cooling, had conceived the idea of drilling holes in the pistons and doctoring up the fragile little engine so that the oil circulation, for cooling the pistons (still novel in 1940), was improved and the machine worked with much greater reliability than before. Literally all one did with that engine was to pour raw gasoline and castor oil into the crankcase and let her go. Now, in 1940, we are about to go into fuel injection in our aviation motors and do away with the carburetor entirely. That Monosoupape motor had all this in 1918. A bullet through one of the cylinders and pistons meant little because the boys would work all night, change the cylinder, piston, and even the crankshaft assembly and the plane would be all ready in the morning.

The second day at Touquin we practiced all day taking off in full squadron formation and the 147th, 94th, and 95th did likewise. Great rivalry developed for speed and perfection. It was astonishing how quickly the squadrons could get into the air, actually in formation and soar off with complete balance and control. Scarcity of planes was our worst trouble. At this time the 27th had only eighteen which was not enough for its pilots and we had none in reserve. And usually only about ten or twelve were really ready for duty.

Having organized our squadron into a smooth, harmonious homogeneous unit, an inspection from up top was in order. To my surprise and delight we were visited by two of America's first fliers—General Benjamin Foulois and Colonel Frank Lahm. I had never met them before but as a young lad had been a hero-worshiper of each. General Foulois was the first chief of the American Air Service, way back, I think, in 1909, when he received a total of five hundred dollars as the first annual Army Air Service appropriation. The modern super-flying fortress carries over four thousand gallons of gasoline now in one loading, costing about $650, or more than "Benny," as we all got to know him, had to spend in an entire year on the whole Army effort! Colonel Lahm, on the other hand, was the man who had flown with Orville Wright at Fort Myer and is today still in active service and one of our most distinguished and gallant flying officers attached to II Corps Headquarters at Governors Island, New York.

They marveled at our being able to get a whole squadron of eighteen planes off the ground from dead cold motors in formation in ninety seconds but they didn't marvel half as much as some of our modern experts today who won't believe that we ever did it. Today it takes about five times as long, at least, if one wants to be sure he won't blow a cylinder head or a spark plug.

And now we came around to an important anniversary in my life, July 1, 1918—just two years after my first really big fight in the air up on the northern front with the RFC. The boys of the 27th didn't realize something of which I was certain. Up to now, although they had acted splendidly and were highly efficient and full of bubbling enthusiasm and courage, they had only been playing at aerial warfare and the few combats we had experienced were only a foretaste of what was to come. I was certain that soon, perhaps on the morrow, we would run into a very long stretch of gory battles with great numbers of enemy machines and no chance to rest between combats. Richthofen had been killed by Roy Brown of Canada but his "Flying Circus," the "Checkerboards" as they nicknamed those waspish camouflaged little ships, had been taken over by Udet, Germany's greatest flier at that moment, and I had had a tip from Intelligence that they were about to swarm the skies and put on a grand show for us.

On the night of June 30, the château seemed snug and "homey." The "bully beef" tasted better than ever and Lieutenant "Bugs" Raymond's violin added to the feeling of repose as he played Mendelssohn's *Spring Song*—now brutally and imbecilically outlawed in Germany because its composer was a Jew. Such childishness! I didn't feel like asking Dudley to bring me my cornet. I was full of foreboding.

Next day I sent the whole squadron aloft for the aerial push I was sure would start on that day. But July 1 came and passed without incident. So that night I called a conference of all my pilots in the main salon of the château and told them the whole story of the great battle of July 1, 1916, of the 20th Squadron of the RFC.

The boys were fairly wild with enthusiasm and frantic to get into a big scrap like that. So, with permission from Phil Roosevelt, I issued the following order:

27th Aero Squadron, S. C.
Operations Office
1st Pursuit Group
July 1, 1918

Operations Order No. 47

1—The following schedule of operations for the 27th Squadron is announced as effective for tomorrow, July 2, 1918, by Group Operations Office

2—The entire 27th Squadron will be on Alerts, viz:

From 4 hours (4 A.M.) to 7 hours 30 and from 12 hours 30 to 16 hours 30 (4:30 P.M.)

This meant that instead of three planes being "on alert" at stated intervals, every pilot in the squadron must be at his machine at four o'clock for three and a half hours, and again in the afternoon, ready to take off at an instant's warning. I had arranged the squadron in two flights, Norton commanding one, Hudson the other.

I believe I dashed five times in a motorcycle sidecar from the Group Headquarters down to the 27th hangar between 3 A.M. and 6:15 that beautiful sunny morning.

"My whole gang's down there, rarin' to go," I said a dozen times.

"Down where?" asked Phil. They were always kidding us about our château. "In the castle—sleeping in?"

"No siree. Give me the order and you'll see the best squadron in the world do a real job."

The conversation was abruptly interrupted by the field telephone. Phil raised his tousled red head.

"All right, Major, do your stuff. French headquarters report an enemy squadron has just taken off from near Fere-en-Tardenois and means business."

I called Lieutenant Dupuy down at the tarmac, or parking space in front of the hangar, and with a mighty roar those nine Monosoupapes, cold, went into action and the whole nine were actually in the air within ninety seconds. This could not be duplicated today starting with cold motors. In them were Lieutenants Norton, Grant, Wanamaker, Hoover, Elliott, Hudson, Schmitt, Rucker, and MacArthur.

It is hard for me to write about a fight in which I didn't participate, and which I didn't even see. But it was a corker, the greatest to date for the 27th. At 20,000 feet, over Etrepilly-Verdilly, north and east of Château-Thierry, Hudson's flight was suddenly attacked by nine enemy ships of the Richthofen Circus and the party was on.

The Germans thought they had a two-to-one advantage but they failed to spot Norton and his crew way above them. They knew about it soon enough, however, when Norton's men dived on their tails like death spitting comets. It was an even fight—nine against nine—fliers of about equal skill but with greater experience on the side of the Germans. To offset this we had the superior maneuverability of our faster and better climbing little Nieuports against the sluggishness of the Boche Fokker D VIIs. Formations broke up immediately and there was a grand mêlée. Around and around they milled, everyone trying to gain altitude for diving and all having a terrible time.

Suddenly a wave of gun jamming set in among our new Marlin machine guns. When Norton caught the second Hun echelon at the old trick of trying to get around and behind our first flight he fairly threw his four planes at them and when he had both his guns practically sticking into the cockpit of the leader he pulled his triggers. What happened? Zero. Ordinarily that Boche and his plane should have been almost instantly on a quick trip to the ground but with both guns jammed Norton was helpless. But he did not quit the fight. As leader, but unable to clear his guns, he continued to wheel and dodge and stayed in the thick of the combat.

This dizzy battle lasted for thirty-five minutes, then both sides, getting low on gas, broke away. Our boys had engaged in thirty-two combats. We had definitely brought down four Boche machines. We got official credit for only two but by this time the boys were getting accustomed to this. It is heartbreaking to risk your life in mortal combat, vanquish your enemy and then receive no credit for it. It is my honest belief that the 27th and, in fact, the whole 1st Pursuit Group, brought down fully twice as many German airplanes as were ever officially confirmed for them, while credit for many of their victories went to French outfits that weren't within miles of us at the time. Every flier going into any future war must steel himself against these disappointments, which will surely happen again and which, in the excitement of war, with battles proceeding on the ground as well as in the air, are inevitable. It must have happened to the German fliers as well.

Almost all of our pilots had seen two American machines go down and they returned home with heavy hearts. They knew whose planes they were: Elliott's and Wanamaker's— two of our very finest officers.

"Cap" Elliott was killed and his death cast a pall of intense grief over all of us for days. After the Armistice I sent Captain Rankin, commanding officer of my park squadron, the supply and mobile depot unit that accompanied the Group, back over the ground to see if he could find any traces of Elliott. And he found him. He was identified by a big gold tooth. At the same time Captain Rankin found the body of his own son, a Marine, who had been killed at about the same time nearby. War is like that.

We mourned equally the loss of Wanamaker. But here we were luckier. A little later we learned he had been brought down by Udet and made a prisoner and spent the rest of the war in various German prison camps. I see Judge Wanamaker every once in a while now out in Akron, Ohio, and we always fight the war all over.

That night I went to Elliott's room in the château. Fred Norton was there with tears in his eyes packing up Elliott's things.

"Yesterday Elliott got actually ill in his plane," he said. "He was deathly afraid you'd find it out and send him to the rear. I wish to hell you had."

Elliott had a Boston bull pup which he had willed to Norton in case he passed on. That night Norton told me I was to take the dog if the Germans got him, too. Eighteen days later the dog was mine. I had it for ten days. Then some passing French troops, of whom I have an excellent picture, swooped him up and I never saw him again.

And so the war moved along its sad, exciting, and bloody way. Almost every day I went out with the entire squadron, with from ten to thirteen planes, especially to spot what the enemy was doing in preparation for his big final push around Château-Thierry. And he was doing plenty. German ground troops were literally filling the salient with piles of ammunition, crudely camouflaged by the roadsides. It was obvious big doings were in the offing. Combats were few and far between and without results.

Everything was quiet around our camp in the early evening of July 7, when suddenly twenty snappy British Sopwith Camels came along and sat right down on our lawn.

"The whole British 5th Pursuit Brigade is coming here in the morning, sir," said one of the young English public school-boys, jumping out of his plane. "What's going on here, anyway? Must be something brewing."

The next morning one hundred ships, the whole 5th Brigade, under the great British flying man, General Sir Hugh "Boom" Trenchard, moved in on us, with Bristol fighters, big Handley-Page bombers and a mosquito fleet of Sopwith Camels. And we moved three miles up the road, nearer to the lines, to a little place called Saints where the airdrome was smaller but plenty big enough for our beloved little Nieuports.

Good-bye, our beautiful château. It was a sad and disturbing move. Some of the other officers and I were quartered in the Hotel de Marie. It looked unoccupied when we arrived but we found this to be a fallacy. It had been used as an Arabian hospital and to our sorrow the Arabs had left behind billions of those overfriendly little things known throughout the armies as cooties. The place was alive with them, and so, presently, were we. The other officers and men were similarly attacked and this, coupled with intense heat, made most of us move outdoors and live in our pup tents. And when a soldier voluntarily sleeps in a pup tent there must be a strong reason for it, very strong. The pup tent, like the overseas cap, is an invention of the devil.

This brings up another point, one of the real horrors of war—the lack of bathing facilities. Nobody in any of the armies ever had enough baths. Perhaps there were armies in which this didn't matter so much, but with the English, American, and Anzacs the absence of proper bathing facilities wherever we went, in all camps and all French towns and cities, was one of the real hardships of the war. It is easy to accustom yourself to a morning shave with a little steel mirror stuck in the bark of a tree and water secured from beneath the ice in a mud puddle or farm cow yard. But thousands of us used to go to sleep at night dreaming, not of the deadly danger in which we were living or even

of our loved ones at home, but of the lost ecstasy of getting
loose in a modern tiled bathroom with real plumbing facilities
and plenty of hot water and soap and big clean rough white
towels. It was the American and British soldiers' idea of
heaven. We hated ourselves. I never want to see another
cement footprint or leaky overhead dripping shower pipe in
my life. Go through the physical activity of war in the field
for three weeks without a bath and you'll know what I mean.

We hated to leave Touquin but I was most happy to find
that my old pal and flight commanding officer in the RFC
20th, Major Reginald Maxwell, was there and I looked forward to spending some pleasant time with him before we
were both bumped off. By this time England was taking
the airplane rather seriously, spurred by a tremendous German daylight bombing raid on the lines, and had organized
the independent Royal Air Force, to which all members of
the old Royal Flying Corps had been transferred.

Maxwell was glad to see me and that went double. Perhaps I boasted a little too much about our snappy little
Nieuports. Anyhow, when I left him, I knew there was a
spectacular demonstration coming of what his Camels could
do.

Sure enough, the next day, July 10, 1918, Maxwell, coming back from a patrol with some of his boys, staged a mock
dogfight right over our airdrome at about 100 feet altitude.
It lasted about five minutes and such diving and hell raising
you never did see. I lost my breath running over to our
hangar and before they were gone I was in the air in my
trusty Nieuport, determined to hang a few raspberries on
Maxwell himself. But they were low on gas and promptly
disappeared. So, to prevent my boys from gaining any impression that the British ships were better than ours, I put
on the damnedest one-man show I ever attempted, before or
since. That Monosoupape was my pet engine and I had no

fear of it stopping if I nursed it closely at every move. At very low altitude but very high speed I proceeded to do everything Maxwell and his crowd had done and then some. Up to that time I had not fully realized what I could do and I did things I had never attempted before. Two loops were literally right off the ground, although I made sure that I had plenty of reserve speed to get out of a dive before coming on down to get into it.

Temporarily I had forgotten I was now a part of the U. S. Army in which much of the authority in the air service lay with swivel chair ground officers behind the lines who knew nothing about flying. As soon as I landed a document was handed to me: COMPLIMENTS OF THE GROUP COMMANDER, MAJOR HARTNEY WILL PLEASE REPORT AT ONCE, ETC.

Unlike the Winchester incident in which I got blazes for not wearing my spurs, I knew pretty well what was coming. As I walked briskly in to see Major Atkinson, I could see a twinkle in the eyes of Phil Roosevelt, the operations boss, and Sergeant Major Cunningham.

"My God!" Atkinson exploded, fairly raging. "Are you crazy?"

"What's the matter, sir?"

"Are you going to set an example for our officers like that? Are you going to let those blighters of Englishmen lead you astray and kill yourself? Don't you know those fellows are just plain crazy? You can't do that."

I could have smacked him in the eye. Maxwell crazy! A veteran of four years of front-line flying and one of the best in the world! But I was very docile.

"Well, sir," I replied, "I know all this is foolish. I know nobody would stunt like that even if he's an expert flier, but this was an emergency and I've warned the pilots that they must not try to do likewise. But those Englishmen came over here. They had been boasting that our tails are too long, our motors unreliable and our ships so logy they couldn't get out of their own way. I just couldn't let our men get the idea we have inferior ships. It would kill their morale. As a matter of fact, our ships are better but nothing will kill a ship quicker than a whispering campaign." (And how true that statement is to this day.)

"Well," said Atkinson, actually shivering. "You just can't do that around here. I'm going to forget it this time but, by God, if you pull that phony stuff again, you're through."

So that was that. Nuts!

CHAPTER 12

Chateâu-Thierry—
Our First Big Test

NOW WE MUST be getting along with the war, because the war was getting closer to us and most uncomfortable. The great final drive of the Germans came just when we expected it, July 15, 1918. On the 13th our Group was inspected by the snappiest and, by the pilots, the most idolized officer in the American Air Service—also the one who knew most what aviation was all about—General Billy Mitchell, and General Henri Giraud, who ranked second to Foch in the French Army. It should have been a gala day. When I had been serving with the 20th RFC and the Prince of Wales, had visited us, caterers were flown over from London with the finest foods and wines and perhaps His Highness thought this was our regular fare. When Maxwell had given the 27th a blowout a few days back he had imported a caterer with supplies from Paris. We could not return his hospitality because our pay checks had been sent to some wild destination through a mistake of some muddleheaded quartermaster. We were all broke and our only affluent officer, Lieutenant O. J. Gude, Jr., had lost his all in a dice game.

When the great French general and his natty staff were dashed into our field by the immaculate Billy Mitchell in one of the latter's beautiful Mercedes cars, we thought, of course, our high command would put on a meal worthy of the occasion and the importance of our guests. Imagine our chagrin when we were ushered into a tent with plain pine tables with no linen, thick sandwiches of army beef and plain thick china army cups full of water. Water for a French general! In a land where every child is taught that unbottled water is practically poison and where sanitary conditions are such that it practically is!

The orderly serving this ghastly meal was in shirt sleeves, dirty, insolent, and slovenly. It was a disgrace to us and to our entire army. I have often wondered since what General Mitchell and General Giraud thought of the 1st Pursuit Group about which they had heard so much favorable comment. The incident simply showed the inability of some of our citizen-officers to grasp the importance of military etiquette. It will happen again.

The next day Lieutenant Quentin Roosevelt of the 95th Squadron, son of the great Teddy, came to my quarters and asked me for the loan of any officers of the 27th who could play musical instruments to help the 95th hold a party in honor of France's greatest holiday, July 14, in the Hôtel de Ville, in Coulumniers.

"How would you like 'Blow-Hard' Hartney to come to your party with his cornet?" I asked.

"Swell," said he. "Who is he?"

"He's the petit major of the best flying squadron in all France and he can blow the insides out of a tootle-horn."

"By gosh," he beamed. "Are you the one who blows that horn at night and plays that old hymn I used to hear so much at Oyster Bay? Can you play marches and popular airs?"

"I'll be there with bells on and plenty of wind," I promised.

The party was a social and musical success. "Bugs" Raymond, with his fiddle, tried to compete with me and we had about a dozen other assorted instruments. Probably the sounds we made would not pass muster at the Metropolitan Opera House but we and our audience enjoyed it and Quentin had the time of his life leading us in imitation of Charlie Europe, the great colored leader of the 365th Infantry Band, by far the best band in the AEF. That was Quentin Roosevelt's last night on earth. He was killed next day in a patrol over the lines and I'll have more to tell about this a little later on.

I shall never forget July 15, 1918, as long as I live. It seemed as if the whole German Army, in desperation, simply hurled itself at our part of the lines around Château-Thierry. Our boys were in the air practically all the time. I had turned my own machine over to one of the pilots. Frantic orders came through asking us, high flying pursuit planes, to skim the ground and try to fix the position and extent of the German advance, to try and determine how far over the Marne the Boche had reached. It was the ultimate of frenzied excitement. Allied troops of all kinds were rushing by us in both directions, French going back on relief, waves of Americans going forward. It was the climax of the war.

Twice I went out myself in the only crates I could find, two new British Camels on which the guns had not yet even been hooked up. With no armament, all I could do, with fully armed German planes dashing at me from all sides, was to take a quick "look-see" and run like hell toward home.

The boys were magnificent. I could not begin to put into words my admiration of the way they acted that day, and for many days after. MacArthur, particularly, appointed himself a committee of one to stop the whole German Army by strafing the troops crossing the pontoon bridges at Dormans and elsewhere on the Marne. I would dearly love to know just what damage he did that day. Time and again he came in, filled up with gasoline and bullets and rushed out again. He flew a total of seven and a half hours, emptying all his ammunition on the ground troops and hurrying back for more.

None of my officers flew less than five hours that terrible day. In fact, the damage to our machines got so bad that I finally had to forbid them to go out any more because all of them had so many bullets holes in their wings and vital parts that I was afraid they would fall apart from bullet-hole fractures and we would be out of the battle entirely. We started work at 3:30 A.M. with fifteen planes and the last machine landed after 9 P.M. A busy day! While our men had constant combats with individual Boche planes and several times saw high flying enemy formations of up to thirty ships, which did not come down for battle, we did not lose a man.

Next morning, July 16, things were very serious. The Germans had broken through our lines and some were reported as far back as Epernay, south and west from Château-Thierry. I could not believe this and, on the evening patrol allotted to the 27th, I decided we would fly both high and low and get at the truth of the matter. In the morning the boys went out with twelve ships and got themselves into a lot of miscellaneous fights. And here we lost a fine officer who had been with the squadron since its early weeks, Lieutenant B. Malcolm Gunn of Chester, Pennsylvania. The spot where he fell was simply pulverized by artillery and, although I exhausted every effort after the Armistice, no trace of him or his plane was ever found.

At 6:30 the evening patrol took off with eleven planes and I followed in my gunless Camel. Fred Norton was leading and the way he handled the boys was marvelous. His ships were faster than mine but by cutting corners and climbing without the weight of ammunition, gear, or guns, I was able to keep contact. And suddenly, over Château-Thierry at 18,000 feet, there was a terrific fight. It was truly a battle royal. I can remember enemy and friendly ships in about equal numbers, whirling around madly with streaking tracer bullets flying all over the place and that familiar and highly distressing *zip-zip-zip* of bullets whistling past your ears. In no time at all we were down to 1500 feet and over Epernay where I didn't believe there were any Germans. And here Lieutenant R. F. "Bugs" Raymond, Jr., made his exit from active service in the jolly old war.

The attack broke off and we started for home. But before I knew it we were again in the midst of a lot of strangers. Suddenly I looked around me. Not one of our planes was in sight, nothing in fact except two mean-looking Fokkers coming at me with guns blazing. Helpless, I immediately went into some diving, circling acrobatics and the two Huns decided to call it a day and dived for home. By this time I was more or less frantic with the excitement and completely forgot I was entirely unarmed. I followed after the Fokkers for five miles or more and years after the war "Bugs" Raymond, now a happy real estate man in Hartford, Connecticut, told me about it. He had been shot to earth by Udet himself. He was positive he was coming down well within our lines. Suddenly, from nowhere, dozens of helmeted German soldiers pounced upon him and he was a prisoner of war.

As they grabbed him he looked up and saw a lone Camel which he recognized. It was his totally harmless CO, blissfully sailing over at about 1500 feet, with the sky flecked with enemy ships. He says he wanted to signal me to go back. Of course that was out of the question. I'm glad he didn't try. I couldn't have seen him and he would have been shot instantly. Anyhow, I came to my senses soon and pedaled for Saints, where I found the remnants of a bedraggled and weary outfit but a victorious one. The stragglers were coming in all night. We suffered no casualties except the loss of Raymond and in the day's work "Red" Miller had officially brought down two German balloons and Vasconcells and Clapp a biplane Rumpler each.

From this time on for more than a week our pilots and mechanics were on the job for eighteen and twenty-one hours a day. The war situation was discouraging and, with the Germans swarming all over the place, it looked as if the Allied cause was about to collapse. At this juncture, July 17, after fourteen of us had gone out on an early morning patrol and MacArthur and Roberts between them had brought down one biplane Rumpler, I took things somewhat into my own hands and packed up two trucks with spare parts and supplies and with a few enlisted men moved them back to Melun, thirty miles away. I was mindful of the manner in which the Germans had broken through the lines up north in the spring and the British fliers had had to take up rifles and retreat on foot, shooting, while whole squadrons of airplanes and equipment fell intact into the hands of the enemy. I was determined to have some reserves on hand in case the worst came to the worst. But it never came.

At 5 A.M. the next day, from a grandstand seat 20,000 feet in the air, while leading a formation of sixteen planes, I witnessed the famous Allied counterattack of July 18, 1918.

No man ever saw a more magnificent or, rather, a more significant sight. Here was the tide of a world war involving twenty million men actually turning before my very eyes. The Americans, fresh, vigorous, and engaging in their first major battle, were sweeping across the Marne, outflanking the famous Prussian Guard and actually setting it back on its heels. It was the beginning of the breakup of what, at the start of the war, had been the greatest military machine ever known—the German Army.

The stirring and bloody events transpiring at that moment on the ground have been pictured in print time and again, in many ways and from many angles. My assignment was in the air and I must stick to that. We could not, of course, tell what was really going on below us except fragmentarily. In future aerial warfare the fliers at the front in a great battle, those who survive, will be fully informed by ultrashort wave radio of the trend and many of the details of events "down there." Until the arrival of aircraft one of the surest ways to defeat an enemy was to "turn his flank." In future hostilities "flanks" will be turned, not at the side, but over the third dimension up top.

We were flying very high, four miles up, when the barrage started, the ground being churned to powder by artillery and the air full of smoke and dust. Strangely enough, although we saw several groups of twenty-five and thirty German planes flying high in formation, they did not give us an argument. Our complete squadron patrols that day were at 5:10, 9:35 A.M. and 7 P.M. with sixteen, fourteen, and eleven planes at an average of 7500 feet. We didn't have a single combat in the air, nor did we have a casualty except that Schmitt and Hunt had to squat in strange but friendly territory. Hunt came home late. Schmitt was slightly wounded and was parked in a French hospital.

The wounding of Schmitt brings up another matter. In modern warfare every flight in every air squadron should have at least one capable, sympathetic but stern doctor. In the 1st Pursuit Group we had only seven doctors for six squadrons consisting of 1450 men and 150 officers. It was not enough. Health standards were not alarmingly low, because the boys were young and leading a clean, outdoor life but many times minor ailments which a flight surgeon could have alleviated and physical defects he could have discovered were allowed to grow into serious matters.

Schmitt was an example. His eyesight was such that he never should have been allowed to participate in front-line activities of any kind. In fact, if he had not faked his tests he would probably have been rejected for any Army service. I did not know this until I observed him in several aerial combats. Huns would slip up on him and he would never know it until bullets began flicking through his windshield or tearing at his gas tank. Although he was credited with helping to bring down two Fokkers on July 2, 1918, I considered him a menace to himself and to the other fliers.

The second day of the great Allied counteroffensive, July 19, I called him to my office.

"Look here, Schmitty, old topper," I said. "You're as blind as a bat."

"What do you mean?" he asked.

"I mean that somehow I've got to send you back to the rear before you get killed," I replied.

"Oh, don't do that," he pleaded. "No one will ever understand. I just haven't been quick enough on the trigger. They won't catch me again. Please let me go on a few more days and then if I come back with any more bullet holes near my head, I'll ask to be sent back; you won't have to order it."

What could I do with a spirit like that? I weakened. That afternoon he flew off blithely with a patrol. A Boche gunner planted a nice clean bullet hole in the seat of Schmitty's pants and he was sent home, a "Blighty," with honors. He is now living happily in Cleveland, instead of resting under the squashy sod of France. An amusing incident, perhaps, but others were not so funny. They could all have been avoided by a qualified doctor exclusively for pilots for each squadron or even each flight.

Thanks to our doughboys near us and the other Allied troops along the line, the enemy was chased so far back, especially in the vicinity of Fere-en-Tardenois that we had precious little aerial fighting to do in the next few days and most of our missions were strafing ground troops and protecting various squads of photographic planes, mostly French.

It is impossible to give a careful report of the dizzy lives we were leading or of the mental condition of the men. The war psychosis was upon us in full force. Officers and enlisted men alike forsook their own thoughts entirely and gave their minds and energies solely to the destruction of the enemy. We lived, fought, and worked as one man—3 A.M. to 10 P.M. and later, every day. Self was forgotten. So were our folks at home, so were death and even life, everything except the job at hand. I have never before or since seen such desperate, unselfish, complete co-operation between human beings. It was superb—a priceless asset in war. Unfortunately, however, this was not the general condition throughout the Army but only in those units where a companion spirit reigned between the commanders and the command. I can go no further with this subject without causing controversy. But I hope, in any future conflict, the War Department will give attention to the vital matter of "public relations" in the various outfits and spend some time inculcating in officers and men a real desire for enthusiastic co-operation, free of military politics and bulldozing, and with some very genuine patriotism. The American soldier, well able to think for himself, will respond to this treatment a hundred per cent.

The next day I wandered over to Touquin to see my old friend, Maxwell. He was nowhere to be found so I paid my respects to the commander of the whole 5th Brigade, RAF, at the front. I called on him, and what he told me set my teeth to chattering.

"We are moving out of here in the morning," he said. "We have suffered losses worse than you will ever know. You probably heard that big German ammunition dump exploding all day yesterday. Well, it cost us dozens of pilots and dozens of planes to get it. One outfit alone lost fifty per cent of its fliers. I hate to leave you chaps here. The enemy now outnumbers us in this salient three to one. When we pull

out they'll outnumber you at least six to one. Your boys
have the guts of the devil. They're too brave. Warn them of
the enemy's superior numbers. Don't let them take unnecessary chances. The Allies need every man you've got."

That night when I repeated the words to my flight commanders they actually beamed. Not a trace of fear or appre-
hension was in their earnest young faces. The next day was
one of the most disastrous in the history of the 27th Squadron.

About seven o'clock in the evening after a busy day testing
new machines and guns, five of the boys went out on a voluntary patrol to practice some new combat formations. I waved
to them as they took off. That was the last I ever saw of Fred
Norton and MacArthur and the last I saw of Miller until after
the war, my three most trusted and substantial officers. From
Roberts and Dawson, the only ones who came back, I learned
the news that knocked me out completely—blown far into
German territory by a storm and attacked by seven Albatrosses, Norton and MacArthur were killed, Miller brought
down and captured.

Good old Freddie Norton, all-American football star (Norton Field at Columbus, Ohio, is named after him), the
very highest type of officer, a wonderful flier—in that sky
battle he received a bullet in the chest but managed to wiggle
away from his attackers and flopped down among our troops
in the front lines. The roads were congested with supplies
and artillery. It took two days to get him to a hospital. During the first night he developed pneumonia. He died in a
truck and just before he breathed his last, he scribbled five
words which I still treasure—*"Twenty-seventh, more power
to you."* That was Fred Norton. He had been an inspiration
to all of us and had brought down two German planes.

MacArthur, an electrical engineer from Buffalo, one of
our first aces, destroyer of seven German planes and count-

less ground troops, was one of the most skillful and most gallant officers on the front. Again I say the most agonizing thing about war, aside from your own suffering if wounded, is the heart pain when your beloved companions are suddenly snatched away from you.

We were cheered, however, by news of "Red" Miller two days later—safely in the hands of the enemy. This young college boy was hard luck's favorite child. One day, back at Toul, returning from a patrol, he actually cut off with his propeller the head of a Frenchman who was mowing our field. Then he accidentally set fire to his machine and burned it up along with one of our hangars. When captured he had been officially credited with bringing down two German planes and one observation balloon. After the war he graduated from Princeton and became a doctor. In 1920 I flew to Princeton and met him and several others of my surviving officers completing their interrupted college careers there. A year later he bought an old Italian Savoia-Marchetti plane and started on a transcontinental flight. Shortly after the start he got into a spin and was killed.

In six days we had lost seven officers and two a few days before that. Nine new ones were sent to us as replacements on July 23 and 25, 1918, splendid boys, all of them, but sadly in need of advance training which we were almost too busy to give them. Among the lot were two of the greatest fliers that ever wore the American or any other uniform— Frank Luke, Jr., and J. F. Wehner. Of them, more later.

I shall never forget the day those nine eager, brave, intelligent American boys lined up before me in headquarters.

"You men stand in front of me today," I told them. "Within two weeks each and every one of you will be dead —cold dead—unless you weigh what I say.

"You are going to be surprised in the first, second, or third trip over the line and, despite all I can say right now, you will never know there is an enemy ship near you until you notice your windshield disintegrating or until a sharp sting interrupts your breathing.

"School is all over. You have a man's job. You hold a commission. You are the right hand of the President of the United States, himself. If when you get up there over the lines you find you want to come back that means you're yellow. I do not ask you to be brave enough to go over, I only ask you to have enough guts to come back and tell me so and get to hell out of this outfit.

"Remember, we are about two hundred officers up here all told. You are now members of the 27th Squadron in the 1st Pursuit Group, the finest flying outfit on this front. Back home there are 50,000 young men learning to fly and eager to be where you are. But you are in the 27th in name only. When you have shown your buddies out there that you have guts and can play the game honestly and courageously, they'll probably let you stay. You'll know without my telling you when you are actually members of this gang. It's up to you."

Nine fine young men saluted and retired.

How true were my words! All of these men became brave, skillful pilots. But when Armistice Day rolled around on November 11, only three, Hewitt, Harkins, and Donaldson were present. All the rest had been killed. But those six had officially brought down 26 German planes or balloons and Hewitt and Donaldson had accounted for one each.

Busy, busy, frantic days. The new boys took hold in splendid fashion and all of them showed the mettle demanded to belong to the 27th Squadron. Much of our time was spent teaching them the technic of formation and combat flying and on "Cook's Tours" over the lines to acquaint them with every detail of our sector. In the meantime, of course, we had our regular patrols, protection missions and countless trial flights for new men and new planes, but no dogfights, because the Germans were being pushed farther and farther away from us and we knew we should have to move soon to a new field where it would not cost us so much gasoline and time to catch up with them. And then came August 1, 1918.

I cannot today look at the reconnaissance report of that awful day without having a lump rise in my throat. The report says, simply enough:

Protection Pat.—7 hours 05 to 9 hours 05 A.M. 18 planes, Lieutenants Grant, Dawson, Martin, Donaldson, Hunt, McElvain, Whiton, Vasconcells, Nevius, Beauchamp, Hudson, Polk, Rucker, Clapp, Roberts, Wehner, Sands, Luke. To protect 2 Salmsons (French photographic planes) in Fere-en-Tardenois region, Altitude 10,000 feet, Lieuts. Hunt, Martin, McElvain, Whiton, Beauchamp, Sands did not return."

That is not quite right. Beauchamp did return, his plane riddled with bullets. Directly over our field his ship went into a spin and he was killed almost at our feet. Sands was killed. Hunt was killed. Whiton was killed. McElvain and Martin were brought down and captured. It was heartbreaking. Here is Donaldson's report of the flight.

"We were attacked by 8 Fokker biplane (2 seaters with two cockpits and 2 men) chasse machines east of Fere-en-Tardenois at 8 h 10. I tried to bank to left and fell into a spin. When I came out of the spin there were four EA on my tail. I tried to turn again but fell into another spin. I was followed by the 4 EA down to 3000 feet. As I was coming out of the spin a Boche machine was headed straight at me. I fired and he turned to the left. I turned a little to the left and turned back again. Being right on his tail I fired about 20 bullets into him. He fell off slowly on his right wing and went into a spin. I turned on the other machines and went into a spin. When I came out they were climbing up. My engine was boiling and I could not climb as my nourice was empty and by using the hand pump I could just keep going. When northeast of the railroad between

Fere-en-Tardenois and Saponay I encountered a Rumpler biplane between 300 and 600 feet away. He passed me on the
right and banked up to give his gunner a good shot at me.
I turned and got on his tail and followed him in a circle firing
right into his cockpit. Suddenly his right wing came off and he
crashed. I was being fired at by machine guns on the ground
and was essing when I noticed another Rumpler under me to
my left. I turned down and fired at the gunner. He disappeared
and the machine crashed just beside the railroad embankment.
I circled the machine once to see if either the pilot or the
gunner got out but they did not. Confirmation for three (3)
requested."

Not bad for a brand new pilot in his first aerial battle!

At this time there was utter chaos at the front so far as
small routine details were concerned. Although there is no
doubt that Donaldson alone brought down the three machines he claimed the balloon crews and infantry officers
were much too occupied following up the fleeing German
Army to bother about such things as confirmations and we
never received them. He is credited on the records of the 27th
with one measly plane which he brought down almost three
months later. It should be explained here that in this battle
the original Fokkers of the Richthofen "checkerboards"
were joined by a very large number of other Fokkers and
Albatrosses, a squadron of stubborn Rumpler two-seaters
and a unit of the new and marvelous two-seater Hanoveranas.
Of whatever number of enemy planes our boys brought
down that day, Hudson, Roberts, Vasconcells, and Nevius
were officially credited with six, of which Hudson alone accounted for three.

The next morning some newspapermen came all the way
back from the front to tell us of the magnificent fight our
boys had put up on that August first before the admiring
eyes of at least two divisions of American troops who, until

then, had pretty generally scoffed at our air service. And then they told me something else that made me frantic.

"The ground up there is covered with busted airplanes and dead American and German aviators and nobody has any time to take care of them," one of them said. "Yesterday I saw two redheaded Americans dead in the wheat fields, still in their planes near Villers-Cotterêts and the heat is raising hell with them. The infantry told me one of them was named Sands and he certainly put on a grand fight for a full half hour and could have ducked out of it half a dozen times. He's in a Nieuport."

Within ten minutes I was in my new plane and off to look for Sands and any other of our boys I could find. I was determined to land right in those trampled-down wheat fields at the front lines if necessary and see what could be done. Flying very low all over the now famous Belleau Woods, north to Cantigny and Villers-Cotterêts, there was an ominous silence. No troops were to be seen anywhere on the ground. This spelled extreme danger to me because I knew they were there and I knew a safe landing and get-away were utterly impossible. So back to the airdrome I flew, took out my old Packard Twin-Six and with a chauffeur and a couple of officers quickly went by road to Villers-Cotterêts. It was now in the hands of the French. Many dozens of captured German cannon were lined up around the market place in the quaint little village. As we stopped, the head of the French staff arrived with a group of his very snappy aides. As much as I find it difficult to understand the characteristics of some individual Frenchmen, I will have to admit that the French Army staff is probably the most efficient in the world. They move mentally as a single mind, thinking the same thoughts, doing the same things in unison, correctly, skillfully, expeditiously, and at the proper moment.

We started to drive east in the hope of finding some of our

ships. It was getting late and on the muddy road about a kilometer out of town the left rear wheel began to drag. A ball race had seized and we could drive no farther. Getting out we began to walk. A little farther on some French officers stopped us excitedly and warned us to get out of there immediately because we were now literally beyond the front lines and without doubt the enemy was going to retake the whole works in a matter of minutes.

We made our way back to the town and then walked some eight miles to the rail head. Many French trucks and cars passed us and we tried to thumb a ride. Without exception the drivers ignored us. We had had no food since breakfast and were ravenously hungry. Near the rail head some French railroad workers were cooking up some stew in a big iron crock for their supper. We asked for a bit of it. Curtly and offensively they refused us any share of it. I met this selfish attitude in a number of other spots in the battle zone and farther back and it has profoundly affected my own international feelings. I am positive that such things could not happen, especially toward wartime allies, in America or England.

Five miles of weary trudging, then we came upon a small freight train which we were told was going back to Paris that night. Like hoboes we climbed aboard and slept most uncomfortably while the toy train squeaked and groaned its slow way to the suburbs of the French capital. Next morning, stiff, disheveled, dirty and unshaven, we walked more miles through labyrinthine railroad yards until we came to the station, the Gare du Nord, where I dashed to a telephone and called up 45 Avenue Montagne. It was like a cool bath and a meal to hear the cheery voice of the American officer at the other end of the line—our first friendly contact since leaving the airdrome the day before.

"Say," I said, with an actual note of apology in my voice.

"This is Major Hartney, CO of the 27th Aero Squadron, with three other officers from the 94th and 147th. We've had a hell of a time getting back from the front lines since yesterday. Will you let us have transportation back to our squadrons at once?"

"You're damn tootin' we will," said the voice. "Anything you want. You boys are doing fine up there."

Within two hours we were home—funny the places a man can call home—and I dispatched a motorcycle and sidecar with a new ball race for my Twin-Six. Two more hours and the car was fixed and on its way home and a few minutes after that the spot where it had sat all night was again in the hands of the Germans.

Again, a few days later, I went back to the front looking for my dead boys. Never in all my days have I seen such a sight. It still wakes me up nights. It was a shambles, a rotting human slaughterhouse. But I am going to postpone further mention of this unhappy and dangerous trip until a later chapter about Frank Luke, because he was with me and it was this trip that determined him on the incredible course of action he pursued afterward.

It was at this trying time that the sterling quality of our enlisted men showed up most brightly. The harmony and enthusiasm of the officers had spread to them, and was reflected back. Even Dudley, my orderly, was obsessed with only one subject—piling up victories. One morning he was so beside himself that he went among the boys who were getting some well-earned sleep and woke them up an hour before their regular time. He was really heartbroken when he was greeted with a shower of boots and profanity.

But the squadron was not in good shape and I knew it. After that battle of August 1, which was so disastrous for the 27th but a glorious one for the rest of the group, the pressure began to taper off as the Germans were beaten farther and farther back. We were deficient in equipment, in seasoned pilots and in the pep which until now had made our squadron a shining example. We were tired and there was no getting away from that fact. When one loses one's best friends in a fight the full force of the reaction does not come at once. When it does it is terrific and weakening.

By about August 5 I could see that the new faces were not supplanting the old. I had made it my personal job to take on every man in mock combat. Our newcomers, those who survived the August 1 thing, were supposed to be the cream of the training camps but without exception, even after repeated warnings, I could sneak up and close in on them so near that it would have been fatal for them had I been an enemy. It was this experience that confirmed my obsession concerning surprise attacks and the need of good eyesight.

And now another catastrophe befell the squadron—they took away our beloved little Nieuports and gave us 220-horse-power gear driven Spads. Both the 27th and the 147th were heartbroken; the 94th and 95th were delighted. Neither of these machines was in favor with the French Army. In fact, the Nieuport had never been accepted by them. The British refused the same batch we got. But we loved them and they performed perfectly for us. This was because both Bonnell and I had learned, from similar machines in England, the frailty of the Nieuport wing structure and the likelihood of the fabric ripping off in a too-sharp dive, and pull out. This was why I sent one boy to the rear for repeated improper dives and why the other men never violated Bonnell's and my orders in this respect. In the whole time we used them no Nieuport of ours ever stripped its wings. Being unwarned about this weakness, both the 94th and 95th had some mean experiences with it before they discovered it and moderated the steepness of their dives. This will not happen in any future war because our ships will have thorough service testing (I hope) and, besides, the pilots will wear parachutes.

An Englishman who flew one of the Spads on our airdrome said, "The thing flies like a bloody brick, you know." That was our opinion, too, and it and the Spads remained with us for the rest of the war. Even our mechanics, the very best in the world, could not keep them as serviceable as the Nieuports. Therefore our "machines available" for each day's work dropped from about ninety per cent to fifty per cent, despite long hours of night work and extra men on each job. I hope that never again will we be so unprepared in a war that we have to take from an ally the cast-off ships which he doesn't want. Major Bonnell was supposedly promoted from command of the 147th squadron, on July 22, 1918, to do some reorganization work at St. Jean de Mont where our gunnery school was located. As a matter of fact, we learned later, he lost his command and was bypassed to other duties because he raised so much hell about risking his men in those Spads. Our mechanics dug into their job with fine spirit. Although it meant four days for a complete overhaul of the new water-cooled engine against four hours on the air-cooled Monosoupape, they realized the additional risks being taken by the pilots and accepted the situation with good grace.

By now the Germans had been driven so far back from Château-Thierry that the front lines were too far away from our airdrome for practical operations—from 50 to 70 kilometers. Therefore a small advance field was set up at Coincy for the 1st Pursuit Group under our Lieutenant Fred Ordway, where the boys could replenish gasoline and oil and make reports. It was a makeshift but it worked all right temporarily. I paid a visit to that field the first day in my car alone with Frank Luke. It was on this trip that I believe I learned to know his character better than anyone on earth. Here we found the cement emplacement of the Big Bertha which had bombarded Paris seventy miles away. And here we saw another sight that I shall never forget.

That field had been the scene of a great tank battle and it was literally strewn with little French two-man tanks, most of which had caught on fire and burned. Beside each of them were two graves, and over each grave was a crude wooden cross surmounted by the steel helmet of the occupant. Why should a steel tank catch fire and burn?

The French specialized on small two-man Renault tanks. They were fine honest little machines. The armor-plating was so honestly made that it would deflect ordinary rifle and machine-gun bullets and nothing less than a 37-millimeter shell (one-pounder) could pierce it. The armor was so strong that when a bullet hit the $\frac{1}{8}$-inch slits through which the driver and the gunner watched the outside world, it would disintegrate into white hot metal and splash harmlessly off their asbestos masks and non-shatterable goggles. But these tanks had one deadly fault. Their fan belts were weak and when the driver would speed up the engine trying to churn out of a shell hole, the belt would break, the engine would overheat, then backfire, and set fire to the oil and gasoline and the crew would have to open the doors and run for it, only to be picked off easily by enemy sharpshooters.

We had 25,000 U. S. Tank Corps troops in France late in 1918. Only three battalions, the 301st, the 344th, and the 345th, all recruited from our troops in France, ever got into action, and they gave a splendid account of themselves. All of them were using secondhand reconditioned tanks, the 301st heavy eight-man British Mark Vs, the others the little two-man Renaults with the weak fan belts.

Shortly before the Armistice three American-made tanks were received at the camp of our Tank Corps at Bourg, near Langres. They bore the name plates of two of our best known automobile companies. In appearance they were exact duplicates of the little two-man Renault tanks. In order to see what stuff they were made of, some of the Tank Corps officers played a Chauchot machine gun on one from each of the companies for 1½ minutes each. The result was astounding. At the end of the test both tanks looked like Swiss cheese. Every bullet had gone clear through. The iron exterior handles of the front doors had been sheered off as if with a knife. The ⅛-inch slits, which were supposed to provide vision and to turn hostile bullets into harmless liquid metal, had opened up big holes and the bullets would have drilled the drivers and gunners through the head.

The history of the 27th Squadron from the disastrous battle of August 1 to August 21 was a period of extreme quietude—testing those damned Spad machines and testing new pilots. Only a few patrols occurred, most of them without important results. Only two of them stand out in my memory. Most vivid are the protection mission of August 16. Eleven of our planes went up at 9:10 A.M. to protect a Salmson photographic ship of the 88th Observation Squadron. In the air, dodging around among the clouds our boys never did find the Salmson but they found a flock of enemy airplanes and had quite a circus. There were no casualties on our side. This was Frank Luke's first aerial battle. I think his report, although pretty routine, is worth repeating for the historical records. Here it is:

Combat report—August 16th, 1918.
Lt. Frank Luke reports:
My machine was not ready so left an hour after formation, expecting to pick them up on the lines, but could not find formation. Saw Hun formation and followed, getting above into the sun. The formation was strung out leaving one machine way in the rear. Being way above the formation I cut my motor and dove down on the rear man, keeping the sun directly behind. Opened fire at about 100 feet keeping both guns on him

until within a few feet of him, then zoomed away. When I next saw him he was on his back, but looked as tho he was going to come out of it so I dove again holding both guns on him. Instead of coming out of it, he sideslipped off the opposite side much like a falling leaf and went down on his back. My last dive carried me out of reach of other machines that had turned about. They gave chase for about five minutes and then turned back for I was leading them. My last look at the plane shot down convinced me that he struck the ground for he was still on his back about 1500 meters below. On coming home about our lines saw four EA. Started to get into the sun and above but they saw me and dove towards me. Peaked for home. Three turned back and the other came on. I kept out of range by peaking slightly, and he followed nearly to Coincy where he saw one of the 95th boys and turned about. The 95th man could have brought down this EA if he had realized quick enough that it was an EA. The machine was brought down North East of Soissons in the vicinity of Joui and Vailly. Do not know the exact location as this being my first combat did not notice closely but know that it was some distance within German territory, for archies followed me for about ten minutes on my way back. My motor was fixed at Coincy and filled with gas and oil. Also found out that our formation had been held up by the Salmson that it was to escort and had just started. So left the ground to find them. Flew at about 5000 meters from Soissons past Fismes, but did not see the formation. Saw one Salmson but no EA. Returned home.

At 5:05 that evening I led a protection patrol of nine planes for one of the 88th's photographic Salmsons. And it was right after this mission that Lieutenant R. V. Nevius, was killed in an accident, taking off from the field. Although he was one of our new men, I had taken a great fancy to him as a hard-hitting pilot, a plugger who never shirked a patrol and who, I thought, was destined to do great things in the air service.

It was during these patrols that I met Captain Kenneth

Littauer, one of the really great officers of the American Air Service and one of the few actual fliers given high command. Commanding officer of the 88th Observation Squadron at that time, he had trained his boys into a highly efficient and valuable adjunct of the American effort in France. Shot down on September 14 with his observer, Lieutenant T. E. Boyd severely wounded, Littauer brought his plane down safely and successfully completed his important mission. He was always a source of encouragement and enthusiasm to his men. It was inevitable that he should go higher and on September 19 he was put in command of the Observation Group of the III Army Corps and about October 25 was raised to Chief of Air Service of the entire III Corps.

The comparative inactivity of the 27th Squadron, and in fact the whole 1st Pursuit Group, continued for ten days beyond August 21, 1918. But on August 21 a revolution occurred—perhaps not a revolution for the 27th but certainly a most emphatic one for me. Maybe you won't believe me but I give you my word that from the day I joined the 27th I had never given one second of thought to the idea of personal promotion. The job was so exacting with the 27th, and, I felt, so incomplete that I never considered I had mastered it sufficiently to give time to personal aggrandisement.

I had met General Mitchell (then Colonel) several times when he came to inspect the squadron. He was always very businesslike in his routine of questions and orders and never relaxed into informality. It did not occur to me that he would give us a second thought after passing on to some other outfit.

On the afternoon of August 21 I returned from a trial spin with one of the new fliers. I had engaged him in mock combat and then given him a thrill by dodging over the lines with him. The air had been very bumpy and I was all in. Old Dudley, my orderly, was waiting for me, evidently excited, pulling in his head in that characteristic manner of his. I knew something was up—perhaps he had purloined a frying chicken for my dinner.

"Major," he said seriously, "I hear we'all is goin' to move over into Major Atkinson's quarters and you is goin' to be boss of the works around here. You ought to tell me these things 'cause you and me is pretty lonesome with all these new caydets and everything and I need cheerin' up jest like you."

He could not have made a more profound impression on me if he had hit me with a baseball bat. Quickly I said:

"Don't be loony, Dudley. Somebody's been stringing you. If I ever get transferred out of this outfit, it will be to go back and organize something, maybe with Bonnell."

He grew positively frantic.

"No, sir, no sir," he almost shouted. "This is the straight goods. They told me about it over at Coulumniers just a half hour ago. Major Atkinson is bein' promoted and you is goin' to take his place. We is on the move, Major. We is on the move."

Before he had finished speaking an orderly approached with a paper—an order. It was true. Lieutenant Alfred A. Grant, one of my steadiest officers and now a successful businessman in Los Angeles, was to take command of my beloved child, the 27th Squadron. And I was made commanding officer of the 1st Pursuit Group, the greatest American aerial fighting unit on the front and certainly one of the finest in the entire war. It was unbelievable. I, the Saskatoon lawyer, was to direct the fortunes of such wonderful fliers as Eddie Rickenbacker, Jimmie Meissner, Reed Chambers, Ham Coolidge, Doug Campbell, Norman Hall, Major David Peterson, Sumner Sewall, John Hambleton, Harold Buckley, Alex McLanahan, Ken Porter, W. W. White, Ralph O'Neil, Francis

Simmonds and many other intrepid aces as well as my own crowd in the 27th. I have never had anything hit me so unexpectedly and so overwhelmingly. Within an hour I was in my new quarters, boss of the 27th, 94th, 95th, 147th, Pursuit Squadrons, the highly valuable 4th Park Depot Squadron, formerly the 213th and later the interesting night pursuit unit, the 185th, the only one of its kind in the U. S. Army. I could not have been prouder or more stunned if I had been elected President of the United States. Sixteen hundred men and officers under my command! To me it seemed like an army. Through my dazed mind one thought kept whirling around—I must make this, by personal example and enthusiasm, the greatest unit of its kind in the world. What a responsibility!

CHAPTER 13

The Group Gets Heavy Action

WELL, here I was, ringmaster of a six-ring circus made up exclusively of star acts performed by actors of the highest ability. The excitement and worries of running a single squadron were multiplied by six. My five new war babies fitted perfectly into my ideals and, although I sometimes almost dropped from the amount and variety of problems and work, I was happy from the moment my additional burdens came to me until they called off the show on November 11—six months too early.

I found in the other squadrons the same ultrafine quality of officers and men of which I had been so proud in the 27th, courageous, well-trained, decent, loyal and intelligent. As the busy war days went on, I grew prouder and prouder of the whole outfit and even today I get many a thrill when I think of countless incidents which helped to make the 1st Pursuit Group one of the most magnificent fighting units of all time.

Take, for example, Lieutenant Wilbur W. White, Jr., of the 147th, a veteran flier with eight victories. He was leading a patrol of three planes with Lieutenants Meissner and Cox, to protect Lieutenant Brotherton in an attempt to destroy an enemy balloon near Dulcon. Just as Brotherton was diving on the balloon, five Fokkers dropped out of the sky above them with guns belching. Brotherton was hit by ground fire and killed. One of the enemy ships was about to pounce upon

Cox, a new pilot, from the rear. To save Cox, White made a beeline for the Hun but both his guns jammed before he got within effective range. He did not stop, however, nor swerve out of the fight. Instead he kept on at full speed, right at the Hun, and crashed into him head on. Both machines plummetted to the ground, totally destroyed. Both pilots were killed instantly. "Greater love hath no man than this, that he shall lay down his life for his friends." Lieutenant White did just that. It was no accident, no error of judgment. It was the deliberate act of a brave man. Who could fail to feel a thrill merely to be associated with such men?

The following note was discovered in the uniform of this gallant officer when his body was found six months after the Armistice in a shallow unmarked grave by Major Reed Chambers of the 94th and White's father who were out searching for some trace of White or his plane. "To Lieutenant W. W. White: Embarkation orders await you at Colombey les Belles. They need you back in the United States to advise there in staff and school work. This is a great honor and you deserve everyone's congratulations. Turn your command over to Ralph O'Neil and come by group headquarters soon as you can. H. E. Hartney, CO."

White had gone on one last voluntary patrol with this note in his pocket.

When I took over the group on August 21, 1918, its pilots were credited with sixty-five official victories and had suffered forty-nine casualties. When the war ended their official score was 201 German planes and balloons destroyed and seventy-two of the group's fliers dead, wounded or missing. In other words, during the time I was with them they brought down 137 enemy ships and lost only twenty-three pilots doing it. It is no wonder I was proud of them.

One of the most important factors in any army is—officers. With proper officers an army can, and frequently does, perform miracles. But such officers must have an instinctive fellow feeling with their men plus a superior knowledge of the work at hand and a definite capacity for leadership. Given those things the men will follow them unquestioningly. The great weakness of the German Army was its professional officers. Trained to regard the German soldier as a cold piece of mechanism and a willing slave with whom it was unthinkable to share thoughts, hopes or feelings, it is no wonder that once the officers' supposed superiority was shattered by the necessity of retreating before the Allies, there was little left of the Army's morale. The German military spirit before a war is fed on boastfulness. In a war it must be nourished on victories. When victories ceased it began to crack and finally collapsed entirely. This is something well worth remembering. The secret of Hitler's power is that he has enabled the Germans to boast again. The complete final discouragement of the German Army was due in large part to officer failure. Iron discipline, even from childhood, is no substitute for real leadership.

The squadrons, at the time of my appointment, were in the hands of the following fine men, all excellent fliers, brave soldiers and capable leaders:

    27th—First Lieutenant Alfred A. Grant (made Captain October 11, 1918).
    94th—Captain Kenneth Marr.
    95th—Captain John Mitchell.
    147th—First Lieutenant James A. Meissner (made Captain October 11, 1918).
    4th Park (formerly 218th)—Captain J. C. Rankin—(later)
    185th—Night Pursuit—Lieutenant Seth Low.

The Group had suffered a loss on July 9, 1918, when Captain Phil Roosevelt, the energetic, intelligent operations officer, was transferred. General Mitchell made him Air Service operations officer of our entire First Army. His place in the

Group was taken by Second Lieutenant Romer Shawan of the 147th who did a grand job and was speedily promoted. Later on, I lost him, too, to General Mitchell's staff, and replaced him with First Lieutenant Arthur L. Cunningham who carried on splendidly to the end of the war.

Naturally, there was a change in my mental attitude when I took over the Group. I had to give up much of the detail work and leave the writing of orders, reports, etc., to trusted officers, most efficient and enthusiastic men inherited from Major Atkinson and Phil Roosevelt, a staff so well conducted by Major Henry Lyster of Detroit, the best adjutant in the whole U. S. Army, that to have interfered with their work would have been foolish. I realized I could no longer take part in all patrols. I was, however, determined to do even more actual flying but only in new and untried equipment or in the testing of experimental air tactics before making them part of our regular setup. By far the most important thing I did was to keep in constant personal touch with the officers and men of every squadron. I was among them all hours, learning their thoughts, their methods and their capabilities. I don't believe any commander ever kept in closer contact with his organization. We had very frequent conferences of officers, in different groups for different purposes —interpretation of orders, explicit plans of attack, and, especially, the free exchange of new ideas.

It was a result of this close contact work and mutual feeling of confidence among officers and men that the Group accomplished during the next three months many things which should be of utmost value in the conflict to come. I might mention:

1—The establishment of advanced interceptor airdromes as close up to the front lines as we could sit down. This worked out wonderfully but it was hard to find fields and difficult to remain there once the enemy got wind of what we were up to. He would shell the daylights out of us right away.

2—The employment of high-flying pursuit planes in low-flying countermeasures against the enemy. We didn't invent this but we did great things with it. General Mitchell called me up to Army Headquarters one day and asked me if we could bring our flying down, from four miles up down to 500 feet or less. This was toward the end of the war when the Germans developed the habit of harassing our ground troops from low altitudes in an attempt to break their morale. The infantry naturally was squawking about it and Mitchell asked us what we could do. I told him our casualties would rise but we could help a lot. The results were splendid—a great increase in the number of enemy ships brought down and a great decrease in their attacks on our troops. Today this would be very difficult for engines are now keyed up for efficient running, "full load," from 8000 feet up. Aviation engineers are thinking only of the higher altitudes including the stratosphere. The next war we get into will include many planes flying below 1000 feet. Fortunately, the casualties did not rise as I had anticipated.

3—The opening up of our flying formations from tight to wide open but closely controlled units. About October 15 we opened up our echelon, flight, and squadron formations. They continued to fly like wild geese in a broad arrow design but each man was at least 200 yards from his next in line, both front and rear, above and below. The head of each echelon (group of three to six planes) was independent but kept in touch with the head of his flight or squadron. Then they would move across country advancing slowly, because each echelon would circle back and forth, still going forward but completely eliminating the danger of being surprised.

In other words, each flight would now fly covering a space of say, one square mile, the whole squadron moving forward gradually. Thus each squadron would cover about four square miles. The whole unit would move over a thirty-mile front and back again in about an hour. Previously, close together and flying straight ahead, the squadron embraced about a quarter of a square mile and moved over the whole frontal area in about eight minutes, as compared with fifteen under the new setup. Sometimes, under the new system, we would not go up to the northern end of the sector and we would make all our moves erratically but always keeping intact the chain of responsibility from the leader on through. This proved very effective the first day.

Next day the Germans came out and did the very same thing. They saw the value of it at once and used it right up to the Armistice. And they are still doing it! I believe this valuable innovation has been missed in all our standard air service textbooks and is entirely forgotten. In all the formation flying I see these days the echelons are close together and fly in more or less straight lines, without feeling their way ahead. In our coming war this will be apple pie for the enemy with his new methods of effecting surprises.

4—The establishment of night pursuit. There will be plenty of this in our next war. In the last one, however, there were only two night pursuit squadrons in the entire conflict, the 1st Pursuit Group's 185th and a British unit, several months ahead of ours.

We were never allowed to forget our primary purpose in being at the front—killing Boche. My main responsibility, I felt, was to keep the morale and the equipment at the very highest possible level, to learn new methods of aerial warfare and to encourage mechanical developments that would make, not only our Group, but our entire air service more efficient. When Lieutenant John Sherman Donaldson invented a gadget for quickly reducing to zero the jamming of machine guns in the air, I sent him to Paris, to 45 Avenue Montagne to perfect it, which he did with splendid results. Jamming guns had been one of our nightmares, especially during July in the 27th when they gave us a lot of defective Marlins of a type of which 200,000 had to be destroyed after the war. It cost us the lives of several pilots.

There is one thing in which I take particular pride in the administration of the 1st Pursuit Group—the complete absence of personalities and politics. I never held a grudge and I don't think any of the boys did, either. Ask any of them and I'll bet they will tell you that when on duty I would strafe the living hell out of a man for some error or some stupidity (never in front of subordinates) but would have him at my mess for dinner that evening and the incident would never be mentioned.

Another point I should mention here is this: I let everybody in the Group know that I considered an officer's commission as something which marked the possessor as a right-hand man of the President, himself. I learned this in the British Army; there a commission is something sacred. It doesn't indicate that an officer is any better than anybody else, but he has been given very special responsibilities, often involving life or death for those around him, and he is entitled to the utmost respect and the greatest help in maintaining those responsibilities.

I believe, and always will believe—and in this I am opposed everywhere—that the commanders of flying units in the field must fly, themselves, all the time. Only occasionally will they lead the men into battle, but now and again they must do that, too. I know, from firsthand experience both as rookie pilot and Group commander, the tremendous effect this has on morale, enthusiasm, and the entire efficiency of the unit. Nothing else will give the commander such a "command" over his men, both officers and enlisted, and gain for him such respect. More important, however, nothing else can possibly give him such knowledge of the problems his fliers have to face and the proper answers to those problems. Let the Kiwis who want to command wartime flying units talk themselves black in the face. I know I am right.

It was lucky for me there was a ten- or twelve-day lull in the activities of the Group. It gave me a chance for an intensive study of the squadrons, their history, their officers, men, and equipment. I met every officer; got to know him. I visited other flying units, both French and American, talked with hundreds of the hard-working mechanics, cooks, office staff, and others. And I spent a lot of time studying the Group's flying equipment. I inspected instruments, dug personally into fuel and lubrication problems, even repair jobs on wings and especially on motors, tried to see every motor that was torn down to find some extraordinary situation, such as a bullet hole through a piston, through a petcock or three-way valve. Often I clambered up on a machine and took a look at the manner in which the pilot had his ammunition placed in the belts leading to his guns.

At the time I took over the Group, on August 21, 1918, the American Air Service in France was assuming considerable proportions. Already we had twenty-four squadrons at the front, of which twelve were for fighting, eleven for observation, and one for bombardment. Not bad, considering that in April 1918, one year after we entered the war totally unprepared after three years of warning, only two American squadrons were in the Zone of Advance—the 94th and 95th.

If the war had gone on for another year, as everyone expected, we almost would have fulfilled that ridiculous boast of some dizzy politicians in Washington to "darken the skies with airplanes." Our greatest of war assets, our capacity for mass production of superior products, of munitions, cars, planes, and other war materials, was just getting into its stride. I was privileged to see the official program which the high command approved August 16, 1918. It called for 202 American aero squadrons and 133 balloon companies at the front by July 1, 1919. Sixty of these squadrons were to be fighters of twenty-five planes each, 101 observation of eighteen planes each, and forty-one bombardment squadrons with twelve big bombers each. This would have meant 3810 planes, 4000 pilots, and a supporting cast of 1000 other officers and 40,000 enlisted men. Quite an aerial army! Contemptible, perhaps, to the Germans, who turned over 15,500 fighters and bombers to the Allies on signing the Armistice and who last April (1939) took over from Czechoslovakia 1535 modern fighting planes but now have so many of their own that they do not intend even to be bothered with those of the Czechs. Or so Hitler says! Even with the vast air fleet they developed in the war their losses were infinitely greater than those of the Allies. The Germans are not natural fliers.

I think we would have come pretty near to having that proposed aerial army in the prescribed time. The progress being made can be judged by the fact that by the time of the Armistice our air force at the front had increased to forty-five squadrons operating 740 out of the 2925 planes which had been sent up to the lines since our first units arrived. This was in addition to the 2948 planes supplied to our flying schools in France. The life of a plane in war time is a matter of only a few hours of actual flying.

Of the total of 6624 machines with which our aerial forces were provided in France by November 1918, 4879 were sold us by the French government, 283 were British, 19 Italian, and 1443 American. Toward the end of the war these latter began to arrive in droves. They were practically all DH4s, a very disgraceful compromise between a budding good engine, the Liberty, and the English Corps Observation plane, the DH. Some called them "flaming coffins." Personally I never did subscribe to this title because I had one for my own use and feel that inexperience killed more pilots on them at the hands of the enemy than did fires flaming up spontaneously aboard. The Liberty engine was a good engine—after it had 286 changes made on it *after* the Armistice. But in the war it was a tragic failure.

I might add here that this attainable schedule of 202 squadrons, approved and adopted by General Mason M. Patrick, our Chief of Air Service in France, and by the War Department at home, replaced a dream program previously worked out by some of our more enthusiastic well wishers with high authority calling for 358 squadrons by July 1, 1919. It is wonderful how many aviators and planes can be put in the field overnight—on paper—by an optimistic politician! Our greatest pacifist said, "A million men will spring to arms overnight." But he forgot a detail—they would have no arms to spring to for at least two years and then it would be too late to do any springing.

Our breathing spell came to an end. All hell started popping on September 1. The United States First Army, 150,000 strong, had been organized as a separate and distinct unit under its own commander, Lieutenant General Hunter Liggett. By Armistice time we had three good "grids" of armies in the field but it was the First Army which stood the brunt of the fighting in the two first great offensives.

On August 21, 1918, orders were received relieving the 1st Pursuit Group from its connection with the Sixth French Army under which it had been operating and making us part of the United States First Army directly under General Mitchell. To be with our own forces and on our own American responsibility, with General Mitchell and the great infantry divisions, our own artillery, signal corps and other services and the fine new aero squadrons which had recently come up to the front, was like a powerful stimulant to the officers and men of the Group.

That night General Mitchell called for me to come up quietly to a new sector on the St. Mihiel salient for a conference. I slipped up in my car to Bar le Duc and there had my first real insight into what goes on at Army headquarters in preparation for a big assault. I was fascinated. They had a large contoured replica of the whole front, complete with trees, hills, trenches, and everything. It was like toy soldier stuff but in deadly earnest. At dinner, with a flock of generals, we discussed the transfer of our group to a new field at Rembercourt where we could take an immediate and vital part in the next big move of the war—the St. Mihiel offensive.

Said Mitchell to me:

"Hartney, I want you to go over to that map and look at that tiny field, then go back and prepare to slip in there overnight when I give the word, without fuss of any kind. The enemy mustn't know we're coming. Can you do it?"

"Certainly," I replied. "Our boys can land their Spads on a dime and if there are small hills, so much the better, regardless of wind directions. But how big is it?"

"Thirty acres," he said. "The only thirty acres left in France, so don't squawk."

"O.K., sir," I said.

Today, in 1940, with our fast landing planes, at least two hundred acres would be required with at least ¾-mile runways as compared with the 1000-foot runways on that particular one-way field.

The next night, by truck and plane, the entire group crept into Rembercourt and within twelve hours our first patrols were flying over the new sector. The first was a two-man excursion of Lieutenant Roberts and Wehner of the 27th, to strafe balloons. Nothing happened. But it was the first aviation activity of America's new First Army. Both of these boys were dead a few days later, protecting Frank Luke. Later that afternoon we established hourly patrols of one plane each, to prevent any stray enemy machines from taking photographs of our new position. Meanwhile many of the pilots were busy ferrying planes over from Saints and Colombey-Les-Belles.

Our field at Rembercourt was unbelievably small and incredibly rough. Group headquarters was in a dilapidated shed. Our barracks were roughly constructed shacks hidden among the trees. The officers lived in tents. I had little fear the enemy would find our new location. I could hardly find it myself. It was a mess. Every man who took off from or landed on that field had to do expert work with the stick and rudder to avoid smashing himself and his plane to bits. And once again, mud, mud, mud.

It was of utmost importance that the enemy should not learn of our presence in this spot. Therefore our patrols were all on our side of the lines and consisted of only one or two planes each. One enemy balloon was annoying the boys because it was flopping about in the wind 2500 feet up, right at the lines, in what they considered a most insolent manner. Lieutenants McLanahan, Curtis, and Sewall of the 95th decided to do something about it. They attacked it on September 3, in the face of lot of machine-gun fire from the ground, but, owing to a scarcity of incendiary bullets and the fact that they were not equipped with the larger balloon strafing guns, it refused to burn. Several other balloons were attacked during the next two days with a similar paucity of results. Our friends, the Fokkers, were nowhere to be seen and were undoubtedly still back around the Château-Thierry area wondering what had happened to us. I shall never forget Alex McLanahan on his return from that flight. Usually quiet and of few words, he came in and demanded for all subsequent balloon attacks the larger balloon gun. He voluntarily mounted it on his ship knowing that all future assignments of this, the deadliest of all missions, would be his.

On September 8, Lieutenant Norman Archibald of the 95th pulled a stunt that caused our Army brass hats to have hysteria, hydrophobia, and the galloping jitters. Not knowing just why they were forbidden to go over the enemy lines, some of the men got the wanderlust and began sneaking over into German territory. Encountering no enemy planes or diving for home when they did see any, they felt supremely safe. But they didn't count on the enemy antiaircraft guns. Archibald's motor was hit by fragments of a high explosive shell at a high altitude and his plane came down crippled in a beautiful spiral well inside the German lines. We hoped he had had time to set his ship on fire. No such luck. Two of our own observers saw him land and get carted off to prison camp. Our bosses were sure the secret was out because the Germans knew the kicking mule insignia of the 95th. Archibald had sense enough to tell them he had become lost on a long flight from our old location at Saints. He always did have an innocent-looking face so perhaps they believed him. At any rate there was no more flying over the lines.

Then came a big day! It was the opening of the St. Mihiel offensive, the first great independent operation of the United States Army. It was only late in the evening before that the officers and men of the Group were told what I had been harboring for days, that "The First Army attacks on the whole front at 5 A.M., September 12, 1918."

From then until the night of November 10 our boys had no cause to complain at any lack of action. From that day until the end of the war we and the other American units at the front literally poured aviation into the German lines and quickly gained complete domination of the air.

On the morning of September 12, our men were on the job long before daylight, but, to the disgust of everybody, the weather was atrocious—pouring rain, with low hanging clouds. This, however, was perfect for one part of our plans

—low flying. The pilots certainly flew low that day—they could not do otherwise—and the success of this new system pointed the way we followed until the end of hostilities. And by low I mean low. The clouds at times formed a solid ceiling of mist at 100 feet and everything had to be done below that. This low flying by an entire group was a revolution in wartime flying.

There were no German planes in the air that day and our fliers had an entirely new and interesting game to play— shooting into trenches, tormenting retreating troops and supply trains, raising hell generally with whatever enemy objects and operations appeared over the sights of the guns. In spite of the miserable weather we sent out thirteen patrols of from two to five planes each from all four of our combat squadrons. I could write at length on the Group's exploits on that first day of the St. Mihiel offensive while our infantry and other troops were doing such a magnificent job on the ground. I think one incident will tell the story. Here is the simple combat report of Lieutenant James Knowles of the 95th Squadron, and, as you read it, please remember that ten meters is a little over thirty feet and that many of the trees in that territory were fifty and sixty feet tall:

Sept. 12, 1918.

Lieut. Knowles reports:

Found German artillery and wagon trains retreating on the road Crue-Vigneulles. Flying at about ten metres attacked and killed several horses in wagon train. Others ran away and piled up among the artillery, causing great confusion and blocking the road. Artillery horses ran away and all piled up in one big heap. Vigneulles on fire and big explosion occurred about 6:10 P.M. Heavy machine gun fire from the ground. No enemy aircraft sighted.

Knowles broke all speed records back to the airdrome. His report was phoned instantly to Army headquarters and in a matter of minutes our artillery got the exact range on the mess Knowles had caused and blew the whole thing to smithereens, horses, men, and guns, making the road completely impassable for German troops or equipment. A little later Knowles was mentioned in orders for this exploit, received a highly laudatory letter from General John J. Pershing and was given our second highest war decoration, the Distinguished Service Cross. He is now a busy executive with a national drug firm in St. Louis.

At the beginning of this drive we had in the 1st Pursuit Group seventy-five pilots and ninety-six planes. Of the latter only sixty-four were available (damn those Spads!). The second day, the 13th, the weather was slightly better, with meager visibility up to 1200 feet. We were able to send out twenty patrols which continued to harass the retreating Huns and to bring back reports of ground movements and conditions, very valuable to the Army staff. A few German combat planes appeared but our fliers completely cleared the air of them.

The St. Mihiel drive was short-lived but completely successful. The Germans, realizing the St. Mihiel salient, which stuck into our lines like a trowel-shaped bayonet, was untenable, had started to withdraw before our offensive began and the doughboys and artillery swept through it like a hurricane. In three days the salient was wiped out, the Germans dug in on a previously prepared line and our high staff went to work on plans for what proved to be the final offensive of the war. But we remained increasingly busy.

On September 16 the German aviation began to get a new grip on itself and we sighted many enemy patrols in flights of three, nine, and thirteen planes. The air was full of Albatrosses, Halberstadts, Rumplers, Hanoveranas, and our little friends from down below, the Fokkers. From then on our lives were a succession of vicious dogfights. On the next day, the 17th, an awful thing happened. A lot of our ships were equipped with those new Marlin machine guns with which we had had such trouble in the 27th. Sure enough, the minute most of our fliers engaged the enemy their guns jammed and thus deprived us of all offensive power. This was especially true with the 95th in which, at one time, all of the guns were jammed at the same time in a battle and there was nothing for the pilots to do but to bluff by flying ferociously at the enemy and then ducking for home when the bluffs didn't work.

Other guns were put into use, however, and all of the squadrons in the Group did magnificent work during this period. The figures alone tell that. From September 12, the opening of the St. Mihiel show, to September 26, when the Argonne offensive began, the Group brought down thirty-four enemy aircraft and suffered only three casualties. Really a superb record. Captain Meissner of the 147th and Lieutenants Hudson and Frank Luke of the 27th added themselves to the growing list of American aces. Luke and Joe Wehner of the 27th accomplished astounding things with their balloon strafing and Lieutenant Rickenbacker of the 94th brought down his seventh Boche plane.

The casualties are worth more than a passing notice. One was Joe Wehner, killed on September 18 in a manner described later. My good friend, Lieutenant Waldo H. Heinrichs of the 95th, now professor of "Contemporary Civilization" at Middlebury College, in Vermont, was the victim of misfortune. If you think war is a jolly picnic, you might read the following excerpts from his personal account:

Sept. 17, 1918:

The second flight of the 95th was ordered up for a 2:30 P.M. patrol. I secured the new spare Spad with new American Marlin machine guns.

Seven Spads left the Rembercourt Airdrome. I was flying in the lower echelon with Capt. John Mitchell (now in the sugar business in Louisiana), who led the formation, and Lieut. Lansing G. Holden (who was killed in a flying accident November 13, 1938). Holden had the squadron 11-mm balloon gun. We sighted seven Fokker D17 biplanes one far behind the rest. We had elevation on them at 9000 feet, and Mitchell gave the signal to attack. I picked on the last rear plane which was evidently there as bait and dived down after him. Only one member of my squadron joined me in this attack. The upper echelon apparently sighted another formation of German planes and entirely disappeared from this formation.

Mitchell likewise dived on the rear man whom we separated from their formation while the other six Fokkers continued on south. After the first dive, Mitchell pulled out of the attack and signalled that his guns were jammed. He was also carrying a pair of the new American Marlins.

I had fired two or three bursts on the rear Boche when both my guns jammed. While trying to correct the jams on a vertical virage, my plane fell into a sharp vrille which dropped me out below my opponent. He opened up on me. By this time the other Fokkers were back in the fight and two of them joined in the attack on me, while four sat over us to prevent any of the 95th planes coming to my assistance.

I turned toward our lines but was cut off by the entire Fokker formation. My first opponent attacked from behind. A full burst of fire from the rear went through my cockpit. I felt one bullet hit me in the left cheek. The bullet exploded in my mouth and seemed to blow out the whole interior of my head. I remember spitting out teeth and blood which were blown back at me by the wind, blinding my goggles. I threw the goggles over my helmet and executed a sharp renversement to escape the fire of another Boche, diving on me from the front. This brought me out directly below him and above the opponent who had attacked me first.

At the top of the renversement my motor stalled and the stick and the propeller went absolutely dead. I looked down to find my left arm hanging limply by my side. I then held the stick between my knees and opened the throttle with my right hand, but there was no response. The motor was dead. I allowed the plane to dive straight for the ground while the three Fokkers dived after me. I looked toward our balloon line to find the distance too great to glide in with a dead motor. We levelled out directly over the tree tops and by good luck right into an open field. I cut the switch to prevent fire in case of a crash and the plane settled down with great speed. The right wing plowed through a field telephone post, about 3 inches in diameter, which it snapped off like a toothpick. The plane settled onto the field for a perfect three-point landing without the motor and came to rest not more than 20 yards from the edge of the woods.

Recalling the orders of the War Department to set planes on fire in enemy territory, I reached into my flying suit pocket for a box of matches and tried to hold these in my left hand, but my arm was quite useless, hanging limp and broken. I then broke the gas lead from the nourice to make a better fire and the gasoline splashed all over the cockpit and myself. Then I tried to place the box of matches in my mouth. I found, however, that apparently the whole inside of my mouth had been shot away (both jaws were fractured and 16 teeth were shot out) so I could not hold the matches there. I did not think to place the box between my knees, which probably saved my life, for I would certainly have burned up with the plane. Many a man has been killed by a bullet, but I had been hit by seven and still lived.

Fully 50 Boche infantrymen ran out of the woods with their rifles lined on me, demanding surrender. I released the safety belt, held up my right hand in surrender, slid out of the cockpit and crumpled up under the left wing of the Spad. The Germans came up to me at once with a Red Cross first aid kit and placed a tourniquet on my left arm above the elbow and one on my left leg, high up on the thigh. They were very considerate. My right hand was bleeding profusely as my little finger had been nearly severed. More than 25 fragments of another explosive bullet have since been found by X-ray in the palm of my right hand. Probably the same bullet also went through my right heel where some two weeks later I was able to extract a fragment of the bullet with an old pair of scissors loaned me for a manicure by a German Sister in the Catholic Hospital at St. Clements.

The soldiers immediately offered me a shot of German schnapps (cognac) which I refused as my mouth seemed to be on fire from the explosive bullet. They asked my name and identification and I pulled out the "dog tag" from around my neck where they read the identification disc on which was inscribed, "Heinrichs, Waldo H., First Lieutenant, 95th Aero Squadron." The man who read it said in German, "Heinrichs. Ich bin Heinrich auch." ("I am also named Heinrich.") My opponent had circled around overhead for five minutes after I had landed and although the infantrymen said he was from Richthofen's squadron, I discovered in 1936 in Berlin at the Air Force Headquarters that he was Lieutenant George von Hantelmann, who was credited with 25 victories in the war and who was killed in Russia several years later. He belonged to Jagdstaff (Pursuit Squadron) #15.

Two stretcher bearers appeared before long, and I was transported to a field hospital. The German orderly at this place stole my clothes, personal belongings and photographs. I was put in a bed next to an American private who was severely wounded in the stomach. We were both parched with thirst and called for water the whole night long, but the German orderly refused to give it to us.

The next morning, I was taken to the Intern Hospital for Allied Wounded in the City of Metz, named St. Clements. There were fourteen officers and some six hundred soldiers more or less wounded. To minister to this crowd of Italians, Russians, Frenchmen, British and Americans there were six nurses, two doctors and one attending physician.

On the third day I was taken to the Information Officer and questioned. The only questions I answered were my name and address, according to War Department instructions. The officer, however, seemed to have more information regarding our Air Service than I had myself and told me the location of my squadron, number of hangars, the officers and other details.

The food at the Metz hospital was plenteous for the officers. The enlisted men, however, received only two soup rations per day.

The medical attention was limited by lack of equipment and personnel. All the bandages were of paper and they seldom used disinfectants. The treatment of British and American prisoners was not only unkindly but often brutal. There were many Russian prisoners who came in in frightful condition and died in great numbers. The French were uniformly well treated. There were many instances among our enlisted men of gross neglect and maltreatment. There were three cases resulting in death which I personally know of where the soldiers died of blood poisoning because the German doctors had not operated in time. They passed this off with the excuse that the soldiers had worried themselves to death.

On November 11th the Armistice was signed. By November 16th all the Germans had left and it was due alone to the kindness of the French people of Metz that we received food and care. One of the prominent physicians of Metz, a Frenchman, came in and inspected every case and every wound. It took him two days and two nights. When he finished he broke down and cried like a child. He said he had never seen human beings who had been left in such horrible condition.

It is a significant fact that the Germans robbed us of all our belongings. I returned to our lines with a Belgian cap, German cavalry coat, French artillery breeches and a pair of Russian boots, covered with a French infantry overcoat which had been left in the hospital by dead Allied officers or men.

The lack of proper medical attention in that German hospital left me with several wounds which have never healed properly and a double fracture of the elbow that never has united.

That night it was the general belief in camp that Heinrichs had been killed. The next day his best friend, Lieu-

tenant Bill Taylor of the 95th, disobeyed orders against
individual flights over the lines and, saying he was just
going to turn his motor over, took off suddenly on a voyage
of vengeance. As he left he held up his hand and said to his
mechanic, "A Boche for every finger on that hand for Heinrichs or I don't come back." He didn't. Alone he attacked
a formation of five Fokkers and brought one of them down
after a brilliant battle which earned him, posthumously, the
Croix de Guerre. But the others jumped him and Taylor's
end was a long dive, in flames, from 2000 feet, in the exact
spot where Heinrichs had been taken prisoner.

By this time the St. Mihiel offensive was a thing of the
past and our lives had flattened out into a busy routine of
killing Boche and destroying their planes and balloons. In
the latter we were especially successful, and on one day,
September 29, the men of the 1st Pursuit Group were credited
with bringing down seventeen sausages without losing a life.
We did have casualties—Wehner and others—but they were
few and far between. After Taylor's death, the 95th did not
lose a man, up to the end of the war while, in the same
period, accounting for twenty-seven enemy planes and balloons. We flew in all kinds of weather and at all hours. Our
men were getting extremely expert in all types of air fighting
in which, as in other activities requiring skill and daring,
experience produces near-perfection. The new men who
joined our group took hold like veterans. Sometimes a rookie
flier would actually be over the lines with us within half an
hour after he had reported for duty and without exception
they acquitted themselves splendidly. The morale was the
highest I have ever seen, both officers and enlisted men working with wild enthusiasm. They led charmed lives. Under no
other supposition can I account for their small number of
casualties.

The 95th opened up a splendiferous bar far from the main

highway with hand painted decorations and a white coated bartender. Almost instantly it became the social headquarters of the entire army in that part of France, not to mention most of the French and British armies as well. I think every Allied general on that front had at least one snort in Château 95, some considerably more than one.

CHAPTER 14

The Final Big Push Begins

THE TIME skyrocketed along to September 25, 1918, a
memorable day in our lives. Then two important things
happened. Lieutenant Rickenbacker was made commanding
officer of the 94th squadron, with the rank of captain, and
an order was received reading:

THE FIRST ARMY ATTACKS ALONG THE ENTIRE FRONT AT
5 H. 30, SEPTEMBER 26, 1918.

It was the signal for the Meuse-Argonne drive, the offensive that ended the war. Side by side, the Allied armies
poured their strength forward. Nothing could stand before
them. For many nights the roar of thousands of motor trucks,
motorized artillery, tanks, and the marching of hordes of
men had drowned out the guns at the front and had told us
unmistakably that something big was coming. It was even
bigger than we dreamed. In this last great drama of the First
World War we played an interesting and active part. To us
was given the job of clearing the lower air, below 2000 feet,
of German regelage and photographic missions, shooting
down pursuit planes which attacked us, burning German
balloons, strafing their troops, horses, supply trains, and
artillery. Above us, at the higher altitudes, the 2nd and 3rd
Pursuit Groups performed miraculous work in knocking out
of the sky the fighting formations which appeared by the
dozens. Some day I hope to write of Carroll Cone, Carl
Dolan, Bill Thaw, and dozens of those fliers who worked

so closely with us all through this show. In this battle almost the entire German Air Service was engaged and it was only a short time before the Allies clearly demonstrated their superiority and secured complete domination of the skies.

When it became necessary to appoint a new commander for the 94th there were several excellent men in line but it seemed the best results would be obtained by jumping Ricken-backer over their heads and giving him the job. There were several reasons for this. He was older and more mature than the others. He had established already a wonderful reputation as an aerial fighter, one whose actual example would be followed by the pilots, and he had a splendid knowledge of planes and engines. Most important of all, the 94th mechanics held him in high respect. In several ways the 94th had been slipping badly. It was absolutely necessary to have more "machines available" in that squadron and I thought Eddie could bring this about.

I'll take my hat off to Reed Chambers and the other flight commanders in the 94th. They were superb sports about it. In a conference I told them my reasons for wanting to put Rick in charge. And without exception and without a mur-mur of disappointment or disapproval they O.K.'d the deci-sion. General Mitchell was surprised and dubious over my jumping ranks this way but he backed me up and the ap-pointment was made. It worked out perfectly. The squad-ron took on a new lease of life, a new, almost fanatical enthusiasm. Rick, with his experience and natural executive ability, straightened things out immediately and led his men so superlatively that between the St. Mihiel offensive and Armistice Day they accounted for forty-seven enemy aircraft, of which Eddie himself brought down twenty. On the day of his appointment, before his confirmation, he went out on patrol and destroyed two Fokkers. Eddie was different from most of our other pilots and I'm going to devote some space to him later on in this book.

They had told me our preparatory artillery bombardment would start five hours before the 5:30 zero hour the morning of the 26th. But at ten o'clock the night before there was a gradual increase in our artillery activity. In a few minutes it had reached a point where there was practically no interruption in the shattering roar which increased to a fury of sound almost beyond human endurance. This kept up steadily all night. I wonder if there was ever such a bombardment in the world before. It was a shrieking, blasting inferno. Sleep was out of the question.

I had no time to sleep, anyway. There was too much to do. I sent one flight of eight planes, of the 27th, under Jerry Vasconcells to a new advanced airdrome almost on the lines at Verdun to work on alerts and the protection of Allied balloons. A flight of the 147th was sent to another advanced spot at Brebant-en-Argonne under Lieutenant A. H. Jones for similar duties. Lieutenant Alex McLanahan later took a detachment of his officers up to a third field and while there captured, with Sewall and Curtiss, the Fokker DVII which is now in the Smithsonian Institution. Our faithful mechanics worked practically all night.

At 4 A.M., long before dawn, our pilots piled out of their warm cots into a cold and noisy world. A quick breakfast, a dash to the hangars and they were off, eighty-one of them. I was frantic to go with them but it was not possible to be in two places at once and my place was at headquarters. Besides, shortage of equipment momentarily gave me a surplus of pilots.

What a magnificent but appalling sight our lads witnessed as they soared into this titanic battle in the inky darkness. The flashes of our guns along the whole front, north and south, had grown into a living stream of fire, searching out with its screaming, metallic messengers of death the tiniest hiding places of the enemy.

With daylight came the realization that the entire German side of the lines was blanketed by a thick fog through which no eyes could pierce and no airplane could navigate. It cleared a little later in the day but this was the forerunner of the worst spell of weather we had ever encountered. Almost every day from then, all through October and the early part of November, there were mist, rain, and low-hanging clouds which, normally, would have prevented any flying at all. But we flew nevertheless. And so did the Germans. The weather was just as bad for them, of course, as it was for us. Occasionally it would clear and at times the sun would come out for a few hours. And in those hours our fliers became the scourge of the skies for the fast deteriorating Huns whose Army was cracking up around them.

On that first day, September 26, 1918, in the few hours allowed us for our low flying, the pilots of the 1st Pursuit Group accomplished nineteen squadron patrols, had twenty-three combats, and wrote a flaming finis for two Boche airplanes and six balloons—without suffering a casualty to plane or pilot. Of these Alex McLanahan brought down one plane and a balloon. The next day in eighteen patrols and thirty individual combats, our men destroyed six planes and two balloons. This day, however, we were not so fortunate in the matter of casualties. Lieutenants Ivan Roberts of the 27th and Alan Nutt of the 94th failed to return. Roberts was killed protecting Frank Luke of the 27th on one of the latter's famous balloon-bursting expeditions. We found Nutt three days later shot to death at La Forge. No trace of Roberts was ever found.

In addition to their constant aerial combats the fliers of the 1st Pursuit Group were worth their weight in gold to the high command for the priceless information they, as pursuit pilots, not trained observers, brought back concerning troop movements and other conditions, not only at the front but fifteen and twenty kilometers inside the German lines. As the Argonne drive steadily pushed the Boche troops back, it became apparent that their Army was breaking up. It was for this reason, I believe, plus a barrel of luck and a growing skill, that so few casualties were suffered by our fliers. From September 12 to October 12 the 1st Pursuit Group accomplished 103 confirmed victories and lost only a handful of pilots doing it. Toward the end there were practically no German balloons in ascension and those few that did appear were speedily hauled down at the mere sound of an American plane, only to be burned in their nests by Luke, Rickenbacker, Woodard, Cook, or one of the other men.

Our flying at extremely low altitudes had proved highly successful, and not nearly so expensive in lives and planes as I had anticipated. In spite of the doubling and tripling of the number of machine guns around the German balloon pits our pilots made it practically impossible for enemy balloons to operate at all, thus depriving the Boche staff of a highly useful source of information. The development of dawn and dusk balloon strafing was one of our most valuable contributions to the Allied cause.

The concentration of our supply and mechanical replacement and salvage problems in the hands of the 4th Park Squadron (formerly the 218th) was a wonderful move on the part of the higher ups. The Group simply could not have functioned without the devoted services of Captain J. Gordon Rankin and his faithful crew of officers and men. Never have I seen a job better done. Rankin had been the Group's supply officer from the beginning. Lord knows how they did it, but they foraged, begged, borrowed, and stole lumber, canvas, wire, and other things to build the Group's first hangar at Vertus in January 1918 for the 95th. And from that time on we had what we needed, no matter how it was obtained. In every possible case, of course, the French made minute notes and secured receipts for every scrap of material they supplied us, for future payments. The manner in which Captain William R. Kales, partner and buddy of Henry Ford in the old Model T days, kept up a constant supply of gasoline and oil, Lieutenant J. C. Beam managed the mounting of machine guns, Lieutenant W. L. Kemp secured cars and trucks and operated our vital transportation system, Captain J. L. McGrath, an old Army sergeant, organized American clerks and elderly Frenchmen into efficient laborers who could put up a village around a new airdrome almost in a matter of hours, Lieutenant J. H. Marshall swindled, hypnotized, and cajoled the authorities into giving us uniforms, flying clothes, airplanes, spare engines, floodlights, flares, guns, pistols, ammunition, and innumerable other items must all go under the heading of "war miracles."

Perhaps the most important job was done by Lieutenant Reade. All he had to do was to create and operate a complete rebuilding and overhauling department for our new and old planes and engines and enemy machines. Once we found ourselves with engines from seven different French factories. No part from one factory would fit the products of another. Every new engine had to be torn down to remove stray nuts and bolts from the crankcase. And they all had to be rebuilt in some semblance of standardization. How lucky we will be if we can standardize some of our flying equipment before we are caught again instead of in the middle of war. The salvaging of crashed planes, both ours and the enemy's, was a highly dangerous task and efficiently performed by Lieutenant J. M. Egan. I shall always have the greatest appreciation for the loyalty, intelligence, and laborious sweat of the 4th Air Park Squadron of our Group.

The work of destroying German planes and balloons went

on apace. By October 12 Eddie Rickenbacker had shot down seventeen Boche aircraft. Five more pilots had become aces, Captain Harold Buckley of the 95th, Lieutenant Hamilton Coolidge of the 94th, Lieutenant Wilbur W. White, Jr. of the 147th, Lieutenant Jerry Vasconcells, Frank Luke, and Joe Wehner of the 27th, bringing our total of aces up to thirteen. Frank Luke died, gloriously, on September 29.

Some of our men, notably Captain James Norman Hall (co-author of *Mutiny on the Bounty, Hurricane,* etc. and at that time a prisoner), Captain David McK. Peterson, Lieutenants Rickenbacker, James A. Meissner, and Charles W. Chapman (killed in action), all of the 94th, had been decorated by the Franch for valor in action back on May 15, 1918. Now arrived some American decorations for the Group, the first of many. The following were honored with the Distinguished Service Cross: Captain Rickenbacker of the 94th, five citations; Captain James Meissner, 147th, two citations; Lieutenant Ralph A. O'Neil, 147th, two citations; Captain Alfred A. Grant, 27th, Lieutenants A. H. Jones, 147th, and Kenneth S. Clapp, 27th. There men were all present to have the medals pinned on their manly bosoms by General Robert Lee Bullard himself.

DSCs were also awarded to the following who were absent on leave or teaching war flying in the United States: Major David Peterson, 95th; Lieutenant Douglas Campbell, 94th; Captain E. W. Rucker, 27th; Lieutenant J. C. Raible, Jr., 147th, and to the following who could not attend the ceremony because they were languishing in German prison camps: Lieutenants Walter T. Avery, 95th; Alan Winslow, 94th (from whom we received a letter announcing the amputation of his arm from a bullet wound, requesting us to notify his mother and to send three cartons of cigarettes); John MacArthur and Robert Raymond of the 27th. Another was issued to dear old Freddie Norton of the 27th, dead these many months.

Several times in this book I have stressed the fact that morale is of prime importance in any fighting air unit. In ground and naval troops the necessity of esprit de corps has for ages been recognized. But this Up and At 'Em spirit must be present in air squadrons from the take-off through the patrols and fighting and even back in the billets at night.

To obtain this, I know of no better incentive than that of decorations both by our own and foreign governments. They arouse a sense of pride and stimulate in the breast of the tyro a desire to make good.

For some time in our Army the acceptance of foreign decorations was forbidden and the award of our own medals of secondary importance. To me this is quite inconsistent with the very spirit of democracy. Initiative, incentive in democratic armies, impel where in the autocratic these factors have no place at all. To call this class distinction and decry the award of ribbons for bravery is quite anomalous.

Believe it or not, it will take more than the willingness of Congress to get some of our boys the decorations which they so gallantly won in the World War. It will take a change of heart on the part of the advisers to the committee of Congress concerned, for invariably in the routine of such bills advocating decorations at this late date, negative reports reach the committee from unappreciative quarters and if the truth were known it has a bad effect on the service by killing the very incentive that would make for morale. I regret this in several instances, but the mention of one should not be amiss in this book and might do good. Captain Alexander McLanahan, a flight commander in the 95th Squadron led his men through heavy air fighting to some twenty official victories, often beyond the call of duty, with the loss during this awful period of but one officer. No one knows the long hard grind, the narrow shaves, the discouragement he suffered, yet he never received the Distinguished Service Cross for which he was recommended because some absent-minded clerk in the rush of front-line work failed to include the facts at the time and now it is too late.

Some day I hope the Congress will rectify this, not so much for the men themselves as for their children, and for the sake of the morale in the great American air force of the future.

By this time a most important new development had taken place—the beginning of night pursuit fighting. For a long time we had had this in mind but the French tried to tell us it was a crazy idea. On October 7, 1918, there was assigned to us the 185th Squadron, under Lieutenant Seth Low, equipped with British Camels. We went energetically to work on what seemed to be one of the most significant of all the new experiments in war flying. Organizing the unit and mapping out its routine and strategy took much of our time and thought but presently we were ready to give it a whirl in fighting off enemy night bombers over our sector. The weather, however, was against us and it was not until October 19 that we were able to establish a night patrol.

Our first two patrols of two planes each found heavy clouds and no enemy bombers. On the 22nd I decided to try out personally this new system of warfare. In close co-operation with our Signal Corps, ground troops, and searchlight units, through the very efficient Colonel Blair, Major Marvel, Captain Brunette, and Major Tomlinson, I went aloft in one of those grand Camels into all of which we had fitted the big 165-horsepower Monosoupape motor, giving us the finest little all-around pursuit ships on the entire front, friendly or enemy. The big Gotha bombers had become an extreme annoyance to us and to the doughboys in the trenches. Every night just after dark they would drone over the lines, apparently in perfect immunity, wander off toward Paris, bomb hell out of it and any other targets on the way, and return about an hour later, saluting us with engine exhaust signals as they sailed over. It got our goats.

The Mono engine had a black eye with many people but we knew it and liked it and its bad reputation gave us a much-needed and bountiful monopoly of spare parts. In the hands of inexperienced pilots this engine would catch fire easily and cause real trouble. But knowing this, it was easy for us to quench such fires simply by shutting off the gas injection feed and whirling the flames into extinction. For co-operation with the searchlights this plane was ideal. The pilot up there could shut off the engine and simply glide about for minutes at a time with absolutely no sound. This would give the searchlight crews a chance to hear the drone of an approaching bomber and shoot their beams from distant sites in its direction. They would seldom pick up the intruder on the beam but the lights would give the Camel pilot a pretty good idea of the location and he could turn on his power and dash over to investigate. The Gothas, we knew, on their way to Paris would generally follow the glinting rivers and streams, so we covered these routes patrolling over such landmarks. This type of night co-operation with searchlights will be followed in our impending war because it is simpler and safer than ordinary radio and subject to no interference except the weather. With the development of the quasi-optical or ultrashort wave radio we will substitute a radio beam for the light and then weather won't bother us, either.

The night of my voyage was hazy. But with a murky but unlimited ceiling it was obviously a grand night for German bombing operations. Presently I was sitting in my Camel, two miles high up over Verdun. We had fitted our night ships with all sorts of gadgets including Holt wingtip flares, which

I hoped never to use because they had a reputation in bad night landings for setting the planes on fire, and Michelin flares, a parachute device which, when I used them, almost invariably failed to light up unless it happened to be over some innocent noncombatant's hay stack, barn, or house, which they always destroyed when they worked at all. But I had forgotten one important thing—we had installed the larger "Mono" engine in these ships which were fitted with gasoline tanks with capacity only for smaller motors. I looked at my watch and realized that I had only gas enough for three quarters of an hour including the reserve tank. I cut down my full-open periods on the engine to about three minutes and opened out the gliding time with cold engine to about ten minutes. But I was losing altitude which in night flying, as in day, is the pilot's greatest asset before and during an attack.

Suddenly, after a long silent glide, on came some ten searchlights with their slanting beams pointing far back into enemy territory to a point halfway between Verdun and the spot where I was hovering. I flashed on one of my two pocket flashlights and got a shock. I had dropped from 14,-000 down to 7000 feet. Turning on the engine full blast I began to climb toward the converging beams as hard as I could go. Engine working perfectly, with steady blue exhaust flames, I tested the two good old fixed Vickers machine guns. They were O.K. I pulled up on the Constantinesco hydraulic gear to make sure the synchronizing pressure was up. Everything was working smoothly. And then I began to watch for the blue exhaust flames of my huge prey.

The searchlights never did pick him up but occasionally they flashed in my eyes and I was afraid the enemy would see me and turn tail. I knew by the searchlights that he was at about 12,000 feet, so I cut corners for Bar-le-Duc and pointed toward home, still climbing frantically.

Suddenly, in the black night, I saw the telltale blue exhaust flames of the bomber, right ahead of me and about a thousand feet higher. "This is duck soup," said I. Without the slightest fear of his gunners, I got right on his tail, underneath in his blind spot, and started to climb for him. He was plowing on with his nose down, going almost as fast as I was but never dreaming of my presence. For five minutes the chase continued and then, in the blackness, I almost collided with him. Suddenly there was a light. The pilot had opened the cockpit window, pointed a flashlight at the port outboard motor, and I could see the bomber's left wing. I was so close that I was on the point of overshooting him from beneath.

And now with too much deliberation, I idled the engine. The machine stalled, my nose being too high, and started to fall off on the right wing. I had clumsily lost my balance (lateral control). This cost me a good four hundred feet altitude and some six hundred feet in distance which I had to make up. Again I drew near the big Gotha and, nosing up, I let him have it with both guns. My aim was correct and I could see the tracers, much scantier in night flying (one in every fifteen shots), entering the big ship.

I was just saying to myself, "Why in hell doesn't he catch fire?" when without warning, my engine quit cold. The propeller stopped dead. Quickly I turned on my reserve gas. But inadvertently I had switched off my engine so, naturally, it remained dead as a door nail. But I completely forgot to turn off the gas jet feed. I was filled with complete chagrin.

"My reserve tank is empty," I thought. "How can I ever sit down here?"

Diving vertically, I flicked and flicked on the stick. Nothing happened. Then leveling out, suddenly I thought of the switch and clicked it on. Instantly the whole cowling in front of me was in flames, blinding and terrifying. Raw gasoline had been pouring into the crankcase. I was badly frightened, although I had sense enough to curse my own stupidity. It looked like curtains for me. There was nothing I could do but let it burn. And this it did merrily, whirlingly, a full minute that seemed like an hour. And then, just as suddenly as it had started, the fire died out. I switched on my throttle slowly. Gasoline from the reserve again surged through the jet into the crankcase. The engine caught and slowly but surely picked up its old hum. It was the sweetest of music to me.

Most present-day aeronautical experts will say, "Impossible. The whole aluminum cowling and engine bearers would burn up." I am here to tell the doubting Thomases that the paint was hardly scorched but I know that many a man lost his head and his life when a Monosoupape took fire like that and the whole front of the fuselage was a whirling flame. I can't blame them. It is an awful experience.

I had only twelve minutes of gas left when I switched to the reserve and I knew that I was twenty miles from home and 8500 feet up. The night was black, the haze below me so thick it almost looked like the rolling top of a cloud. Suddenly, off to my left, there was a blinding flash from the ground. Then another and another. Someone was getting bombed. The searchlights flattened out and pointed to a spot to the south. I couldn't worry about it just then. I was in trouble.

The plane was sinking too rapidly. An occasional easing on of the throttle and the engine would come on and pull me up and ahead but it seemed to be using so much gas that I could not leave it on. I could not see the vertical beam of the searchlight over our dummy airdrome, placed to fool the Germans but also as a beacon to tell us where we were. This worried me terribly. I looked below. I could discern things directly beneath but nothing to the sides. I was passing over a flint road. "I'll gamble that's the *Sacre Via*," I said to myself, meaning the beloved road which saved France when the brave poilus at Verdun said, *"Ils ne passeront pas"* and they didn't. It had saved France; now it saved me.

Veeering abruptly to the left I followed it along and in two minutes there was the good old vertical beam of our dummy airdrome. I pulled a parachute flare to send a message to my gang. Nothing happened. "Damn those war contractors who sell us dud stuff," I murmured.

Still 200 feet in the air and expecting the motor to quit any second, I kept what altitude I could as I arrived smack over our own field. Flashing my recognition signal I obtained instant response from the flimsy control tower on the headquarters roof and I saw the men, who we had arranged to line up on the airdrome, each with a flashlight and flat piece of wall board to give me perspective, start flashing their little pocket lights againt the surfaces of the wall board. On flashed our dummy airport boundary lights three miles away. Haywire stuff? Certainly, but so was the first Bell telephone, the Morse telegraph, the Duryea automobile. But like those classic things, our plan worked. Can you imagine the scientific improvements in this system we and our enemies will have worked out by the end of the next real war?

And then, for no good reason, I turned on my right wing magnesium flare. Why I did it I don't know, because I was scared to death of those things. But I did many foolish things that night.

The flare, affixed below the lower right wing tip, lighted the whole place and, at the risk of my skin, I circled again around the field to let it burn out. Time told me I was out of gas but I left the switch on and now and then slowly opened the throttle until it would catch and give me headway, then shut it right off again. I landed without a single drop of gas left and the men had to roll the machine across the field to its hangar. In those uneasy minutes in the air

I learned more about night combat flying than I could have learned in ten years sitting at a desk with spurs on. And I was now ready to really co-operate with the 185th Night Pursuit Squadron with some personal experience to back it up.

Here, however, was the amazing dénouement of my night voyage. When I landed, a swarm of officers and men surrounded me to ask if I had got anything. Two or three raiders had dropped bombs in the vicinity. I did not answer. I was disgusted with myself—and did not even put in a combat report. Had I done so I would have had an official victory of a very unusual nature. About November 20 after the Armistice, they found a big German Gotha in some woods right under the spot where I had encountered the bomber. It was riddled with bullets from underneath. It did not burn and was not smashed up much. Its motors were undamaged. There was no sign of the crew and no one has heard of them to this day. No other pursuit ship ever encountered a bomber in that vicinity. There is no doubt it was mine but I was too late to claim it. I would certainly like to meet one of its passengers and compare notes.

Now I had a pretty good idea what the 185th could do and we went about the job of doing it. The night after my Camel trip we sent out eight night patrols of one plane each on 1¼ hour flying duty, flying at 6000 to 10,000 feet. The following night we varied it with six patrols of three planes each. And for many nights afterward our men from the 185th were in the air looking for trouble. No trouble came to them. For the rest of the war the night work of our night pursuit squadron and, equally, of their prey, the Gotha bombers, was cramped by impossible weather. So we found other work for them to do—strafing.

On the afternoon of October 23, 1918, Lieutenants Kelton and Benson dropped four 20-pound bombs on Longuyon and reported good bursts—whatever that might imply. A few nights later Kelton machine-gunned a German train wending slowly in the darkness from Spancourt to Longuyon. How surprised its passengers must have been! Undoubtedly military, I hope they were generals. On October 28, the 185th had a sad event. Lieutenant Ewing crashed and burned to death returning to the field. He made a hard landing, was penned in, the gas flowed slowly down the wing and the Holt flare still blazing ignited the whole craft before Ewing could extricate himself.

After the Armistice, Phil Roosevelt and I at Chaumont prepared a complete line of activity for future night pursuit squadrons and groups. I hope it may be useful if ever needed, and it will be needed, never fear. I think we have the correct answer on this question.

So the jolly old war rolled along dizzily to its inevitable end. The doughboys down below us in the Argonne were having a terrific time but the better they did their job the easier ours became. The 1st Pursuit Group by this time had adopted another innovation—concentration patrols, in which we would send over every available plane in a single wave from twenty-four to seventy-five strong, flying at 1000 to 1500 feet, right over the heads of the infantry as they went over the top. In fact, toward the end, after a year or more of contempt on their part when, for months, they didn't even see an American plane, the infantry and artillery really began to like us and to realize we were legitimate players on their team. Every day they would wave to us as we went over. It pleased us immensely. Once we dropped them a lot of copies of that day's Paris edition of the New York *Tribune*. They sent hearty thanks back to us.

All sorts of things happened—exciting, tragic, significant, ridiculous. Waldo Heinrichs of the 95th, before his capture, was soaring along placidly one afternoon when he was passed by a balloon going in the opposite direction, with no basket, observer, or cables. He turned and gave chase, pouring incendiary bullets into it. It refused to be annoyed, kept galloping on its way and presently soared off for some mountains to the south. Heinrichs acknowledged himself beaten and came home to dinner. The bag is now probably somewhere off Australia.

It was on October 19 that one of our boys shot down a Fokker whose pilot reached the ground safely with a parachute on our side of the trenches. So far as I know this was the first use of parachutes from combat airplanes. Now, of course, every military aviator has a parachute strapped to him and the percentage of casualties in the coming war should be thus lessened, but the losses in planes may rise because some pilots bail out too readily, losing a ship that otherwise might have been landed intact. Believe it or not, the pilots during the World War felt it was "sissy" to wear chutes. In 1920, in the office of the Chief of Air Service, I helped to prepare the orders in the steps to make their use compulsory.

On October 24 one of the boys brought down a German plane well behind our lines—the first armored plane we had ever seen. The motor, pilot's seat, and gas tanks were armored with sheets of slate about 1/8 inch thick. This plane had two guns pointing directly downward through holes in the floor in addition to the usual guns for observer and pilot. A troop strafer, undoubtedly. In the war that is just around the corner for us most of the military planes on both sides, especially the bombers, will be armored. But not with slate. It will be beryllium alloy, tougher than armor plate and almost as light as aluminum. Liquid cooled engines in England are already armored. With beryllium we will armor our air-cooled motors, too.

In the month from September 12 to October 12 the 1st

Pursuit Group shot down fifteen balloons in dawn strafing, twenty-four in dusk strafing, and two in broad daylight. During the same period the concentration patrols developed by the Group shot down thirty-nine enemy planes. During this time our casualties were negligible but highly tragic when they happened. On October 30, Lieutenant Garney of the 94th was killed when jumped by twelve Fokkers.

The boys evidently thought they were not doing enough at the front to win the war. On October 27 I was proud to post a list showing the Group's contribution to the Fourth Liberty Loan—$20,800, led by the 27th with $7150. I occasionally throw that in the teeth of some of my commercial acquaintances back home.

Confirmations had been slow in arriving. After October 30, however, they came in increasing volume and some of them covered victories won months before. It always rankled that some of our most spectacular and hazardous victories, amply witnessed, were never confirmed, but such is war, an ungrateful proposition at best. Here is a table showing the percentage of our casualties in comparison with victories from our starting point in April up to November 11, 1918.

On October 24, 1918, Lieutenant Ham Coolidge was returning home from a late afternoon patrol deep in German territory when, over Dun, he encountered a man serenely sailing toward the earth under a white billowing parachute. Coolidge swore there was not a German plane or balloon within miles. A visitor from Mars, perhaps.

On July 7, First Lieutenant Stuart McKeown of the 95th had been shot down over the enemy lines. He was a steady, intrepid flier. The men of the 95th grieved mightily and constructed an ornate cross which they carried around for the rest of the war, hoping to find his grave. After the Armistice, we found a wreck of a man terribly wounded, lying in filth and vermin in a German prison camp. It was McKeown. He

Month	27 Sqdn.		94 Sqdn.		95 Sqdn.		147 Sqdn.		185 Sqdn.		Total		Totals	
	Vic.	Cas.	Vic.	Cas.	Vic.	Cas.	Vic.	Cas.	Vic.	Cas.	Vic.	Cas.	Vic.	Cas.
April	Not Attached		3	0	0	0	Not Attached		Not Attached		3	0	3	0
May	"		13	5	5	3	"		"		18	8	21	8
June	4	3	1	2	1	0	0	0	"		6	5	27	13
July	9	8	1	4	9	8	10	3	"		29	23	56	36
August	5	7	1	1	2	3	1	2	"		9	13	65	49
September	18	0	8	3	4	3	5	2	"		35	8	100	57
October	9	4	27½	3	9½	2	10	3	0	1	56	13	156	70
November	10	0	12	0	18	0	5	0	0	2	45	2	201	72
TOTAL	55	22	66½	18	48½	19	31	10	0	3			201	72
Percentage of victories to casualties	{ 27th 250%		94th 369%		95th 255.8%		147th 310%		185th 310%				Group Average 279%	

was nursed back to health and today is a useful and valuable citizen.

On October 8 we had started a series of daily mimeographed news items, summarizing the events of the past twenty-four hours. It was highly successful. So on October 26, at the instigation of Sergeant "Jack" Mursell of the 95th, today employed in the Government Printing Office in Washington, we established a regular weekly newspaper, entitled *Out of Control,* for the Group. Lieutenant Ward D. Fowler of the 94th, formerly sports editor of the Los Angeles *Times,* was made editor-in-chief, with Lieutenant Paul Lockwood of the 4th Park Squadron, formerly an editor of the Boston *Globe* and New York *Times,* as managing editor, and Lieutenant Fred Ordway of the 27th, circulation manager. For subeditors we had a distinguished and imposing list of fourteen of our officers and enlisted men. The success of this publication in raising morale and riveting the attention of the men on squadron matters was immediate. This is the type of internal public relations work which must be carried to considerable lengths in the forthcoming madness in order to promote enthusiastic teamwork.

Early in October we received at Group headquarters the first radio message telling of the location of enemy balloons. They were most helpful. The present war is being directed largely by radio. Presently we shall have ultrashort wave with sending stations in helicopters and directed beam transmission, subject to no static interference.

On October 25, Lieutenant Low was peremptorily snatched from me for other staff duties and I placed Jerry Vasconcells of the 27th in command of the 185th Night Pursuit Squadron. I have never seen a finer, more enthusiastic and intelligent officer. If the war had lasted you would have heard great things from the 185th and from Jerry.

As the days ticked along October drifted into November

and it was apparent to everybody that the end was near. The German Air Force was shot to pieces but who can blame them? You cannot keep up flying morale when your equipment has been captured or gone haywire and all the other military units around you are scuttling for home and safety. The air was full of rumors but we were actually getting some facts.

Up to November 11, 1918, there were trained in the United States on Jennies, with one or two Thomas-Morse scouts, a total of approximately 12,563 American pilots. Of these, about 3441 had so-called advance training on American planes at home.

In France, the United States Army produced a total of about 4961 pilots, exclusive of a comparatively small number trained in England. Of our pilots trained in France, 1854 got no further than primary training, 1881 took advanced training. Of the latter, 57 took additional courses in specialized work on observation ships, 782 on pursuit planes and 335 on observation craft.

On November 1, 1918, we learned that Turkey had quit, then that Austria and Italy had agreed to an armistice. Our First Army was sweeping along on its whole front as were our gallant Allies, the British and French.

On the following day the sun was out and for the first time in such flying weather, since we arrived on the front in April, no enemy balloons or airplanes were sighted by our patrols. The same condition existed on the 3rd. But on the 4th of November the enemy suddenly came to life and the air was full of German biplanes protected by formations of seven to nine Fokkers. We hurled seven patrols at them including one concentration patrol of twenty-four planes. The Group brought down four planes and two balloons without a death or injury.

Big sheets of confirmations of previous victories were now arriving daily, materially boosting the Group's morale, its score and its number of aces. We could thank the American balloon service for ninety per cent of our confirmations. It was one of the most efficient and hard working outfits in the army, under Colonel Chandler and Major Paegelow, "Jack" Jouett and the most efficient citizen-officer I ever met, "Bill" Carthy. Our balloon companies, fifteen in number finally, performed Herculean labors during all three of our offensives and lost thirty-two balloons in the process with only one death. Lieutenant C. J. Ross had his parachute burned by sparks from his flaming balloon and crashed to earth. Only one in ten of the enemy's plane attacks on our balloons was successful and the balloon companies brought down four German planes with machine-gun fire. During the St. Mihiel and Argonne offensives American pilots shot down fifty-eight Boche balloons, of which forty-eight were confirmed.

There is not much to tell of the last five or six days of the war. From our radio we learned of the dispatch of the German delegation to negotiate an armistice. On November 10 we sent over the usual patrols and Major Maxwell Kirby, a Regular Army officer, of the 94th, brought down a German plane. It was the Group's last victory of the war—the last of the 285 enemy aircraft shot out of the sky by our four squadrons, of which 201 were officially confirmed. It is a proud record. The Group lost seventy-two fliers in action, killed, or seriously wounded, and by accident or capture. Only two enlisted men lost their lives with us, Private Albert D. Boughman of the 27th, killed in a motorcycle collision, and another who was struck by lightning.

A great mark of distinction for the Group is that it supplied twenty-four aces of the total of seventy-one in our entire Air Service. America's three leading aces, Rickenbacker of the 94th with twenty-six official victories, Luke of the 27th with eighteen, and Lufbery of the 94th with seventeen, were members of the 1st Pursuit Group. It should be stated here that all of Lufbery's official victories were achieved with the

French Lafayette Escadrille. He was, however, the first flier in American uniform to bring down a Hun plane, which he did on April 12, 1918, while he was commanding the 94th at Toul, shortly before he was killed. He never received confirmation on this machine.

It was Lufbery who led our first patrols over the German lines—on March 28 and 29. In the very first were Lieutenants Eddie Rickenbacker and Douglas Campbell; in the second, the next morning, were Lieutenants Thorne C. Taylor and John Wentworth. There were no combats on those patrols but a flying fragment from an archie shell passed through Rickenbacker's ship a few inches from his head. That slight miscalculation cost the German Army the lives of fully three score of its flying men. Two pilots of the Group received the only Congressional Medals of Honor won by American airmen during the war—Luke of the 27th and Rickenbacker of the 94th.

The first enemy plane brought down by an American-trained pilot was vanquished on Sunday morning, April 14, 1918, by First Lieutenant Douglas Campbell, of the 94th, but he was only seconds ahead of Second Lieutenant Alan Winslow of the same unit. This was one of the most remarkable incidents of the war. Heavy clouds were hanging low over the field at Toul. The sound of motors was heard above and Campbell and Winslow, on alert, leaped into their planes for a look-see. They had barely left the ground when two German ships plopped down through the clouds looking for trouble. Instantly Campbell and Winslow were on them like a couple of tigers. In less than two minutes both Boche machines were lying destroyed on the edge of the airdrome, one aflame, and their pilots were captured, one badly burned, the other grievously wounded.

Campbell came through the war in great shape with eight victories. On May 31, 1918, he had brought down his fifth

German plane, thus making him the first American-trained ace. Quiet and stalwart, son of the head of the Mount Wilson Observatory in California, he has since done a beautiful job in helping to make the Pan American-Grace Airways in South America such a whale of a success. Poor Winslow did not have such a happy time of it. After bringing down another enemy ship, he went on patrol on July 31, 1918, was shot down badly wounded and made prisoner. His treatment in the German hospitals was terrible. He never got over it and finally passed on about five years ago.

On the night of November 10, we intercepted on our radio the instructions to the Geman envoys at Foch's train, telling them to sign up on his terms at 11 A.M. the following day. The war was over. We knew it. We had won. I leaped to the telephone and notified every squadron. And then all hell broke loose. Most of us repaired to the 95th mess and bar. Laurence La Tourette Driggs, a war correspondent, afterward president of the ill-fated but timely and beneficial American Flying Club, made a speech and insisted that I get up on the bar and talk. Everybody was milling around. They hoisted me up.

Suddenly, outside, there was a terrific racket. It was Captain Rankin's brass band. There was a rush for the doors. Everybody started firing pistols and guns. The air was full of flying bullets and rockets. Someone turned on the searchlights and swayed the beams back and forth. I started across the airdrome but had to lie down to avoid the whizzing bullets. A great weight was lifted from us. We had lived through it. We had lived through the war.

Next morning some of the boys wanted to go out on a final patrol. Nothing doing. The war was over, or would be in a few hours. If I had let them go out and any of them had been killed or if they had killed any Germans I would never have got it off my conscience. I often wonder what the secret thoughts are of the officers who were rushed up to the front on November 11, 1918, so they would have it in their records that they commanded troops at the front in the war, and then ordered the boys over the top. The Greeks had a name for it; so have we.

CHAPTER 15

Frank Luke, Jr., and Joe Wehner— Flying Tops

THE MOST EXTRAORDINARY flier ever produced by the United States Army was Frank Luke, Jr. His bare official record of achievement at the front is breath-taking and unequaled— fifteen enemy balloons and three Boche planes in seventeen days. This included one exploit in which he destroyed three planes and two balloons in ten minutes. These are fantastic figures to anybody who knows the intricacies and difficulties of wartime flying, especially the balloon strafing. But some of the details of Luke's flying adventures are still more fantastic. They are absolutely incredible, and if I hadn't seen some of them with my own eyes I should refuse to believe them, even if told me by the Archbishop of Canterbury. In addition, I personally know that he brought down several more balloons and planes for which he received no credit.

Parts of Frank Luke's story have been told in print—a few of the highlights. Therefore, I shall only relate some of the facts that have not been written about him, some of those intimate moments in which I got an insight into his curious character and a few of the unbelievable exploits he performed within my own sight or knowledge.

Although of German ancestry, Frank Luke, Jr., was a perfect American, of the rugged cowboy type, strong, blond, energetic, and highly individualistic and self-confident. Born and bred in Arizona, one of nine children, he grew up in the rough and tumble of frontier life on the plains and in the mountains, witnessing several bloody battles with the Indians. His parents saw to it, however, that he went through school and college, which he completed just as we plunged into the European holocaust. It would be difficult successfully to regiment a boy like Frank in a routine branch of service. It is not surprising, therefore, that we discover him, almost immediately we entered the war, as one of the first students at the ground school at Austin, Texas. From there he went to San Diego, California, and presently found himself among the fledglings at the great and muddy training center at Issoudun, in France.

He was bashful, self-conscious, and decidedly not a mixer. It unquestionably caused him many heartburns when his reticence was interpreted as conceit. In fact, this preyed on his mind to such an extent that he became almost a recluse, with an air of sullenness, which was not that at all. When he arrived, with eight other replacements for the 27th Squadron at Saints, on July 25, 1918, he had found a buddy, and only one, who was to be his confidant and sidekick and who, on September 18, was to give his life for his pal. This was Lieutenant Joseph Wehner, one of the greatest fliers that ever graced the American uniform.

Luke's self-confidence caused most of the pilots in the group to regard him as a boastful fourflusher and many of them never liked him, even to the end, in spite of his extraordinary accomplishments. You could not altogether blame them. Frank was unfortunate in frequently giving the wrong impression. One day George Jordan, a veteran sergeant of the 147th, told me he had been chatting with Luke as a German plane flew over. Looking up, Luke said, "Gee, that plane would be a cinch for me." This and many similar remarks would certainly indicate a high degree of boastfulness but I really believe they were nothing of the sort. I think they were simply the honest confidence of a zealous but not-too-diplomatic boy. He was a clean-looking, towheaded youngster, with piercing steel blue eyes and quick motions. He practically never entered into general discussions around camp or in the mess. To him miscellaneous conversation was a waste of effort and words. I took him on in mock combat and general training as I did the other newcomers. He was far from perfect as a war flier at that time and I had no more trouble in taking him by surprise than I had with the others. Having lost many of my best men and not being very enthusiastic about the progress of Luke and the other replacements, I was pretty discouraged for a while.

The first time I really took much of an interest in him was about three days after I had lost six of my officers and Don Hudson had shot down two biplane Rumplers carrying four men on August 1, 1918. I had already been up to the lines to see if I could find any of my boys who, newspapermen had told me, were still lying in their planes dead with no one taking any care of them. That first day I could not get any farther than Villers Cotterêts, not far from our small advance airdrome, although farther north, and had to return by foot and freight train via Paris.

A couple of days later Luke came to my tent and said, "Major, Lieutenant Clapp says it is all right for me to go up with you this morning if you can take me." I shall never forget that journey. Frank, one enlisted man, and I went along in my Packard. On this trip he talked freely, of his days on the plains back home, of incidents of his training, of his ambition to be an outstanding flier. He was extremely serious always. Walking to the top of a hill we found the two German planes Hudson had brought down. They were actually interlocked. Hudson had crowded one into the other in the scrap. The two pilots and their observers were still there, their faces black, the summer sun getting in its rapid work. One of them had on very light patent leather low shoes. This impressed Luke. "Wonder where he was the night before," he murmured. Rumor had it among the ground troops that one of the Germans was a girl but this was not true.

Three hundred yards farther we came to the top of another knoll and looked down the other side, a smooth space of about a hundred acres. Never have my eyes rested on such a sight. May they never again behold one like it. The hill was literally covered with dead men, side by side, head to head, little or no space between, practically all of them American doughboys. They had died in droves charging German machine-gun nests left behind to cover the retreat. Right in front of us were a German and an American who had actually pierced each other with their bayonets and neither bayonet had been withdrawn.

Frank stooped over and picked up some unmailed postal cards fallen from a pocket of one of the dead boys. The one on top was addressed to his mother out in Iowa.

"Leave them there," I said. "That American padre over there is busy picking up such things to send back to the next of kin."

Carefully and reverently, Luke replaced the cards in the pocket of the dead Yankee.

"Boy!" he exclaimed. "I'm glad I'm not in the infantry. They haven't a chance, have they, Major?"

Hiking back to the road, we got into our car and made our way farther along toward Fismes, on the Vesle, where somebody had told us the front line lay. We noticed some peculiar stares in the eyes of several small detachments of American troops marching on the road. Presently a young second lieutenant stopped us.

"Sir, do you realize you're beyond the front lines? The last car that went up there didn't come back. It was captured."

Things were so quiet it seemed incredible.

"Have you seen any planes around here shot down?" I asked.

"Oh, yes," he replied. "My men have seen several Frenchmen still in their planes but we don't have time even to look at them. All troops are on the move." Frank spoke up. "Where is one?" "There's one about a mile over there," pointing toward Chamery, back southward. Slowly we turned the big Twin-Six around and went back about two miles, parked the car and got out. We walked along the ridge of a hill, watching every clump of stumps or anything that might conceal the wreckage of a plane. We found several, including two enemy and several British Camels. Most of them had bullet holes through the head rests. On one we actually found a rifle lying on the wing. The plane seemed intact and only a splotch of blood and a torn helmet indicated what had happened to the pilot.

"These men were all diving away when they were hit, weren't they, Major?" asked Luke.

"Yes," I replied. "It's what I've told you and the other boys a dozen times. That's about the only time one gets hit."

"By God, they'll never catch me that way," said Frank.

As we came to the brow of a small hill we heard an American antiaircraft gun firing at a couple of enemy ships 'way out of range. We turned and walked down for a chat with the crew, then continued up the hill at a different angle. If we had kept going straight ahead in the first place we would have been among the first Americans to find Quentin Roosevelt's grave, with fragments of his plane, right at the apex of the angle we had missed. Today, on the spot where that gun was firing is one of the few single-person American cemeteries in France. Over Quentin's new grave is erected a beautiful classic granite monument, about the size of an

automobile, to the memory of the brave 1st Pursuit Group
boy who fell on top of the hill nearby.

We walked farther and saw other wrecks but none of them
ours. Then we went back to the Packard and drove toward
Fere-en-Tardenois. Luke asked permission to go over and
take another look at the two crushed, interlocked German
two-seaters. We got out and I strolled over to glimpse again
that terrible slaughter field where so many men lay dead for
economic and political reasons beyond their comprehension.
It was getting dark. Except for the rumble of distant guns
there was absolute silence. Silhouetted against the evening
skyline on top of that hill was one moving figure. It was the
steel-helmeted padre. Slowly he would stoop over and pick
up something and put it in his pocket. I did not disturb him.

Again in the car we were almost to Fère-en-Tardenois
when something attracted our attention. It was a group of
American soldiers watching something in the sky a little distance away. We got out and joined them. It was a single
German plane. He had dropped from the sky like a bullet
and poured some incendiary bullets right into one of our
observation balloons. The sausage, full of hydrogen, was falling in flames. The occupants had bailed out in their parachutes. Even as we watched, the heine pilot dipped into a
swift attack on a second balloon nearby. He caught it as it
was being dragged down by its winch. It, too, went up in
flames. The rattle of our machine guns were terrific but it
meant nothing. The Boche Albatross went blithely hedge-
hopping homeward. All was still again.

The sights and experiences of that day must have had a
profound impact on Frank Luke. A less intrepid boy would
certainly have lost any further desire to go into such gory
and savage doings and would have found ways and means
of getting himself sent to a safer part of the war zone. But
with Luke it was different. All the way home he was silent.

And I am positive that on that homeward trip he laid out his future course and made his plans to become our most spectacular flier and the world's greatest strafer of enemy balloons.

Several days later, August 16, 1918, to be exact, I had my first real feel of Frank Luke's dependability in the air. Our advance airdrome at Coincy was ready for us, camouflaged gas trucks and everything, and we got orders to use that as the starting point for a protection patrol. We were having great trouble with the new Spads and the boys of the 27th and 147th had no confidence in them. A poorly housed reduction gear which would get out of line with the slightest nick in the propeller was constantly causing us mechanical difficulties. It would vibrate and soon the various pieces of plumbing would start to ease loose and the engine would begin to miss or quit completely.

At 5:05 P.M. I led a gang of twelve of our planes and three from the 94th out at 9000 feet to protect one of Ken Littauer's photographic Salmsons from the 88th Squadron. We soared up in perfect formation. From Fère-en-Tardenois to Fismes, however, our boys began dropping out with engine trouble. Finally there was only one plane left besides mine. By now we were at 18,000 feet and already had had several minor brushes with the enemy.

It was one of those grim, heat-hazy days when it was particularly difficult to spot enemy ships. The first intimation of their presence would be the streaks of tracer bullets and that nasty click-click as hostile missiles snapped menacingly past your ears. Only this one plane stuck by me. Things got too hot for me and I "piqued" for our Coincy field. As I pulled in, there were thirteen of our ships sitting on the ground. When I had taxied to a stop a lot of the pilots came running over to tell me they thought I had been lost and to utter loud and violent blasphemies concerning the Spads and the French "who had wished those crocks on us." I am told that no man ever cursed as loud and as vehemently as I did at that moment.

I was still ranting and giving everyone hell when a lone Spad came in with the pilot goosing his engine and causing a terrific racket.

"Here comes your boy friend now," said one man from the 27th. "He said he was going to get his first Boche today or never come back. Let's see what the blowhard's got to say for himself. Bet he claims one."

Some of the others beat me getting over to find out what had happened to Luke. One came running back to me.

"What did I tell you? He says he shot one off your tail."

I took Frank by the arm and walked him away from the others. From what he told me, the way he described it and from the fact that I was there, I believed then, and always will believe, that he did shoot a German plane off my tail. However, although I used every resource I could muster, both before and after the Armistice, in trying to get him a confirmation, that victory is unconfirmed to this day.

"I never pulled until I had my gun right in that baby's cockpit," he said. "And I didn't leave him until he hit the ground and rolled over on his back, with me not more than two hundred feet in the air."

He was not lying and I know it.

Frank Luke was a lonesome and despised man from that day until he brought down his first balloon near Mariculles on the St. Mihiel front on September 12. In the whole group he found only three men who believed in him—Joe Wehner and Ivan Roberts in the 27th and Norman Archibald in the 95th. A few days later, just as we shifted to St. Mihiel, Archibald, a green but gallant pilot, was captured by the Germans. Luke spent most of his spare time on the machine-gun range perfecting his already excellent marksmanship.

There was a peculiar reason, unknown to most of the fliers, why Wehner should be attracted to Luke. He, too, was hiding a personal grief. Like Luke, and Rickenbacker earlier in the war, he had been suspected of being something he wasn't. In Texas this private secretary from Everett, Massachusetts, son of a poor German cobbler, was arrested as a possible enemy agent. Again, at Garden City, Long Island, he was picked up and subjected to long questioning. Somebody evidently was reporting his slightest remarks. Even in France, the Secret Service men took him for a long chat. Nothing came of it. If I know anything about men nothing could have come of it. Wehner died, an honored ace, on September 18, 1918, after destroying two German airplanes and six balloons. Like Luke, he harbored a burning desire for vindication. Both received it bounteously—at the cost of their lives.

Frank Luke never got over his chagrin at having his story about that first plane doubted and he adopted a quaint and determined method of getting his own confirmations. Picking out the letters with one finger, he typed a lot of personal confirmation blanks for witnesses of his deeds to sign. On September 12, in an early morning patrol of eight planes, flying at only 600 feet, Luke had adventures best described in his own words in his combat report:

Combat report—Sept. 12, 1918

Lt. Frank Luke reports:—

Saw 3 EA near Lavigneulle and gave chase following them directly east towards Pont-a-Mousson where they disappeared towards Metz. Saw enemy balloon at Marieville. Destroyed it after three passes at it, each within a few yards of the balloon. The third pass was made when the balloon was very near the ground. Both guns stopped so pulled off to one side. Fixed left gun and turned about to make one final effort to burn it, but saw it had started. The next instant it burst into great flames and dropped on the winch, destroying it. The observer, Joseph

M. Fox, who saw the burning said he thought several were killed when it burst into flames so near the ground. There was a good field near our balloons so landed for confirmation. Left field and started back when my motor began cutting out. Returned to same field, and there found out my motor could not be fixed, so returned by motorcycle. Attached you will find confirmation from Lt. Fox and Lt. Smith. Both saw burning.

In other words, Frank knew he had destroyed that balloon and he wanted the rest of us to know it. So he flew toward the nearest American balloon, picked a small field nearby and landed. Leaving his machine with propeller slowly ticking over, he jumped out to meet a man running toward him. In reality he was not on our sector. He was encroaching on territory of our troop's below our front.

"What's the matter?" asked the runner. "Are you hit? Better get your machine under cover or they'll open up on it."

"Here, sign this," said Luke. "You saw me get that sausage over there, didn't you?"

"I'll say I saw it. We all did," replied the soldier. "That thing's been spotting us for three days and our whole gang's waiting to give you a hand."

By this time a considerable group was around Luke. The senior officer and another read the carefully prepared note Luke offered them, filled in two or three blanks and signed it with an indelible pencil. They wondered why Luke murmured, "Guess that'll hold 'em."

Despite that signed official memorandum, I was unable to get confirmation of this victory from GHQ until September 26, but I never told Luke or anybody else about that. I suppose it was because we had poached on Colonel Johnson's preserves and this caused the delay. When his plane reached the squadron, it was literally filled with bullet holes and was a complete "wash out." The guns and special gadgets were transferred to a new ship.

And on September 14 Luke and Wehner had another big day. Colonel Milling, General Mitchell's right-hand man, called me up.

"Hartney," he said, "we can't wait until dusk to try out that new scheme your man, Luke, is putting forward. There's a saucy sausage over there at Boinville and another at Buzy which you must knock off in the next hour or two if you can."

Hurriedly I called in the squadron commanders and explained my plan for a three-cornered attack on the balloons, allotting the 27th to do the actual firing on them. Within ten minutes after issuing the hastily prepared operations orders, four officers of the 27th appeared before me: Captain "Ack" Grant, commander, Captain K. S. Clapp, flight commander of Luke's flight, First Lieutenant Leo H. Dawson, one of the two or three flying officers of the World War still in the service, and Lieutenant Tommy Lennon, now a Wall Street broker.

They had an astounding proposition to put up to me. It was Clapp who voiced it.

"Maj', we've been elected today to get that balloon. Evidently you don't like your old gang in the 27th any more and want to get rid of us. You've detailed us to do the job and to name the man to go down at that sausage. Now, here's the proposition: Grant and I are going to put your boy friend, Luke, on that assignment. If he gets it, he stays in the 27th. If he fails, you'll O.K. a transfer to some other outfit or to the rear. He's a menace to morale."

"'Gonny,'" said I. "You're on. It's a deal. But we've got to land that gas bag this morning and if you have any doubts about doing it I'll let the 95th have a chance. Besides,

I'm going on this party myself just to see that you're all safe."

Instead of one, we had two patrols, one at 9:30 A.M., the other at 2:30 P.M. I went up with the second; so did Wehner. Luke went with both. Here are his reports:

Combat report—Sept. 14, 1918.

Lt. Frank Luke reports:—

Left formation at Abaucourt and attacked an enemy balloon near Boinville. Dove at it six times at close range. Had two stoppages with left gun which carried incendiary bullets, and after fixing both, continued the attack. After about 75 rounds being left in right gun, I attacked an archie battery at base of balloon. Am sure that my fire took effect as the crew scattered. After my first attack on balloon, the observer jumped. The last I saw of the balloon it was on the ground in a very flabby condition. Confirmation requested.

Combat report—Sept. 14, 1918.

Lt. Frank Luke reports:—

I and Lt. Wehner were to leave with formation, dropping out at Buzy to attack enemy balloon. By orders of the CO. On arriving at Buzy left formation and brought down enemy balloon in flames. While fixing my gun so that I could attack another nearby balloon, eight enemy Fokkers dropped down on me. Dove and pulled away from them. They scored several good shots on my plane. I saw Lt. Wehner dive through enemy formation and attack two enemy planes on my tail, but as my guns were jammed did not turn, as I was not sure it was an allied plane until he joined me later. You will find attached confirmation of balloon.

After the second patrol I had scarcely landed and made my way to Group headquarters when Grant, Clapp, and Dawson came galloping up, highly excited.

Dawson was the spokesman: "Listen, Major, we want to take that all back. Boy, if anyone thinks that bird is yellow he's crazy. I'll take back every doubt I ever had. The man's not yellow; he's crazy, stark mad. He went by me on that attack like a wild man. I thought he was diving right into the fabric. Then, even after it was afire, I saw him take another swoop down on it. He was pouring fire on fire and a hydrogen one at that."

Clapp had brought down one of the enemy machines. Everyone in the formation saw him do it. But to this day the confirmation has never come through. Luke had not returned. There were tears in Clapp's eyes.

"Gosh, Maj'," he gulped. "Who spread that dribble around that Luke is a fourflusher? I'd like to kill the man that did. He's gone, the poor kid, but he went in a blaze of glory. He had to go right down to the ground to get that second balloon and they've got the hottest machine-gun nest in the world around it. They couldn't miss him."

The telephone rang. It was the 27th Squadron headquarters. The operations officer was much excited.

"Major, you'd better come down here quick and ground this bird, Luke. He's ordered his plane filled up with gas. He's just run over to Wehner's ship and he says they're going out to attack that balloon at Waroq. His machine is full of holes, two longerons are completely riddled and the whole machine is so badly shot up it's a wonder he flew back here at all. He's crazy as a bedbug, that man."

We ran all the way, a quarter of a mile, to the 27th. On the way over, all of us puffing from the exertion, Captain Grant, who always had more or less of the West Point attitude toward fliers, grunted to Clapp:

"You're his flight commander, Clapp. I hold you responsible. He's making a burlesque of the 27th and I'm just not going to stand it. Balloons or no balloons, we must have discipline."

The mechanics, who idolized Luke, had already stymied

him. They had pulled at least two square yards of fabric off the fuselage from the cockpit back and a like amount off one of the wing panels, to lay bare the punctured spars, fittings, and cables. Luke was standing by, sheepishly.

"Wehner wants me on this next patrol, Major," he said. "Won't you let me have Hoover's ship over there? It's all gassed up and Hoover told me I could use it in a pinch. Come on, Major, please."

Grant then stepped up, with very stern mien.

"Who's running this outfit, Major? You or I? I need Hoover's ship for the next patrol. We've got two balloons already today and this next one Wehner is after isn't so important."

Grant was Luke's immediate commanding officer. He won out. Luke slunk away, giving Grant a disdainful look, and made his way over to Wehner.

I followed and caught him by the arm.

"Listen, Frank, old boy," I said. "I appreciate all you're doing. I'm so proud of you I hardly know what to do. It's only a few hours since the Army called for the destruction of those balloons and you did it. No outfit can beat that. The famous French Cigone group, with their great aces, Fonck and Garros, is over the hill there and they can't even get their new '220' Spads into service, let alone shoot down balloons. Have patience. In flying, patience is the best virtue you can have if you want to live to be an old man."

He looked at me with a strange, inquiring gaze. Maybe he was not intent on living to be an old man. I know he liked and trusted me. I added quickly: "Besides, Frank, you've got to make out a couple of combat reports. What's the use of shooting them down if you don't get credit? Moreover, I want you to try out that dusk idea of yours. I think you'll get them easier and with less risk in the evening when the Huns are afraid to fly."

It worked. As his Group commander I could easily have given him strict orders and court-martialed him out of the service if he disobeyed them. But by this time I was getting quite wise in the peculiar mental processes of war pilots and how to get the very best out of them. My little piece of flattery saved him from disgrace, because Luke was simply not susceptible to ordinary Army discipline. And it cost the Germans at least one dozen balloons and three airplanes.

Wehner was standing by his machine. A big, athletic six-footer, he had a decided poise coupled with cool, calculating sense. He was rubbing his goggles.

"How many's he got, Major?" he asked, smiling.

"Two more!" I said.

"Well, leave him here on the ground. There's only one balloon left up there and even if I get it I still can't catch up to him."

Wehner took out his map, a piece of paper cut down to about three inches square mounted on stiff cardboard which he could easily hold in his hand as he flew.

"I'm going to climb to the ceiling, today, Major. It's so hazy I doubt if I'll be seen from the ground. Then I'm going ten miles directly south over the lines and from there I'll catch him unawares in a swoop from his side. Nothing will stop me."

I could see that Luke was fairly aching to go along. Wehner leaped into his cockpit and was off in less than sixty seconds.

"Remember your promise, Major," said Luke as we parted, he to his tent, I to answer a call from Army headquarters. Major Lyster and my splendid Sergeant Major Cunningham met me part way there. If the latter ever reads this book I hope he will get in touch with me. Lyster was excited.

"There's great rejoicing up at 'Swilly' (Souilly)," he announced. "General Mitchell is on his way over to congratulate the outfit."

Presently Mitchell came along with Tommy Milling, the latter one of the first Army pilots, who won $10,000 in a flying meet at Belmont Park in 1911, and who knew his stuff thoroughly. Mitchell's talk was certainly encouraging to the boys. It was wonderful. Afterward he said to me:

"Hartney, if you can spare a moment, I want you to go over and talk to the French 'Stork' group. Garros has escaped from Germany and rejoined them. They say the '220' Spads are no good and want to know how you keep them from throwing carburetors and plumbing."

Just then the telephone rang. It was for the general. He came back hurriedly.

"Fonck has got that balloon over Waroq," he yelled. I was just about to say, "Fonck, hell, it's Wehner," but restrained my enthusiasm for a moment planning to hold him there until Wehner returned. We didn't have long to wait. In almost no time the 27th was on the wire, advising that Wehner was back safely and had bagged two Fokkers over Waroq just as a French Spad had pulled in and burned his balloon. It was true. Had Wehner taken off one minute earlier or had he not taken time to climb to a great height and get in behind, he probably would have been trapped himself by the same Fokkers that attempted to trap the Frenchman whom Wehner had saved. But the sand in Wehner's glass had not quite run out yet.

Mitchell was proud as punch. He then questioned us about the plan for strafing balloons in the dusk of evening. I called for Luke—it was his idea. Poor Frank was quite flabbergasted as he came before the general in his untidy uniform and cloth puttees. He was bashful and silent. Colonel Milling, a great diplomat, soon had him at ease. And Luke put forth his plan, worthy of a veteran flying general. In his Arizona twang he explained part of it:

"Tomorrow heinie's going to replace those two balloons near Boinville. They're going to keep a constant patrol up there and they think I'm going over to try and pick them off and then they'll jump me. Not me, no siree. Wehner and I are going to try out our dusk stuff on them together and if you gentlemen will come back here just about dusk Major Hartney will give you the exact time when they are going to burn up."

Next morning, however, Luke pulled a stunt that was entirely in keeping with his character. He joined two of the 27th's patrols and, watching for chances, swooped down like a comet and sent both balloons flaming to the ground, as the patrols acted unwittingly as his escort and engaged the balloon-protecting Fokkers overhead. Wehner was also busy on his own hook. Leaving after the patrols, he bagged two flat balloons to add to his score. In addition he shot two Fokkers down in flames off Luke's tail.

About two o'clock Mitchell called me up again.

"Hartney, the French got your two balloons at Boinville so you won't be able to stage that show tonight, will you?"

I went right after him in a kidding way.

"Sorry, sir, begging your pardon, sir, but it was Luke who got both of those balloons and Wehner got two others and a couple of Fokkers for good measure. Luke wants to present his compliments and asks permission to substitute for this evening's special performance for you the following two balloons: one northeast of Verdun, near Spincourt, the other north of Verdun near Chaumont."

I heard Mitchell turn away from the field telephone and speak to Bill Sherman. "Are there two balloons near Verdun? I thought they were all down." Sherman replied, "Yes, that's correct, sir, but they are not very active and we've issued no orders on them yet."

Mitchell, coming back to the phone, asked me, "Then you want us over, don't you?"

"Yes, sir, I certainly do," I replied. "But get here at six o'clock and don't be late. The action takes place at 6:58 and 6:59 and we've got a grandstand seat for you."

And now, reader, I want you to recollect the most dramatic stage play you ever saw and mentally compare it with this show put on, with human lives at stake, by Lieutenants Luke and Wehner of the hastily thrown together United States Air Service.

General Mitchell arrived with Colonel Milling, Colonel Sherman and Inspector General T. I. Donaldson in Mitchell's Benz. Evidently our beloved general switched his cars each day. He had quite a fleet of them. The day before he had had his Mercedes. Mitchell disliked the Germans but he liked their automobiles. We had a spot of coffee, then, looking at our wrist watches, sauntered slowly out in the evening shadows to the brow of a nearby hill. Slowly the hands on our watches crept up to zero hour. Darkness was beginning to fall and a strange sort of peace, broken only by distant rumbling of artillery, was settling over the countryside. The balloons, swinging lazily yet menacingly in the evening breeze, could be discerned through the gathering mist off in the distance, over Verdun way.

Mitchell murmured, "Colonel Barnes is going to do a little extra shooting tonight with his artillery and his gunflashes will probably make the balloon line more active." This was proved correct almost immediately. To the accompaniment of the increasing roar of the good colonel's guns the balloons slowly but surely rose higher and higher, as their observers reported to the German artillery on the locations of Colonel Barnes' guns and their flashes.

General Mitchell shook his head. "Hartney, it's impossible. To get a balloon at all is a feat. To time its demise five hours ahead is beyond reason. And to do it at night is just not in the cards."

Yet he watched his timepiece religiously.

"Twenty seconds to go," said Grant. "They're going after the Spincourt bag first because Luke said they would attack down wind and then . . ."

He never finished the sentence. At exactly 6:58 a tongue of flame shot into the sky over by Spincourt followed by a huge burst of fire as the fast-burning hydrogen practically exploded the entire balloon. I knew the observer was somewhere out there in a parachute, trying desperately to reach the earth before the sparks caught him and the crew on the winch were running for their lives lest the flaming bag settle quickly over them and roast them alive. The second bag was going down rapidly as the winch crew worked feverishly to save it.

"By God, there she goes!" yelled Mitchell. For once in his life the general lost his poise and danced up and down in his excitement as a burst of red and yellow fire shot up from the second balloon. Milling, Sherman, and Donaldson were actually shouting wildly, exultingly over the superb performance of my two brave boys. And well they might.

"That's perfectly magnificent. How can they get down in the darkness, Hartney?" asked Mitchell, when he had regained a little of his composure.

"You watch them," I replied. "We have a system all worked out—something brand new. Come on up to our new control tower and watch it operate."

And I led him to what I honestly believe was the first control tower ever erected in the world for the control of night flying, a rough two-by-four scantling affair on top of the Group headquarters shack.

"Explain this setup, Grant," I said to Luke's commanding officer. In spite of his usual severity, Grant's hands were trembling with excitement as, in his high-pitched Texas voice, he told the Air Chief what we had done.

"You see, it's this way: We have a lighted dummy airdrome four miles down the road. Don't ever try to land on it. It's a blind, solely to receive Jerry's bombs as he follows our boys home at night and thinks they land there while they're really on their way home. He's bombed hell out of it already. We leave the lights on most of the night. When one of our planes comes along, the pilot gives a secret blinker recognition signal to this tower and he is given one minute to land on our real airdrome here but with only a limited amount of indirectly lighted surface in perspective to guide him in. If he misses, he must go up and wait for ten minutes. Meantime, the old Boche, if any, wastes his bombs on the dummy field."

"Very smart stuff," said the general. "We'll have more of those."

And in the present war you may be sure the landscapes in several countries are dotted with brilliantly lighted, entirely phony landing fields to lure the enemy to his destruction.

Kr-Kr-Kr-Karump-Karump! It was the intermittent roar of two big Gnome-Rhone Monosoupape motors, one very much higher than the other, krumping as the pilots turned on and off their selector switches. It was Luke and Wehner "coming home to roost."

Suddenly complete, dead silence. Then in the darkness the sound of a heavy bump and the *Kr-Kr-Karump* of the old Monosoupape as Frank Luke taxied to a stop some distance away from us. Above, at about 3000 feet, the prearranged height, we could hear Wehner patiently waiting his signal to come on in. Again a sullen silence, then, in the dim light of the field, a bump, and Wehner came in with a perfect landing without a single bump. This time both of them taxied not up to their own 27th tarmac but right up the field and stopped in front of us.

Both pilots jumped out and ran toward each other. By the time we reached them they were in an animated conversation. And what do you think they were talking about? Their double victory on which they had called their shots to the second? Not a bit of it. They were heatedly discussing the thousands of bullets which had been fired at them *from our side of the lines.* They had been shot at by American troops all along the route as they made their way home at low altitude. Here was something we hadn't counted on. It happened many times during the war. It would be revealing to know the number of our fliers who lost their lives by being brought down by "friendly" rifles, field guns, and archie fire and the number of doughboys who were engulfed in our own barrages. This is how Ham Coolidge, one of my best officers, died. Honest mistakes will happen and there are probably many boys now alive who will die from this cause in the next war, in which the fire power will be many times greater and faster than in the so-called World War. I know of no suitable remedies being prepared for these human errors.

Eddie Rickenbacker joined us on the field which was rapidly filling with officers and enlisted men. Luke and Wehner were embarrassed by the congratulations heaped upon them but I know Luke was greatly impressed by Rickenbacker's words of praise. He had pulled ahead of Rick and for the moment was the American "Ace of Aces." But he had a tremendous admiration for Rick and his own leadership was not to last long.

"Are their ships shot up at all?" inquired Milling. "Let's look."

General Mitchell took his swagger stick and with a zip pulled huge chunks of fabric off of Luke's left lower wing and then off Wehner's fuselage. Literally those planes had been all but shot out from under them. Each had at least fifty bullet holes and was useless for further service without a complete overhaul. To appreciate the charmed life these boys were leading it is only necessary to realize that any two of those bullets could have ended their careers instantly and that these ships were the fifth that Luke and the third that Wehner had had rendered unfit for further work on account of bullet holes.

Already Luke was talking about two balloons near Reville Romagne and Reville Magines which he and Wehner had spotted that afternoon and which they wanted to bring down in broad daylight the next day.

"We'll burn 'em up as fast as they bring them along," he announced, and he was in dead earnest.

I walked to my billet that night in a sort of daze. Things were going a bit too fast for me. I had a strange feeling that something was going to let go. But one thought stuck in my mind—I was letting two comparative newcomers run away with the entire group.

"After all," I said to myself. "You've got 124 other flying officers in this group besides Luke and Wehner. The others brought down four enemy planes today and a lot of the boys are aces. From now on there will be no more voluntary missions for either Luke or Wehner and I'll transfer Luke from the 27th to the 94th if he doesn't stick with his formations and have more patience, balloons or no balloons."

I prayed for rain or fog the next day, September 16, 1918, to give us a breathing spell, but, although it poured all night, I knew I was not to have my wish. Major Blair, of the good old efficient Signal Corps, one of our most completely reliable branches of service, had assured me there would be plenty of flying the next day and, as usual, he was right. I issued group orders for the day's work—normal patrols and alerts with a final balloon strafe in the evening. We had pushed the front line back behind St. Mihiel. I knew this from a peculiar circumstance—the music in our mess halls. Every one of our squadrons had sent up a truck with a crew which stole back from the Germans the pianos they had stolen from the French châteaus. The sound of ragtime was again in the air.

Some eight miles beyond St. Mihiel the front line of the enemy had more or less taken root for the moment but our Army had secured a most commanding position on some high hills overlooking the flat ground beyond. Two balloons were bothering us. They swayed menacingly in the distance but their crews were obviously jittery. The mere appearance of one of our patrols or a salvo of their own archie, indicating an Allied plane, started their crews cranking them down frantically.

About 6:30 in the evening of the 16th, with the sergeant major of the 95th and two pilots from the 147th who needed a rest, I made my way by Fiat truck to a French balloon company situated nearby on the hill overlooking the flat enemy terrain beyond.

"Voyez-vous les deux drachens la-bas?" I said to the French officer in command. *"Ah, oui,"* he replied with dignity and politeness. *"Eh bien,"* I announced, *"Regardezbien, parcequ' à cinq minutes apres sept heurs ils seront brulees, à ce moment precise."*

The officer's face took on a startled look. *"Tous les Americans sont fous*—all Americans are crazy." That's what he was thinking. It's what most of the French thought, especially of our highly individualistic aviators. He peered at me with eyes that bespoke amusement and pity and my crude French aroused his disdain. He told me there was an American officer up in the balloon basket swinging about 500 feet above our heads. I strolled over and telephoned up to him.

"CO 1st Pursuit Group talking. Keep your eye on the balloons over there at Reville Romagne and Reville Magines," I said. "The 1st Pursuit Group is going to burn them up at 7:05 exactly."

He was all excited.

"But there are dozens of enemy planes over there laying for you or me, I don't know which. Don't try it."

"The orders are out," I said. "Keep your eyes on them carefully. We want your signature after they go down."

"O.K.," he replied.

Then we went back, literally kidnapped the haughty French commander and led him, quite against his wishes, over to the hill under some nice trees. Presently he was joined by some of his officers. I pointed at my watch because zero hour was fast approaching. Both balloons were hanging not more than 200 feet up. Now and then, like fish in a muddy gold fish bowl, we would get the flash of light on the belly of an enemy ship. We estimated at least five of them were lying in wait for our boys at about 8000 feet.

From Mount Sec, Verdun, and Rembercourt three echelons of the 27th were to set out on split seconds so as to arrive at the balloons at exactly 6:55, allowing for wind velocities. Under no circumstances were they to engage the enemy before the balloon strafe, even if they should, by a miracle, come upon some enemy training planes without guns. Luke and Wehner were to attack the bag at Reville Romagne first.

By now the Frenchmen were more convinced than ever that we were quite daft and in a stream of staccato jabbering indicated that we were making a farce of a perfectly good war. God help them if we hadn't been in there! Presently, we began to get serious as the watch hands indicated that the big event was almost on us. So the Frenchmen sobered down and decided, perhaps there was something in this wild Yankee plan after all.

Through the evening haze it was just barely possible to see the weaving sausages. We knew we could not see anything of the actual assault. But it was not necessary. As certainly as the hands of the synchronized watches crept up and arrived at the appointed moment I knew just what Luke and Wehner were doing. And sure enough, at exactly 7:05 the graying sky was split by a long tongue of flame. Balloon Number One, not more than fifty feet from the ground, had succumbed to the joint attack of two of the most intrepid boys that ever lived. And before we could summon speech to voice our acclaim a sudden red glow announced the doom of the second balloon. Immediately the distant air was ruptured by the riveting-machine echoes of dozens of machine guns from the ground and the air as the waiting Fokkers came down, too late, for a dogfight with our protecting patrol, while Luke and Wehner, flying like demons, made their getaway.

The Frenchmen broke into excited palaver but suddenly they seemed very unimportant to me. I went back to the telephone and called up the basket.

"Did you see them go down? Did you see those two balloons burn up over there?"

"No," was the astonishing reply. "There was a formation of enemy planes (our own 27th) went dashing over us just then and I was sure we were attacked and couldn't look."

C'est la guerre!

"Oh, hell!" said I. "Come on down here and get these Frenchmen to sign up then. They saw the whole show."

Slowly we wound down the basket and we got the confirmations for Luke and Wehner duly attested. From where we were we could, of course, only guess at what was going on. Here is the inside picture in the official words of the two principal actors:

Combat report . . . Sept. 16, 1918.

Lt. J. F. Wehner reports:

Patrol to strafe balloons. Flew North-East passing over Verdun and attacked a balloon in the vicinity of Reville with Lt. Luke at 19 h 05. We each fired one burst when I observed that it instantly caught fire. The observer jumped but was burned to death by the flaming balloon before reaching the ground. I headed towards the Meuse river trying to pick up another balloon; could not locate one so headed towards Verdun. On the way back saw a fire in the vicinity of Romagne which evidently was Lt. Luke's second balloon. While waiting for Lt. Luke near Verdun saw red flare near Mangiennes. Thinking it our pre-arranged signal from Lt. Luke, I headed in that direction. Saw balloon just above the tree tops near Mangiennes and brought it down in flames with one burst at 19 h 35. Anti-aircraft very active. Two confirmations requested.

Combat report . . . Sept. 16, 1918.

Lt. Frank Luke reports:

Patrol to strafe balloons. Everything very carefully arranged. Lt. Wehner and I left airdrome passing over Verdun. We attacked balloon in vicinity of Reville at 19 h 03. Both Lt. Wehner and I shot a burst into it. It burst into flames and fell on observer who had jumped a few seconds before. We started for another balloon in vicinity of Romagne. I attacked and destroyed it. It burst into flames on the ground, burning winch. The anti-aircraft guns were very active scoring several good hits on my plane. The last I saw of Lt. Wehner he was going in a south-easterly direction after the first balloon went down. I shot at supply trains on my way back. Two confirmations requested.

It was two days later that Wehner died. It was a hero's death that filled me with unutterable woe and broke Frank Luke's heart. Wehner and Luke, alone with no protection, shot down two balloons. Just as the second of the sausages was streaking to the earth a mass of fierce-burning hydrogen, six Fokkers swooped down on Luke. Wehner saw them and in a desperate effort to save his friend fired a bright Very signal of warning. Luke, busy with his balloon busting, failed to see it. So Wehner piled into the mess. But a seventh Fokker, lurking high above, made a sudden dive with guns belching. And in between the flaming ruins of the two gas bags there came another and smaller spiral of flame mixed with billowy clouds of black smoke from burning gasoline. Then a sickening crash. It was the end of Joe Wehner. He died for his friend and his country. German agent? Ha!

An observer on the ground told me that Luke flew like a swallow as he fought back and forth, avenging his pal. Two of the enemy planes were sent spinning to earth, one in flames, in the viciousness of his attack. Then with his gas running low, he broke away. Barely had he reached the lines when he saw the puffs of friendly archie up toward Verdun. This meant an enemy plane on our side of the lines. Frank, still at 8000 feet, had some 5000 feet altitude on the intruder and could hardly believe his eyes. It had been weeks since we had seen a Boche plane in our territory. His main tank was about out and he knew he had barely enough gas in his nourice to get back to Rembercourt. Yet he swerved abruptly.

Let me quote as well as I can remember from the lips of a private in one of our infantry divisions, the famous Rainbow Division (42d), who had seen the whole thing. I talked to him as we stood alongside of the crashed LVG German plane around which, for some strange reason known only to themselves, the French had thrown a guard and refused to let Luke even take a closeup look at it. The bodies of its pilot and observer were still in it.

"What's the matter with them frogs? They won't let that

kid peek at his own trophy. Three French planes were just toying with this Boche plane and another, afraid to come near them. One got away and this one would have, too, because they were shooting at it from so far away they didn't have a chance. Just then this guy, Luke, came busting out of the sky like a rocket, streaked past them Frenchmen and closed right in on the Hun. I thought he was going to ram him 'cause I never heard his shots until after the German began tumbling. He took this Boche from right under the noses of the Frenchmen who had only been playing with him. Boy! Did you ever hear a whole American division cheer?"

Five confirmed victories for Luke in ten minutes! That's the official word I received that evening—two balloons and three planes. It was an incredible achievement. But Luke was a changed boy. He did not come home that night. He and his plane spent the hours of darkness parked under one of the big "Mothers"—the 16-inch American naval railroad guns— Frank grieving for his friend.

Eddie Rickenbacker, Mrs. Welton, the Group's wonderful YMCA girl, and I drove up next morning in my Twin-Six. Luke was disconsolate.

"Wehner isn't back yet, is he, Major?"

His eyes seemed already resigned to what he himself had seen, but in air battles there is always the off-chance that an outside plane may have joined in.

Here is Frank's official report on the incident that robbed him of his only real friend:

Combat report . . . Sept. 18, 1918.

Lt. Frank Luke reports:

Lt. Wehner and I left the airdrome at 16 h 00 to spot enemy balloons. Over St. Mihiel we saw two German balloons near Labeuville. We maneuvered in the clouds and dropped down, burning both. We were then attacked by a number of EA the main formation attacking Lt. Wehner who was above and on one side. I started climbing to join the fight, when two EA attacked me from the rear. I turned on them, opening both guns on the leader. We came head on until within a few yards of each other, when my opponent turned to one side in a nose dive, and I saw him crash on the ground. I then turned on the second, shot a short burst and he turned and went into a dive. I saw a number of EA above, but could not find Lt. Wehner, so turned and made for our lines. The above fight occurred in the vicinity of St. Hilaire. On reaching our balloon line, flew east. Saw archie on our side, flew towards it and found an enemy observation machine. I gave chase with some other Spads, and we got him off from his lines, and after a short encounter he crashed, within our lines, southeast of Verdun. Lt. Wehner is entitled to share in the victories over both the balloons. Confirmations requested, two balloons and three planes.

We took him back with us in the car. He hardly spoke all the way. Presently, while the rest of us were talking in generalities, he turned to me, looked me in the eye, and said:

"Major, I'm glad it wasn't me. My mother doesn't know I'm on the front yet."

Figure that out psychologically and you will have the key to Frank Luke's character. The next day, almost by force, we sent him off on a leave to Orly from which we knew he would make his way into Paris. It was a vacation of a highly unsuccessful nature. He wanted no hilarity.

And then, with the St. Mihiel drive a complete victory for the U. S. First Army, a vindication of General Pershing's claim that both our staff and our troops were now of age and could co-operate with our gallant allies as a self-contained and self-managed unit, we began preparations for the next big push. This was the text which was to bring such glory but such immense casualties to American arms, the battle of the Argonne Forest. And naturally, in the hectic hurly-burly of operating six air squadrons, I forgot entirely about Frank Luke.

After an eight-day period of comparative quiet, there were terrific air battles for our group on September 26, 1918, and in the day's reports of the destruction of five enemy balloons and six airplanes I was astonished to find one telling of the bringing down of a Fokker biplane by Luke. He had returned two days ahead of time from his leave and had plunged immediately into the furor of the war.

In this and his previous fight against enemy planes, Luke's ship, strange to say, came home without any bullet holes. Kenneth Porter of the 147th, one of the very best flight commanders in the group, undertook to kid Luke in his usual "put-you-on-the-spot" manner.

"What's the matter, Luke? No bullet holes must mean no balloons. Are you slipping?"

Luke came back in characteristic fashion.

"Oh, you'll see. I'm letting everyone take a crack at that bag over Bethenville and if, by the day after tomorrow, you all fail I'm going on over and bring it in."

And he did just that.

The sand was now running very low in the hourglass for Frank Luke. He had to have someone to take Wehner's place with him; someone to take the desperate chances he took, to count on the same luck, to protect him without flinching and someone for him to protect in tight places. So he picked out Lieutenant Ivan A. Roberts of the 27th, a stocky, heavy-set boy from Massachusetts, and a very fine pilot.

At 5:18 on the evening of September 27 he and Luke set out alone to strafe balloons. They did not find any. Instead they found a formation of five Fokkers and immediately went into battle with them. Luke reported later that after firing several short bursts one of the Hun machines went down out of control. This victory, if completed, was never confirmed. Two other EA jumped on Luke's tail but he turned and fought them off. Then he broke away and came home. The last he saw of Roberts was in combat with several Fokkers in the vicinity of Consenvoye and Sivry, too far away for Luke to render aid.

That was the last ever heard of Roberts. We searched for him or traces of his plane at the front but to no avail. In 1929 his father, head of a boys' school in Massachusetts, invited me up to talk to his boys and the men of the village. I went there, talked too long and contracted a septic sore throat. In the school medicine chest I found some argyrol and kept dousing my throat with it. I thought I was going to die but the next day I was better and came back home. That day an epidemic of septic throat poisoning broke out in the town and scores of people died from it. It was one of the worst epidemics in the history of the state. But I, who was Case Number One, recovered and lived. The old Hartney luck again!

At this time Luke got the idea that he could take on the entire German airplane and balloon services singlehanded, without support of any kind. He was certainly the most reckless, unafraid, and self-confident flier in the United States Army. And his amazing successes had done nothing to upset his feeling that he was invincible nor had the hundreds of bullet holes he had picked up in his succession of planes taught him any caution.

It was about this time that we had established an advance base only four miles from the front, near Verdun, under command of the very efficient Captain Jerry Vasconcells. That appealed to Luke. He came to me and pleaded to be allowed to operate independently from that field. His CO, Captain Grant, was frantic at his inability to control Luke's activities. Almost every pilot in the Group had had a crack at the balloon over Bethenville. But it was still up. While Grant and I were discussing the advisability of letting Luke operate as a lone wolf out of the Verdun field, Frank went out, all by himself, at noon on September 28, and burned up the Bethenville balloon in its nest.

I don't know if you know what it means to destroy an enemy balloon in its nest. It means that you have to come down to within 100 feet of the ground, pour incendiary bullets from a special high-caliber machine gun into it with sure, steady aim and maneuver your plane so it will not hit the ground, or the balloon or surrounding trees. All this, plus the planning of a successful getaway over the tree tops must be performed almost on the muzzles of from ten to twenty ground machine guns and countless rifles which are pouring death at you at the rate of several hundred shots a minute.

Luke took this balloon in his stride. Here is his report on it—the last report he ever made:

Combat report . . . Sept. 28, 1918.

Lt. Frank Luke reports:

I flew north to Verdun, crossed the lines at about five hundred meters and found a balloon in its nest in the region of Bethenville. I dove on it firing both guns. After I pulled away it burst into flames. As I could not find any others I returned to the airdrome. One confirmation requested.

Then he went out on another patrol with his squadron. With motor trouble or something he landed near a French balloon company and stayed all night with its crew. My, was his CO, Grant, angry! He came galloping into my headquarters in the morning of the 29th, all hot and bothered.

"Major, this man Luke is going hog-wild," he complained, "I can't handle him unless you'll back me up. He thinks he's the whole Air Service. Rumors are about that he no longer intends to go out with the squadron on patrol. Says he is going on a balloon strafe alone and claims you'll O.K. it. What about it?"

Luke had not asked me, but knowing his mind and his ability, I said:

"Yes, Luke is going up to the Verdun field for a balloon strafe but I have issued absolute orders that his plane is not to stir off the ground until 5:56 P.M. That will bring him over the balloon after dark when all the heinies have gone home to roost." Soon afterward orders came from Vasconcells, confirming my previous talk with him, that Luke could take a crack at the enemy balloons on the upper Meuse near Milly about dusk. I thought it unwise to assign anybody to go with him. Already two excellent men, Wehner and Roberts, had died in Frank Luke's junkets. But Luke was not to stir off the ground until 5:56. I knew that up until then the German pursuit was lying in wait for him and he knew it, too. He left immediately for the advance field where Vasconcells saw to it that he stayed grounded all afternoon by commandeering Frank's Spad and not allowing him near it.

Almost wild with impatience to get going, Frank paced around the field like a caged lion. The dugout at this field was almost under the muzzle of one of the big U. S. Navy 16-inch railroad guns. Vasconcells knew when the next round was to be fired and prepared to play his favorite prank on Luke. Inviting him into the dugout, he poured him a cup of coffee. Just then the snooping commander of the group showed up at the door. I had become nervous over the situation up there and had flown over in the only machine available for such use—an English Camel without guns. And immediately I added myself to Jerry Vasconcells' victims.

Luke's cup of coffee was at his lips and I was standing holding mine in my hand when that huge naval gun went off with a colossal roar right over our heads. Luke hurled his cup, coffee and all, and it hit the ceiling. I jumped about seven feet and dropped mine on the floor. And Vasconcells, the blighter, roared his head off.

We pulled my Camel into the shed. Luke's Spad was a little further in. The watch said a good thirty minutes before Luke would be released. I put on my goggles and climbed back into my machine, intending to fly back to the Group at Rembercourt. The engine just would not start. It was quite a scene. Concealed in that shell-torn shed, even the mechanics wore gas masks at alert. We all felt the enemy was just over the brow of the hill. This was almost true because this was the nearest field to the front on the whole battle line from Nieuport to Nancy.

The engine was stubborn as a mule. Even Sergeant Major Albaugh and Vasconcells himself couldn't get a peep out of it. The clock moved around to 5:40. Luke still had sixteen minutes. I glanced back at him and what do you suppose? Some thirty feet behind me, he was already in his machine with his "Hisso" ticking over. Highly exasperated I reached out of the cockpit and grabbed Vasconcells by the arm.

"Do you see that?" I yelled. "Go over and pull him out of that ship and tell him if he doesn't obey orders I'll stop his flying and send him to the rear."

In a moment Luke's propeller stopped and Vasconcells made him get out of his ship. Luke looked at me sheepishly, grinning. I shook my fist at him. Frank knew he couldn't get away with it. The Le Rhone caught and I was off down the field for Group headquarters.

That gesture, a shaken fist, was my parting with Frank Luke. He never returned from that patrol. And for the rest of his short but vivid story I must refer you to the following documents which reached me in the course of events:

From: Graves Registration Officer, Neufchâteau Area No. 1.,

To: Chief of Air Service, APO

Subject: Grave, Unknown American Aviator.

1. Units of this service have located the grave of an unknown aviator killed on Sunday, Sept. 29, 1918, in the village of Murvaux.

2. From the inspection of the grave and interview held with the inhabitants of this town, the following information was learned in regard to this aviator and his heroism. He is reported as having light hair, young, of medium height and of heavy stature.

Reported by the inhabitants that previous to being killed this man had brought down three (3) German balloons, two German planes and dropped hand bombs killing eleven German soldiers and wounding a number of others.

He was wounded himself in the shoulder and evidently had to make a forced landing. Upon landing he opened fire with his automatic and fought until he was killed.

It is also reported that the Germans took his shoes, leggings and money, leaving his grave unmarked.

CHESTER E. STATEN

Captain of Infantry

G.R.S. Office.

AMERICAN RED CROSS

Inter-Office Letter

Jan. 7, 1919.

From: Capt. M. C. Cooper, Air Service, Am.E.F.

To: Capt. C. P. Williamson, Dist. Mgr.

Subject: Mrs Clarkson Potter, 12 Ave. President Wilson, Paris, and Capt. M. C. Cooper, Air Service, formerly 20th Aero Squadron, have been enabled by the aid of the American Red Cross to obtain the following facts concerning missing Aviators:

10. UNIDENTIFIED AVIATOR

This officer was killed at Murvaux (5 kilometers east of Dun-sur-Meuse) on Sunday, September 29, 1918. The Germans stripped him of all identification, but Captain McCormick of the 301st Graves Registration station at Fontains near Murvaux was so interested in the story told by the French people of Murvaux concerning the death of this aviator that he exhumed the body and stated that it was that of a man of medium height, heavy set and with light hair. On his wrist he found an Elgin watch ✗20225566, which was under the sleeve of his combination and which the Germans who had stripped him of all papers and identification marks had evidently missed. The village people of Murvaux told Captain McCormick that this aviator first shot down three German balloons and two German planes, then descended low over the ground and killed eleven Germans with either hand bombs or machine gun bullets. While flying low his plane was hit from the ground and he himself was apparently wounded. He made a successful landing, got out of his plane and when the Germans called on him to surrender he replied by drawing his automatic and opening fire, thus standing he continued to defend himself until killed. The description of this aviator by Captain McCormick and the fact that Lieut. Frank Luke dropped a note to a balloon company that day stating he was going to shoot down the balloons which were shot down make it almost certain that this officer was 2d Lieut. Frank Luke, Air Service, whose nearest relative is Frank Luke, 2200 West Monroe St., Phoenix, Arizona. If the Air Service wishes to check this case it is suggested that a representative of the Air Service be sent to Murvaux and obtain sworn statements from French people of that village.

A check was made by the Air Service. Murvaux is not far from Rembercourt by car. It is on the north bank of the Meuse close to an airdrome which the Germans themselves had set up and occupied. I had been close to Frank's grave about two days after the Armistice when I went up to look at this airdrome and particularly at some new type ground antennae for directional uses in night bombing which they had laid out there secretly. The residents of Murvaux were proud, still are, of Luke and were glad to give the following sworn testimony:

AFFIDAVIT

The undersigned, living in Murvaux, Department of the Meuse, certify to have seen on the 29th of September, 1918, toward evening an American aviator followed by an escadrille of Germans in the direction of Liny, descend suddenly and vertically toward the earth, then straighten out close to the ground and fly in direction of Briers Farm, where he found a German captive balloon which he burned. Then he flew toward Milly where he found another balloon which he also burned in spite of incessant fire directed toward his machine. There he apparently was wounded by a shot from rapid fire cannon. From there he came back over Murvaux and still with his guns he killed six German soldiers and wounded as many more.

Following this he landed and got out of his machine, undoubtedly to quench his thirst at the stream. He had gone 50 yards when seeing the Germans come toward him still had the strength to draw his revolver to defend himself. A moment after he fell dead following a serious wound he received in the chest.

Signatures of the following inhabitants:

PERTON	VALENTINE GARRE
RENE COLON	GUSTAVE CARRE
AUGUSTE CUNY	LEON HERNY
HENRY GUSTAVE	CORTINE DELBART
EUGENE COLINE	GABRIEL DIDIER
ODILE PATOUCHE	CAMILLE PHILLIPS
RICHARD VICTOR	VOLINER NICHOLAS

The undersigned themselves placed the body of the aviator on the wagon and conducted it to the cemetery:

CORTINE DELBART
VOLINER NICHOLAS

Seen for legalization of signatures placed above, Murvaux, Jan. 15, 1919

THE MAYOR
AUGUSTE GARRE

(Seal of Murvaux)

Frank Luke never did get confirmation for the two machines which he had shot down just before he broke off and attacked and burned up the three balloons. But he did get the Congressional Medal of Honor. The only other flier to receive it was Eddie Rickenbacker and his did not come through until twelve years after the Armistice. Until then, Luke was the only Air Officer to whom it was awarded, "For conspicuous gallantry and intrepidity above and beyond the call of duty."

Thus was brought to a close the life of one of the bravest but one of the strangest men that ever wore the uniform of the United States Army. Did I treat him right? I think so. Did I give him too much leeway? I think not. In any other branch of the service requiring routine discipline he would have been unhappy, unruly, totally lost. In the Air Service his dynamic, rebellious, reckless, fearless individuality found expression. And what expression!—eighteen enemy aircraft destroyed officially in seventeen days and at least ten others not officially confirmed but destroyed nevertheless. In any other branch he would probably have been disgraced for insubordination. In the Air Service he became one of the country's great heroes, an ace whose record will be on the books as long as America has a written history. In wartime flying service there must be discipline but it must be adjusted to the individual and tempered with reason.

I forgot to mention that Frank had a deep religious streak. Every Sunday he would go to Mass and frequently he and Joe Broz, now with Baldwin Locomotive Works at Philadelphia, would pour into the plate their entire winnings from the previous night's crap games.

Anyhow, this is the story of Frank Luke as I knew him. I often think of him. I shall never get him out of my mind. His promotion to first lieutenant came through on November 9, 1918. He had been dead forty-one days. *Sic transit gloria mundi.*

CHAPTER 16

Eddie Rickenbacker—
America's Leading Ace

IN THE PROGRAM of the Indianapolis 500 mile sweepstakes race of 1912 there was a driver named Eddie Rickenbacker. He had been driving racing automobiles since 1906, mostly at county fairs. In his first year in the "big league" he earned $40,000 and from then on for five years he was one of America's most consistent and most popular racing drivers.

Today, in addition to other important executive duties, Captain Eddie Rickenbacker is president of the company which owns the 2½ mile brick oval at Indianapolis and is chairman of the Contest Board of the American Automobile Association which controls the Indianapolis race and all other American racing in full-sized motorcars.

The transition of his name from Richenbacher to Rickenbacker was natural. His country was at war with Germany. His paternal ancestry was German but in all the land there was no more loyal and patriotic American than Eddie. He wanted to go into his country's service but he felt the Teutonic nature of his name might be an obstacle, so the "h"'s came out and the "k"'s went in. It didn't work completely. Like Joe Wehner, he was pestered on numerous occasions by Secret Service men, both amateur and professional, looking for some sign that Eddie had leanings toward the Fatherland. As in the case of Wehner, they looked in vain for something that just wasn't there. No man who kills more than a score of German aviators in a war and destroys thirty-three German planes and balloons, although receiving credit for only twenty-six, is doing it to conceal a secret yen for his victims or their homeland. It was all hooey but it weighed on his mind and I fully believe enhanced the quality of his remarkable work at the front.

A while back I said Eddie Rickenbacker was different from most of our fighting pilots. This was true in several ways. In the first place he was older and more mature. In his work Eddie was usually serious, as he is today. The average age of our war fliers was around nineteen and twenty. They were reckless, daring, brilliant, and often foolhardy. When Eddie started to fly he was twenty-eight and remarkably mature even for that age. He was daring, fearless, often brilliant but never reckless and never foolhardy. An army of Rickenbackers in the sky would be invincible.

His experience as an automobile racing driver was priceless in his work as an aviator. It gave him two great assets— patience and a marvelous judgment of speeds and distances. I have said before that patience is a war flier's greatest friend. Faced with a sudden emergency many aviators get impatient, lose their heads, do the wrong thing and frequently pay for it by losing their lives. A man with patience will somehow find the time, be it only split seconds, to analyze the situation and figure out the right thing to do. It allows such men to stay alive and, in wartime, to become aces.

Nobody will long continue to exist in automobile racing who does not acquire uncanny judgment of speeds and distances. Where an ordinary motorist may be able to judge what his car will do in a space of ten or twenty feet at moderate speed, a racing driver can calculate correctly to a fraction of an inch at high speed. Flying, of course, helps to develop the same ability. A racing driver has a great asset to carry into aerial warfare and a good aviator can pilot a car through congested traffic infinitely faster and more safely than the motoring dub. Rick had patience and experienced judgment of pace to a remarkable degree.

Rick had something else, too—a calm, calculating mind. Most of his victories in the air were won in exactly the manner he had worked out in advance. He couldn't, of course, anticipate just what would happen on each patrol but he figured out a number of possible situations and when they occurred he applied the methods he had determined would cope with them.

Eddie got his air training in France at Tours, and it took less time than usual because of his mechanical knowledge and automobile racing experience. Assigned to the 94th Squadron, the first American trained flying unit on the front, which had been organized at Kelly Field, Texas, August 20, 1917, and was commanded by Major J. W. F. M. Huffer, a beloved and respected officer, Rickenbacker went with that unit to Villeneuve-les-Vertus, on the Marne on March 5, 1918. On March 18 the first planes were received and on March 19 Rickenbacker went with Major Raoul Lufbery and Lieutenant Douglas Campbell on the first patrol of American aviators over the German lines. They met no enemy fliers but as I have already told, a piece of shrapnel from an antiaircraft gun hit Rickenbacker's machine and missed him by only a few inches.

Eddie's first contact with an enemy plane was on April 25, 1918, and his second on April 29. His combat report for April 25 reads, simply: "Saw one enemy monoplane with orange tail and white circle and black center cocards. Had a few shots when two more came out of the mist."

The encounter on April 29 was more serious. Rickenbacker and Captain James Norman Hall attacked an Albatross and after Hall fired 350 bullets at it and Rickenbacker 200,

brought it down in flames. This victory was credited entirely
to Hall. Sometimes Rick thus yielded credit to tyro pilots
to encourage them. In this case, of course, Hall was no tyro.
Before the next month was out the 94th Squadron had produced America's first two flying aces—Douglas Campbell and
Eddie Rickenbacker, each of whom brought down five of the
swarming little Albatrosses before the first of June. Rick was
in the group of American aviators decorated on May 15 in
the presence of a distinguished gathering of Allied officers
when General Gerrard of the Eighth French Army pinned
the Croix de Guerre on him and four others of his squadron.
Today Eddie has practically every decoration available, including the most coveted of all, the Congressional Medal of
Honor. He and Frank Luke were the only aviators to receive
it.

Then Rickenbacker suffered a great misfortune. He was
stricken with mastoid infection, was hustled off to a hospital
near Paris and there spent the months of July and August
in misery. In the meantime, Major Huffer was needed for
other duties in the AEF and the senior officer, Captain Kenneth Marr, became squadron commander of the 94th. We
do not find Rickenbacker's name again in the list of victories
until September 14, 1918, but when he started again he set
a terrific pace. I really believe if he had not been taken ill
he would today be credited with twice as many enemy ships
as he actually destroyed. It is possible that, with his sure, careful methods, he might have continued his aerial combats for
several years whereas the speedy end of such reckless dare-
devil fliers as Frank Luke was inevitable.

In Captain James Norman Hall of Colfex, as flight commander, Eddie had an excellent flying partner. Together they
executed several brilliant exploits but presently, on May 7,
1918, Captain Hall was taken away from the squadron—
by the enemy. I think his experience was the most hair-

raising and amazing in the whole war. With Rickenbacker and Lieutenant Edwin Greene of the 94th, Hall, with three official victories to his credit, had shared in an inconclusive battle with four enemy ships. Suddenly Hall's plane was seen to go down in a *vrille* (spin) and land behind the enemy lines. There it was found that an antiaircraft shell had stuck in his Monosoupape motor just where a cylinder stood normally. The cylinder was gone and in its place was the live, unexploded archie shell. He was promptly captured. Since the war, with a writing partner, Captain Charles Nordoff, also a fine U.S. pilot in France, he has become one of our most successful authors.

From the moment I appointed Eddie Rickenbacker commanding officer of the 94th, on September 25, 1918, that squadron went out and did a real job led by Rickenbacker himself. He was kindhearted. The death of one of his pilots affected him deeply. He was a paragon at team work, better, I believe, than Fonck, Bishop, or even Richthofen. His officers respected him greatly and he not only led them always but ruled them with a rather firm hand and they liked it. He talked little and never dissipated. At our wildest party one of the boys demanded a swig from the bottle Rick was carrying under his arm. It was water.

He never bothered with the details of his paper work but he saw to it that it was carried on accurately and promptly by good men. He never shunned publicity but, on the other hand, he never deliberately sought it. He had a genius for doing things in such a way that they created news.

Rickenbacker's record after he recovered his health and assumed command of the squadron was a noble one. To celebrate his return he brought down two enemy ships on September 25, 1918—his sixth and seventh. Then he went to work in earnest. His twenty-sixth victim fell before his skill and courage on October 30. Here is an excerpt from the official but never published history of the 94th Squadron:

Captain Rickenbacker furnished, by his example, an ideal squadron leader. He and the three other squadron commanders in the group were the type of squadron commanders it was absolutely necessary to have in pursuit aviation. It is useless to send out from the rear officers to command squadrons who have not had experience at the front. It is absolutely essential that squadron commanders be experienced and daring pilots. It is their duty to lead their squadrons into battle and to furnish them always a most glorious and enviable example. Captain Rickenbacker obtained results himself and his pilots could not help but emulate him and do likewise. A squadron commander who sits in his tent and gives orders and does not fly, though he may have the brains of Solomon, will never get the results that a man will, who, day in and day out, leads his patrols over the line and infuses into his pilots the 'esprit de corps,' which is so necessary in aviation and which, so far, has been so lightly considered by the military authorities.

To that I say a devout "Amen."

During May 1918, Rick's five victims were all the lively little Albatrosses which skipped about in the skies at that time. When he came back from sick leave in September and went to work on the enemy again, things had changed. His list from then on reads twelve Fokkers, two Halberstadts, one Rumpler, one LVG, and five balloons. All but one of his balloons he caught in their nests, the other at 300 feet. This means he took the extreme risk of diving into the very teeth of the machine guns and antiaircraft cannon with which the balloon locations bristled. Many bullets entered his various planes but they never came home looking like Swiss cheese, as did those of Luke and Wehner.

For some peculiar reason Rick's victories were frequently double ones. There were several dates—September 25, October 2, 3, 9, 10, 27, and 30—on which he went out and bagged himself a brace of enemy aircraft, frequently before breakfast at six and seven o'clock in the morning or in the cool of the evening from seven-thirty to nine, and he did it at all altitudes from 10,000 feet down to almost zero.

When Eddie Rickenbacker returned to the United States after the war, word of his deeds had preceded him and he was rightly the great national hero. It was a responsibility he took very seriously. He was bombarded with rich offers from various motion picture companies. Just leaving the service, the large amounts of money they waved at him must have been tempting but he turned them all down. He felt the love scenes the movie moguls insisted upon were not in keeping with the character expected of him by the youth of the land.

The real tragedy of the Air Service did not fall upon Eddie Rickenbacker. This tragedy was the inability of many of the greatest of our war fliers to adjust themselves successfully to the commercial aspects of the business they thought they knew best—aviation. This is equally true of some of the postwar fliers who have performed miraculous achievements in the air and have had only bitter drafts to drink in commercialized flying.

Eddie has been one of the outstanding exceptions. Immediately after the war he went into the business of aerial mapping on the Pacific Coast with Major Reed Chambers of the 94th. This was successful but Eddie felt a yen toward his first love, the automobile. He secured backers and placed on the market one of the mechanically finest cars ever seen up to that time—the "Rickenbacker." In it Eddie incorporated the first four-wheel brakes and the first fine engine balance we now find in all our good cars. Eddie partly solved two of the problems which, structurally, stood in the way of engine perfection in motorcars. I refer to the problems of high stresses in the crankshaft and vibration throughout due to the rough explosion of such engines. The continuation of development on these two points has given us the dynamic damper and dynamic suspension, two features which have contributed more than any other material design factors to our marvelous modern aircraft engines which weigh about one pound per horsepower and have such economy and extraordinary life between overhauls.

The car was acclaimed by automotive engineers and its ideas widely adopted. The vehicle was a success but the company could not stand the acrobatics of Wall Street and the fact that it had embarked upon national distribution without adequate working capital. It passed on to join the ghosts of 1200 other American automobile companies. And Eddie passed on to other and more constructive things and more appreciative customers.

As president of the Indianapolis Speedway he has kept it up as a great one-day-a-year show. Most of the automobile companies have abandoned racing in favor of their own proving grounds for testing cars and gadgets, but Eddie has felt a fatherly responsibility in the racing game and has done much to improve it. His speed in 1914 at Indianapolis was 70.83 miles an hour. In the 1939 Indianapolis event the boys were making from 120 to 125 until they were slowed down by the accident that killed Floyd Roberts.

When Eddie really went into commercial aviation he found his true métier. He has done tremendous things to enhance the advancement of safe operations of commercial airlines. First he went with American Airlines. Then General Motors took over Eastern Airlines and put him in charge of operations. It was a losing venture but Rickenbacker built it into a profitable one and then arranged to purchase the interest of General Motors when that company decided to remain in the manufacturing and not the operating end of the business.

He is now president of Eastern Airlines and its record for safety and earnings is a most enviable one. Its route mileage has about doubled since he took over.

Eddie goes to Washington less than almost any airline chief executive. He is trying to make his line economically self-supporting and does not want anything that carries the taint of subsidy or the tricks of patronage. He flies all the time himself, seldom as a pilot and then only to check on the new gadgets and navigating instruments before entrusting the lives of his pilots and passengers to them. He is still thoroughly familiar with all phases of the intricate flying technique.

Truly our most successful aviator—in war and peace.

CHAPTER 17

American Aviation
in the Coming War

I HAVE now written many pages about the past. What of the future?

The future is always vitally connected with the past. As an American citizen who has made loyalty to the United States a fetish, a religion, and aviation a life work, to me the most important and most distressing prophecy of the future lies in an incident of the past—the Wright brothers had to go to Europe to gain acceptance and development of the world's first successful airplane.

This was not an isolated case. Americans are the most ingenious people on earth. We are forever creating new things for others to steal, develop, or benefit from. Hundreds of our priceless industrial and military inventions have been completely neglected here or have been adopted only after they have brought acclaim, riches or other advantages to foreigners more adept than we in appraising the potentialities of mechanical brain children.

To me it is stark tragedy that our Ordnance Department rejected, in their infancy, not only the Wright airplane but, likewise, the rifling in gun barrels, smokeless powder, the breech loading rifle, the nickel-steel high velocity bullet, the automatic pistol, the Hotchkiss, Maxim, Lewis, and Thompson machine guns. Foreign countries quickly grabbed these

American creations and gave them aid and the irresistible pressure exerted by our own line officers eventually made for their adoption here. The world is now trembling over the threat of Hitler's (or, rather, Goering's) air fleet. No weapon of war has ever been resisted and kicked around by our military and naval greats as has the airplane. It would have been so easy and so inexpensive for us to have possessed today the world's greatest defensive armada of modern flying machines and to be able to laugh at the Fuehrer's shouted totalitarian blusterings. One wonders at times how we ever progressed from bows and arrows and war canoes.

Apparently everybody has forgotten a book which attracted incredulous attention back in 1912 or 1913. It was called *Germany and the Next War,* by General Friedrich von Bernhardi. In it he said in effect, "Germany will probably lose the first war. She may lose the second. But the third she will assuredly win and gain her rightful domination of the world."

The old general knew whereof he spoke. He knew the arrogance, the dumb, stolid determination of the Teutonic race to impose its rigid will on all other peoples of the earth. It has been so since Arminius the Great, welder of the savage Teutonic tribes, brought the first emphatic defeat to Rome and annihilated the legions of Varus in the battle near the Elbe in A.D. 9. The Germans have always been, are now and always will be the great disturbers of the world. They have been kept in check only by the superior numbers and more nimble diplomatic brains of their opponents. This may not always be so. They may lose the second war but with the present setup it will be a close decision and unless the Allies, whoever they are in the coming conflict, do a better job of subjugation than they did the last time, old von Bernhardi's words concerning the third war may come true and our grandchildren, if any, will be goose-stepping and heiling this and that by the count all their lives.

My particular interest is in aviation. In the war which I feel is just around the corner for the United States—unless we can stop it—aviation is going to dominate the life or death of almost every person on this earth. Aviation is such a terrific war weapon that few, even of the experts, fully realize how awful it is. It is the greatest war development since the adoption of gunpowder. And yet, believe it or not, aviation could, within a few months, end all threat of wars and keep them ended, allowing humanity to go on to its ultimate happiness and prosperity. After the war I worked out a plan which, some day, may produce that happy result but this is not the place to discuss it.

America at the moment might be the natural leader of nations. In her lap lies the hope of civilization. But she is not leading. She can lead, quickly, decisively and to the glorification of all mankind—through aviation. Having devoted every minute of my time since the war to aviation, I know many things I am not at liberty to mention. I can, however, by inference rather than by direct statement, reply to those who ask, "What about aviation in our next war?"

There are so many frontiers open for development in aeronautics. Take that of one element—a mineral which today is where aluminum was when they made jewelry out of it in your grandparents' time.

If we get beryllium in quantities and at a price, the engine, pilot and all gas tanks in our next war will benefit. In fact, if beryllium can be produced cheaply enough so that we can use 60 per cent of it in an alloy with aluminum we will build most parts of our planes of this material and performance will be extraordinary. This alloy is lighter than pure aluminum and yet is as strong as the finest tungsten steel used in armor plating. It has, also, all the other desirable properties of ductility, Brinell hardness, elasticity, and elongation.

In the development of beryllium the great drawback is

the scarcity of beryl, the ore from which beryllium is de-rived. Some day somebody will find a mountain of high grade beryl (I hope it is in this country, right under our noses), and then we will go ahead into a new era in aviation metallurgy. Parts of the engine, propeller, all instruments and gadgets, in addition to wings and armor, will benefit and will be much stronger and lighter and not so subject to wear and corrosion.

Most attacks in the present, certainly in our coming war will be in "concentration patrols" of great numbers of planes. I believe the 1st Pursuit Group pioneered this principle in the closing days of World War No. 1, but apparently it has been entirely overlooked. I have pleaded with authorities to study our aviation and that of our Allies and enemies covering only the last three weeks of the war and to forget everything that went before. But it looks as if mine has been a voice in the wilderness. Attacks in the impending hostilities, whether on cities, troops, or enemy aviation, will be in waves of pursuit and bombing planes, hundreds of them. They will ferry bomb loads, trip after trip, night and day and only be limited by the capacity of the industry back home. The individual flier will be forgotten in favor of the mass. This has been partially proven in Spain and China. It will be multiplied a hundredfold six months from now, or next year, whenever the present conflagration spreads.

What of the civilian population in the next war? Well, it will have a mean time. Men's standards change and the modern idea of the sanctity of noncombatants will be com-pletely upset. Mr. Mussolini started it in Ethiopia. Both sides proved it out in Spain and the sacred Hirohito's minions have carried it to its ultimate of savagery in China. Germany and Russia did it in Poland and Finland. It is nothing new. The curses of the centuries have followed similar activities of Genghis Khan, Atilla, and many others.

The mere killing of women, children and non-fighting men will not, of course, be the main idea. The objective will be partly to implant in the minds of civilian survivors the invincibility of the enemy and the futility of supporting an army and navy for further resistance, and, more important, the destruction of the life-giving arteries, nerves, and sinews of complex cities and the sources of military supplies.

Take New York, for example. Hostile ships will float over the city dropping high power bombs all over the place. These will kill and maim thousands on the streets and in the hotels and business buildings. The primary object, however, will be to deprive the city, and its defenders, of the gas mains, electric cables, power houses, subways, water mains, bridges, automobile roads, railroads, air fields, and other facilities without which the city and its defending army cannot function, cannot receive food, water and other necessities, and the population must starve.

The great objectives of an enemy over New York will not be the city itself. They will be the oil refineries in Bayonne, the Ashokan, Croton and Kensico Dams, the Brooklyn Navy Yard, Governors Island, the Jersey City railroad terminals, the Newark, Roosevelt, Floyd Bennett and La Guardia Air Fields and other important military assets of our greatest city. Enlarged photographs of all these "bomb spots" are hanging on the walls of the War Office in Rome, snapped during General Balbo's "good will" flight. They have been snapped and resnapped by every Zeppelin that ever flew over New York and you may be sure are part of the archives of every important war office in the world, friendly as well as potential enemy. The modern newspapers almost daily let our potential enemies look into our latest defenses. This, of course, is nothing for which to blame them. It is news. It is up to the government to protect our secrets.

The first thing an enemy of ours will do will be to destroy

the locks of the Panama Canal, by sabotage from land, or airplanes, probably the latter. We have only one fleet. It can protect only one coast at a time. The Canal is our naval lifeline, our time saver. Conceivably we can be conquered while the fleet is going around Cape Horn. It will only require one plane to do the Panama job. Surely, with a wave of planes let loose, probably in advance of any declaration of war, from a raider aircraft carrier or a secret "rice field" or "sugar plantation" nearby, although our air force may be out on patrol one of these planes will get through, drop a couple of 1100-pound bombs on the Canal locks and our name will be mud.

Never let anyone fool you by quoting statistics involving small bombs. In the coming war bombs will be real bombs— no more pea-shooting with small twenty and hundred pounders. One large bomb can do as much damage as a couple of hundred small ones. Now that fliers can hit from 15,000 feet with accuracy equal to, if not better than, naval gunfire at average range, the whole picture changes, provided we have fast load-carrying bombers and missiles of 1100 pounds. This is about twice the size of the largest bombs dropped in the World War or in China and Spain more recently.

We owe our flyers and our populace the protection of larger antiaircraft guns. We are still sticking to the three-inch guns and we have pitifully few of those. The late Senator Royal S. Copeland almost had a fist fight in June 1938 trying to put through a measly appropriation for antiaircraft guns. In the First World War we had little fear of the archies. In fact, they were of considerable help to us. If they fired at us we knew there were no enemy aircraft around. If they were silent as we went over them it was a danger signal. Hostile planes were probably right on our tails. There was one gun that I hated, though, a big, converted naval 6-incher up at Dunkirk in my RFC days. That's why I am a little worried about the larger calibers, four and six inch, displayed by Hitler in a parade not long ago. We have raised the muzzle velocities of our 3-inchers from 1800 to 2800 feet per second. This will help but we should move right along up into the higher calibers with the rest of the folks.

Luckily we are getting more active fliers on our General Staff. This bodes well for our war aviation, although for some time yet they will of necessity be in the junior grades and have little voice in policies. For a few years, 1926 to about 1931, we had an Assistant Secretary of War and an Assistant Secretary of the Navy for air. Provided for by the Morrow Board, men of the caliber and experience of Trubee Davison and David Ingalls responded and served splendidly but their row was not an easy one to hoe. Both of these were exceptionally good men. Such officials, however, are hardly necessary if you have enough experienced fliers of high rank on the General Staff of the Army and the Navy Board of the Navy. The older officers in both branches resented the assistant secretaries giving all their time to air developments. Now, since the Baker Board of 1934, we have an independent air arm, called the General Headquarters Air Force. This is a step in the right direction. Ultimately we may have a Department of National Defense with one secretary and three undersecretaries—for Army, Navy, and Air. It will probably take another emergency to bring this about. So few people, comparatively, in high places, have enough interest in this to study it and appreciate that it must come. Our reserve corps, of which I am a proud member, is a joke.

Good aviation defense depends upon good staff work, whether the air people are a separate unit or not. But in a country with a standing army as small as ours it is unwise to hope for very brilliant staff work until we are into the war a year or so.

Personally, I have always found our brass hats, both in

France and Washington, most sympathetic and reasonable. It is difficult to sell anyone higher up on an idea or plan unless he knows and appreciates both its possibilities and its limitations. A person of authority, with these qualifications, is not easy to find. On the other hand, aviators are likely just to hit the high spots in outlining a proposition and to get impatient with people who do not understand their problems and ambitions. In such cases they are too impetuous to sit down and calmly work the thing out. This makes the brass hats angry, they get to calling names and nothing is accomplished.

If we don't get away from some of the old Prussian practices in dealing with air force personnel, we will never get anywhere, no matter how good our planes may be. There must be flexibility of mind in anything connected with aviation. Colonel Lindbergh testified recently that quality is everything in flying equipment, not quantity. I cannot quite agree with him. Quality is such a comparative term when considering planes, material, instruments, performance and many other things. Give me fifty planes of 300 miles per hour with maneuverability and I'll take on a similar number of planes of 350 mile speed that cannot turn "on a dime" and win the scrap. The 148th U. S. Squadron serving with the British in Flanders proved that. This principle also was definitely proved in Spain. All the same I am for the very best equipment it is possible to obtain—and lots of it. I have no commercial interests whatever in the airplane production industry. I am thinking solely of the country's answer to the tremendous aviation developments abroad. It is next to impossible to find a real expert who has no prejudice or preconceived ideas.

When we returned from France at the end of the war, the army and navy were demobilizing. Both had cradled the orphan child, "aviation," during the conflict and it had become a lusty, promising youth. They had no more love for it, however, than most foster parents whose charges grow up to be too active, too bright, too impetuous and too threatening to the old order of things. The enemy was shorn of his air power—15,000 planes, 20,000 airplane engines and his Zeppelins and forbidden by the Versailles Treaty to build anything much bigger than a glider. This proved a blessing in disguise for Germany. Her air-minded people learned valuable things from it.

With the foe rendered temporarily helpless there was no great urge on the part of army and navy people in this country to encourage the new enterprise that might some day grow too big for them to control. Others in authority, however, with a wider perspective, took the continued conquest of the air more seriously. After I had returned and been assigned to the office of the Chief of Air Service, Washington, there was organized the so called Crowell Commission. This body, which included some of the most distinguished, brilliant, disinterested and public-spirited men in the entire United States, went to Europe in June 1919. Its instructions were to make a thorough survey and to prepare a report, containing recommendations, for Secretary of War Newton D. Baker.

In all the countries they visited they found aviation the chief concern of both soldiers and statesmen. Clemenceau, Foch, Tardieu, Duval in France, Churchill, Haig, Admiral Beatty, Lord Trenchard, Sykes, and Brancker in England, gave freely of their observations and their advice. The vanquished Germans even co-operated in revealing their war secrets and outlining what aviation, in their experienced opinion, portended for man and his civilization.

The Commission did its work superbly. A comprehensive, far-seeing and constructive report was prepared and signed by Assistant Secretary of War Benedict Crowell, Howard E. Coffin, Admiral Mustin, Halsey Dunwoody, James A. Blair,

Jr., George H. Houston, C. M. Keyes and S. S. Bradley. And it was promptly thrown into the nearest wastebasket, thus giving American aviation a blow from which it has hardly yet begun to recover.

Briefly, the report recommended a separate government-sponsored entity for this great new contribution from science and urged its most complete development, in organization, in commercial, military and technical progress. The carefully considered plan was that this grave responsibility would be placed in a new agency of the government, nestled there so that, under the normal processsess of democracy, private initiative would be stimulated and we would forge ahead, developing the benefits of commercial flying as a great auxiliary to our transportation media and as an inexpensive adjunct to our national defense. If, perchance, another war should break out, America would be truly "First in the Air," and hence, possessed of a big margin of safety.

Both the Army and the Navy, busy mustering out four million citizen soldiers and sailors, slightly dizzy with victory and postwar security, seemed either too preoccupied to study the report or were fearful that the proposed new "baby" would actually threaten their prerogatives. Two resumés were written for Mr. Baker and Admiral Mustin. Both documents damned the whole report with faint praise, contradicted the experts by conjuring up the old prewar chestnut that military and civil aviation were two separate lines of endeavor, that the airplane's radius of action was sharply limited and that flying machines could never occupy territory. (Italy occupied Albania in two hours with 2000 men by air in 1939.)

I saw eye to eye with the Crowell Commission but I was helpless, as were all of the other people who knew most about the growth of the airplane through long and agonizing experience. I had the same vision of its future and wanted to be a helpful part of that future. In my wildest dreams, however, I never pictured the modern power plant of 2000-horsepower and one pound weight per horsepower. I knew we would some day be flying on instruments and that our engines would eventually equal the reliability of our little automobile motors. It never occurred to me that 100 immense bombers from England would ever fly over France in my lifetime and in slightly more than six hours cover 1400 miles at more than 200 miles an hour, each plane loaded with two 1100-pound bombs with more explosive power in each bomb than a naval torpedo and each capable of sinking any battleship afloat or obliterating any building on the Wilhelmstrasse.

I could and did envision some of the technical details of the airplanes we are coming to today and in an article in the *U. S. Air Service Magazine* for July 1921 I pictured the plane as an internally braced monoplane, described in general, but not in its huge horsepower and low weight, the present aviation engine, instruments and radio and laid out the airways with their lights, beacons, landing fields, and ranges almost identically as they exist at the present moment. My reward for this flight of fancy was a chorus of loud and raucous laughter. But not from General Billy Mitchell. He, of all my flying friends, glimpsed the future as I did and was willing to bet I was right.

We knew it was folly, however, to seek private capital for such an altruistic enterprise as building up America's commercial aviation to protect us in case of a possible war. There are generally no dividends in such an activity until the production for war actually is on us and we are ready to pay any price for rush work. Uncle Sam was the only source from which funds might be expected in exchange for incalculable benefits in the speeding up of commerce and passenger travel, the air mail and the backlog of national defense. So we went to work on Uncle.

Starting in the army, using General Mitchell's prestige, we began a campaign to sell the idea of using army appropriations for the fostering and encouragement of commercial flying. Today I wonder at our nerve. At every turn it was a fight, a real battle. But progress was made.

We organized the so-called Civil Affairs Division, later called the Airways Section, still later the Bureau of Air Commerce. Now we have the Civil Aeronautics Authority. Some of the original personnel with little or no salary increase have stuck through all the changes and are doing excellent work in the CAA today. In the beginning aviation was just a despised orphan. By only three means could we make headway. We could point out what other nations were doing. We could indicate coyly what splendid publicity would accrue to individuals who aided the cause. In a very few cases we secured substantial co-operation by enlisting the sympathies and patriotism of citizens of understanding and vision. It all worked, but, oh, so slowly.

General Mitchell, gallant, enthusiastic, intensely fond of his country and solicitous for her welfare, lacked one of the basic fundamentals of a successful airman—patience. He could not understand why all the agencies of the government, the departments of the Army and Navy, commerce, and others, would not forget their own particular responsibilities and seize this greatest of all opportunities—flying. Perhaps he went too far. It is certain, however, that many people did not go far enough with him. Much of his work was nullified by bureaucratic and service jealousies, commercial greed, departmental politics and a lot of good, plain ignorance and dumbness. Year after year, permitted to crusade to the public in speech and writing and to appear before Congress freely until the final report of some vital committee was being prepared, he would frequently feel his goal had been reached only to find his endeavors brought to naught by some ignorant or self-seeking office holder or politician.

Billy Mitchell foretold practically every aviation development that has occurred up to the present moment but he was hamstrung by those very people in the services and in the aviation industry who have since personally benefited and who should have been more sympathetic with his shortcomings and helped him in his ambition—to make America a leader in the air. He died broke, in semi-official disgrace, a martyr to the cause, while, in aviation we lagged behind six other countries, three of them almost certain future enemies.

In 1921 I felt so keenly that the safety and much of the prosperity of the United States lay in the development of aviation that I resigned from the regular army and gave my whole enthusiasm to the building up of air consciousness on the part of the public. As I look back now I am afraid I tried to do too much at one time. With Caleb Bragg and others, we decided to reorganize the old American Flying Club which was heavily in debt but which had been of great help to many pilots in aiding them get back on their feet upon their return from overseas. This did not work so well so I set up in Washington a "preliminary organization committee of one hundred" to start the National Aeronautic Association. Aiming at one hundred, the patriotism reflected in the people of the United States is clearly indicated by the fact that in response to one hundred and fifty invitations I received acceptances from more than my quota of one hundred, included in which were high-minded men from coast to coast, many of whom are still loyal supporters of that organization.

Having participated in the New York-to-Toronto and the Path Finding New York-to-San Francisco Reliability Tests mentioned below, actually flying in the latter a captured single-seater Fokker over and back safely, racing had gotten into my blood. It was good for developing better motors. A year before I had won second place in the Pulitzer Speed Race. The same annual event was to take place at Omaha, Nebraska, in October 1921, just after the American Legion Convention at Kansas City.

Trying to organize the National Aeronautic Association, fly at Kansas City at the American Legion Convention and again in the fast race at Omaha, I began to crowd things too much. At Ithaca I tested the fastest airplane in the world at that time—the MB-3 Thomas Morse gull-winged monoplane. We "souped up" the Hispano-Suiza motor, using benzol instead of tetraethyl lead to take care of the compression. A fuel pump which I had been fighting for two years let me down in the race and I had to make a forced landing in a small field in Iowa. Had I fallen out of the air before landing, it would have been all over, but I didn't actually fall until I was hurled from the ship after a 60 foot running when the undercarriage let go. (For nine years I was the only one who had ever landed a racing plane in a forced landing outside of an airport and lived.) This laid me up for some time and in the interim my secretary carried on from the Mills Building in Washington.

Richard Hoyt of Hayden-Stone had started an underwriting to help organize the Association. I contributed $1000 myself to this and took "French leave" from Walter Reed Hospital. I was determined to have the organization ready for a convention we had arranged at Detroit for September 1921, working in co-operation with Harvey Campbell, Howard Coffin, Harold Emmons, Bill Stout, and some other patriotic men out there.

Possibly the highlight of all this frantic activity covering several years was my participation in that first transcontinental air reliability test in 1919. I'm glad I went in because it was the path-finding effort that established the present middle air route to California. In that "sporting event" I flew a captured German Fokker and got safely to San Francisco and back to New York winning first place in my class, while nine of the contestants were killed.

One of the most important things I helped initiate is practically unknown to the public today. I refer to the sinking of the supposedly unsinkable flagship of the captured German navy, the *Ostfriesland,* with bombs from a plane high in the air. It was so easy it was child's play—when large bombs were employed. The report of this exploit was squelched as were the later bombing tests on the obsolete American battleships *New Jersey* and *West Virginia,* now resting peacefully on the ocean bottom off Hatteras, the victims of airplane bombs. I wish someone would tell me who has removed all the facts of this really important development from all morgues and files likely to be searched for evidence on the old controversy—"can airplanes sink battleships?" They can with utmost ease provided 1100-pound bombs are used. I'm afraid we shall find that out, all too soon and not in peacetime tests.

A year before Lindbergh made his great flight across the Atlantic, I looked about for some bait that might help the cause. I saw dangling, unchallenged for eight years, the Raymond Orteig prize of $25,000, which Lindbergh subsequently won, for the first pilot to fly from New York to Paris, nonstop. Then, in the survey of Atlantic Ocean air currents, compiled for Fred Hardesty, who was developing a lighter-than-air line to Europe, I observed that there were strong prevailing winds from west to east. It dawned on me that with a reliable machine, especially one with three motors, one could throttle down and literally be blown across the 3660 statute miles, even though the normal cruising range of exceptional planes at that time was only 2000 miles. So I organized the Argonauts, Inc., and we had an all-metal 3-engined plane built by Sikorsky. But I resigned, at great personal sacrifice, from that activity because they insisted that the pilot be a man who, I knew, would crash the ship on the take-off. He did exactly that.

Presently aviation began to find encouragement in both services and in civil work. We have made real progress since then. Today we have planes and pilots that are second to none in the world for military and commercial work—the much vaunted Germans included. We have approximately 2500 planes of all types ready for military duty. We have 11,100 so-called "commercial planes," approximately 300 of which could quickly be adapted to various forms of war work. We have 26,144 commercial pilots, many of whom could jump from their present work to military flying in a minimum of training time and we have 1000 fairly well-trained war fliers. This looks like a sorry spectacle when we see what Hitler, Russia, Italy, England and the others are doing. It is. We do not have nearly enough. With the developments going on abroad we should quadruple our air forces as fast as we can, consistent with reason and sound technical improvement. Then, and then only, can we sit down and contemplate our coming war in the air with any degree of comfort.

Ten or eleven years ago the "whoopee" period in frenzied finance arrived in the United States. Securities soared skyward as people kidded themselves and each other that stocks could go up indefinitely without earning power to warrant it, much as the real estate promoters did in the Florida land boom of 1925. I am happy I was not a part of this wild speculative movement. Fortunately, two years before that I had started a business and was getting on so well that some people became covetous, especially those who foresaw that the speculative gentlemen of Wall Street soon would cast their acquisitive eyes upon the aviation business. I was the victim of a conspiracy which cost me a fortune and ruined my organization.

I was discouraged. A lawyer myself, but always mindful of the fact that it is dangerous for a lawyer to act for himself, I employed what I thought to be competent counsel. But I lost everything. I am glad. It enabled me to sit on the sidelines and not be responsible for one nickel of the one billion dollars poured into crazy aviation enterprises in 1928 and 1929—and lost.

During this period the science of flying, passing now on the airlines from "contact" to "instrument navigation," began to get a bad name with the public. Too many crashes. Too many deaths. Appointed by one of our most honest, sincere and hard working statesmen, the late Senator Copeland, to urge and conduct a Senate investigation, we soon found the trouble, secured the funds for more intensive airway aids and weather reporting, fixed the future responsibility in the government where it belonged and helped to enact Senator Pat McCarran's and Honorable Clarence Lea's bill creating the Civil Aeronautics Authority. Thus, for the first time, was American civil aviation taken out of the category of unwanted orphans and moved ahead to a spot now almost equal in rank, authority and accomplishment to that of a government department, the much needed separate agency for aviation. America is at last taking to the air with equipment that is good and pilots who are the best in the world.

So what of the coming wars or the spread or speeding up of the present one?

Well, using against the Navy every argument it formerly used so long against us, the radius of action of the airplane is relatively low because we have to come home every ten hours to refuel. Therefore, there cannot be maintained anywhere in the world a long air supremacy such as the sea supremacy enjoyed by the Allied navies during the World War. That being true, whole swarms of bombers, carrying great, deadly bundles of explosives capable of sinking the largest of battleships will make things unendurable for the navies of the world, thus gaining a temporary supremacy. It will be utterly impossible for the British Grand Fleet, America's first line of defense, to bask as a unit in the Firth of Forth awaiting a sortie of the enemy fleet to challenge its sea supremacy. Some, if not most, of the massive battleships will be sunk or rendered impotent from above and the snug rendezvous will be made useless.

During such temporary air supremacies of the enemy nobody will be able to send food, men, equipment or gold overseas. The sea lanes will be the most dangerous roads in the world, safe only for future marauders. This is what is worrying Mr. Chamberlain. It is Mr. Hitler's hope. It is the vital point at issue. No longer is it possible to stabilize a war as we did with navies in the last one. The conflict of 1914–18 was just a practice war in preparation for the real conflagration which now impends.

During the year 1918, 485 enemy planes made twenty-eight raids on Paris. The largest raid, on March 11–12, comprised seventy planes. And how many bombs do you suppose they dropped on the city? Exactly 296 bombs weighing 26,196 pounds—only 13 tons! Thirteen of the low-flying visitors were brought down by antiaircraft guns.

During the entire war, the Germans made fifty-one Zeppelin and fifty-two airplane raids over the whole of England, including London. They dropped 9000 bombs, total weight of 280 tons.

These authentic figures from the office of the Chief of Coast Artillery as published in the *Coast Artillery Journal* of January 1926 and from *The German Air Raids on Great Britain 1914–18* by Captain Joseph Morris, simply emphasize the point I make—that, in the present conflict, bombing from the air can be intensified beyond all previous conceptions in speed, number of raids and bombing planes and in number and weight of bombs.

According to an official test made recently, three of our new "Flying Fortresses" could drop on a city *in one raid* an equal quantity of bomb explosives as were dropped on Paris in all of 1918. And they could make at least two raids per night, flying half as high again and more than twice as fast.

The French and English can do this to Berlin and Munich from French bases. The Germans can do it to Paris. But they cannot do it to London until they get bases in Holland or Belgium. Meantime, German raids on London with light bomb loads can be highly damaging but not devastating. Neither side in the present war can conduct great mass long distance bombing raids because they haven't the long distance pursuit planes to protect the bombers.

I have no use for the rumored Hitler Blitzkrieg plan which contemplates the obliteration of civilian populations by bombing from the air. To me, in addition to being a reversion to the wild animals which ruled the world before temporary dictators were thought of, it does not seem valuable in any way. Why kill noncombatants when they will have to surrender if their fleet is sunk? They'll be helpless.

I do not advocate weakening the army and navy and spending everything on aircraft. This would be silly. I am no militarist but I sincerely believe, in the last analysis, the poor old doughboy will still carry the war on his strong aching back. The more strength we have in all branches the better. They will all be useful in the big war, the really big one coming. In fact, it is largely because we are so deficient and so woefully unprepared in both the army and navy as to numbers of fighting units that I seek refuge for defense in so powerful a weapon as aviation, so unappreciated by our sincere but misguided isolationists. There is no isolation left in the world when heavily-armed airplanes can fly in tremendous numbers from country to country, or from well-protected airplane carriers, far into any land on earth.

If you wonder, in the face of the substantial figures I have quoted as to our present aviation setup in the United States why I still recommend a vast increase in our aerial strength, I will tell you. With the flying background of the entire World War to back me up, I say:

In our coming war . . .

We will fly in all kinds of weather. In the last we never flew much on dud days when fog or rain made flying dangerous and inefficient.

We will fly both night and day.

We will travel at least three times as fast, twice as high, with more powerful guns and more of them and loads of large bombs undreamed of twenty years ago.

On an active front we will lose every plane in each squadron every ten days; the average life of a plane in a fighting squadron will be ten flying hours only.

In a big push we will lose all our unit flying personnel every thirty days.

We will have to back up our aviation with mass production of superior products—not profiteering junk or crackpot experiments. Our mass-production capabilities will be our greatest national asset in the coming war if not sabotaged through our unintelligent and lethargic attitude toward foreign spies and agents.

Our strategy will be part and parcel of the whole campaign.

Our tactics will be entirely different.

We will have a morale among the young pilots of our

democratic air force unequaled anywhere in the world. An army travels on its stomach, an air force on its morale.

Our patrols will cover 2000 miles in flight as against 200 in the last war. Exceptional patrols will fly and return from objectives 3000 miles away with big bombing loads and plenty of fuel in reserve.

Aviation is now and will be our main means of defense. Neglect it and we die or do the goose-step the rest of our lives.

Do we want that? Think it over.

APPENDIX

THE U. S. AIR SERVICE
IN THE GREAT WAR*

The achievement of Army aviation and the American aircraft industry in World War I was never as great as the promise. The task that the Army air arm set itself, at the insistent urging of the Allies, proved to be beyond the capabilities of the country because it was not possible to overcome in a brief nineteen months the effects of almost a decade of neglect and unpreparedness. Not until 1917 did America fully realize the extent to which it had fallen behind Europe in aeronautics. The resources on hand were not a broad enough base on which to build the enormous structure projected.

The resources in April 1917 were indeed meager. The Aviation Section had 131 officers, practically all pilots and student pilots, and 1087 enlisted men. It had fewer than 250 planes, none of which could be classified higher than trainer by European standards. Its balloon strength totaled five. It had no bombers, fighters, or any of the other combat types that had been fighting the air war in Europe. It had only one fully organized and equipped combat squadron. The American aircraft industry had delivered to the Army in 1916 only sixty-four planes out of 366 ordered—and this represented the output of nine different factories. Furthermore, the performance of these planes, especially the engines, could not be compared with that of their European counterparts.

* Reprinted from the USAF ATC Pamphlet 190–1, *History of the United States Air Force,* dated June 1, 1961.

"Clouds of Planes"

Even more embarrassing than the almost complete absence of any tangible air strength, which, after all, could be blamed on the repeated failures of Congress to appropriate money for Army aeronautics, was the absence of plans and programs for building an air force that could fight in Europe. And perhaps most embarrassing of all was the lack of knowledge on which to base the program. According to one Army flier, "Not a single air officer in Washington had even seen a fighting plane." The Army had failed to send trained observers abroad to gather even the limited information that could be gotten about technical and operational aspects of the war in Europe. Much of the fault here lay with the Allies, who exercised strict censorship of aviation information and refuse to permit American air observers to visit the front. The British did not repeat this mistake in World War II, and the exchange of technical information between the United States and Great Britain was of great mutual benefit in 1940–41.

The idea of planning for a war before it began was still new to the Army and alien and repugnant to much of the public. There is a story that when newspapers published accounts of war planning by the War Department in 1916, President Wilson himself was indignant and outraged. The Chief of Staff and the Secretary of War had to explain to him that such planning was necessary and proper. Actually, at this time "The War Department was concerned only with the mobilization of manpower."

The effort to provide a General Staff that would pull together the uncoordinated and often conflicting agencies of the War Department had been none too successful in the thirteen years since this change was made. Congress was suspicious of this "foreign innovation" and limited the number of General Staff officers stationed in Washington. In 1917 the number was twenty. It was little wonder that there was a lack of coordinated planning and that it took the War Department the better part of a year to put its house in order. If the Aviation Section did not know what it needed to fight the war, neither did the Army or Navy—nor the country as a whole—have any notion of what was required.

The original Army mobilization plan, which concerned itself only with manpower, contemplated an Army of 1,000,000, of which aviation would be "a relatively insignificant part." And the initial appropriations for aviation after our entrance into the war—$10.8 million in May and $43.4 million in June— appeared to confirm the minor role planned for aviation by the General Staff. On May 1 the Chief Signal Officer proposed to add six aero squadrons and two balloon squadrons to the seven aero squadrons already formed, but even this modest increase would have to await legislation. Fortunately, there were already forces at work that would lift Army aviation out of its obscurity and raise it to the highest priority among American war programs.

Although the press and the public were enthusiastic about expanding the air arm, it was the insistent urgings of the French and British that tipped the scales on the side of aviation. The Allies rejoiced when the United States entered the war on April 6 and hastened to place their technical knowledge at our disposal. Within three weeks, large and well-staffed missions from both France and Great Britain had arrived in Washington to appeal for full American participation in the fighting in Europe. They felt that the United States could help most effectively by sending a powerful air force to help the hardpressed Allies on the Western Front in 1918. In a cable to President Wilson, received on May 26, 1917, Premier Alexandre Ribot of France proposed a program that became the initial basis for the expansion of Army aviation. Ribot asked that an American "flying corps" of 4500 planes, 5000 pilots, and 50,000 mechanics be placed in France during 1918 in order to "enable the Allies to win the supremacy of the air."

This proposal called for producing 16,500 planes during the first six months of 1918, far more than anyone had previously considered. The National Advisory Committee for Aeronautics had taken the lead in coordinating plans for aircraft production, and on April 12, 1917, it had recommended a program for producing 3700 planes in 1918, 6000 in 1919, and 10,000 in 1920. But the War Department disregarded this plan in preparing early in June a detailed program for Army aviation based on the French recommendation. A group of officers headed by Foulois drafted the program in a few days in an atmosphere of great pressure in which the "one thought was the supreme opportunity and the supreme need for haste." The program provided for 22,625 airplanes and almost 44,000 engines, plus 80 per cent spare parts, which equaled another 17,600 airplanes. Although 12,000 were to be for use in France, the exact types were not yet known.

The magnitude of the program was enough to give pause to all but the most optimistic aviation enthusiasts. From the first Wright plane in 1903 through 1916 the American aircraft industry had produced fewer than 1000 military and civilian planes; now it was being asked to produce 22,000 military planes in one year. France itself, in three years of war, had not produced as many planes as it was asking the United States to produce in one. The French had 1700 airplanes at the front and 3000 training planes behind the lines.

But Secretary of War Newton D. Baker approved the program before formal action by the General Staff and submitted legislation to Congress. It was greeted enthusiastically by the press and the public. The thought of great fleets of American planes turning the tide of battle in Europe fascinated almost everyone for awhile. The Chief Signal Officer, Brigadier General George O. Squier, was so carried away by the dazzling vision that he appealed to the country to "put the Yankee punch into the war by building an army in the air, regiments and brigades of winged cavalry on gas-driven flying horses."

Secretary Baker announced on June 18: "The War Department is behind the aircraft plans with every ounce of energy and enthusiasm at its command. The aircraft program seems by all means the most effective way in which to exert America's force at once in telling fashion." Caught up in the atmosphere of fervor and buoyant hope, Congress rushed through an appropriation of $640 million for aeronautics in fifteen days, and President Wilson signed the act on July 24. It was the largest sum for a single purpose ever appropriated by Congress up to that time. It provided the foundation for the aircraft program, but it came a full three and a half months after the declaration of war.

With ample money, and hope for the future, the Aviation Section secured approval in August of a program for raising 345 combat squadrons, 45 construction companies, 81 supply squadrons, 11 repair squadrons, and 26 balloon companies. Of these, 263 combat squadrons were intended for use in Europe by June 30, 1918, and the remainder in the United States, Panama, and the Pacific. But the high hopes of the summer faded rapidly as all production programs fell far behind.

Aircraft production lagged badly, and by December 1917 both civilian and military officials realized that we owed it to our Allies as well as to ourselves to lower the goals to more realistic levels. After consulting with General Pershing's headquarters in France early in 1918, the War Department approved a new program of 120 combat squadrons to be at the front in Europe by January 1, 1919. In August 1918, Pershing and the War Department agreed on a final program calling for 202 squadrons to be at the front by July 1, 1919. There would be 60 pursuit, 49 corps observation, 52 Army observation, 14 day bombing, and 27 night bombing squadrons, plus 133 balloon companies. Although only 45 combat squadrons got to the front by November 11, 1918, the final program of 202 might have been met by July 1, 1919, if the war had lasted.

Emergence of the Air Service

U. S. Army aviation never fulfilled the promises made on its behalf by civilian and military leaders alike in 1917—whether it was producing planes, raising squadrons, or "crushing the Teutons." But it underwent profound changes during the war that decidedly improved its position and pointed the way to future greatness. From the standpoint of the future, one of the most important changes occurred in the organizational structure.

The existing aeronautical organization at the beginning of the war was completely inadequate to meet the demands made upon it. The War Department had neither the knowledge nor the experience to direct the huge air program, and lacking precedent to serve as a guide, defense officials tended to think of the air setup as semidetached from the rest of the war effort.

The key problem from the beginning was production. To help the Army and Navy in this field, the Council of National Defense established the Aircraft Production Board in May 1917. Congress gave this agency legal status as the Aircraft Board on October 1. Under the chairmanship of a leading industrialist, Howard E. Coffin, the board advised the military services on quantity production and all related materiel problems. After October, when it came under the Secretaries of War and Navy, it tended to advise rather than "supervise and direct" as the law provided. Nevertheless, the Aircraft Board and its growing staff did the basic planning of the aircraft production effort and saw it through the first year of the war.

Within the War Department the General Staff had no real experience in air matters and was busy with other more familiar problems. The Signal Corps, under pressure to produce results, expanded the Aviation Section quickly and reorganized it into a number of divisions, all of which were individually responsible to the Chief Signal Officer himself, General Squier. This officer found himself in the unenviable position of personally supervising two major programs, of which the air was by far the larger. As Arnold later recalled, "The situation . . . was more a state of affairs than a chain of events."

By the spring of 1918 the aviation program was in great trouble. Production had not begun to approach the widely heralded goals, and the public optimism of the preceding year quickly gave way to painful disillusion. With this hard swing of the pendulum came investigations and charges that the agencies handling the program were inefficiently organized and administered.

The outcome was a sweeping reorganization of the whole aeronautical structure of the War Department.

After preliminary steps, on May 21, 1918, President Wilson transferred aviation from the Signal Corps to two agencies under the Secretary of War: the Bureau of Aircraft Production and the Division of Military Aeronautics. The latter, under Major General William L. Kenly, just returned from France, was responsible for training and operations. The new Bureau of Aircraft Production, formed from the old Equipment Division of the Signal Corps, was assigned "full and exclusive jurisdiction and control over production of aeroplanes, engines, and aircraft equipment" for the Army. Since its head, John D. Ryan, former president of the Anaconda Copper Company, was also chairman of the civilian Aircraft Board, a close and helpful connection existed between the two agencies. On May 24, the War Department officially recognized the Division of Military Aeronautics and the Bureau of Aircraft Production as constituting the Air Service, but it did not choose to appoint a chief of the Air Service to coordinate their activities.

The absurdity of not providing for close coordination of two such interdependent agencies soon became too obvious to be tolerated. On August 27 the President appointed Ryan as Director of Air Service and Second Assistant Secretary of War, the latter position assuring him enough prestige to make his weight felt. While the appointment was a step toward representation of aeronautics at a higher level, it may also have been designed to forestall creation of a separate department of aeronautics, for which there was a good deal of sentiment in Congress.

The new organization emerged late in the war when many of the worst difficulties had already been, or were about to be, overcome. The end of the war prevented the Air Service from making a record in 1919 that would have at least partially vindicated the original claims on behalf of aviation.

The Planes

American airplane production during the war was a failure when judged by original goals and promises. But it was a substantial achievement when compared with the records of the other warring countries. During its nineteen months in the war, the United States produced fifty per cent more planes than did Great Britain during its first thirty-one months of war—and Great Britain was the largest Allied producer.

The large appropriations for aircraft and the extravagant production programs of 1917 created rose-colored clouds which temporarily obscured the fact that the American aircraft industry could not produce 22,000 planes in the first year of war. In March 1917 there were only twelve companies capable of producing planes for the government, and their total production during 1916 had been fewer than four hundred planes of all kinds.

Other factors were scarcely less important in their effect on production. Raw materials were often inadequate to meet the enormously increased demand. Drastic action had to be taken to ensure an adequate supply of spruce—the tough, resilient wood that was superior to all others for the construction of airplanes. The government, in effect, took over and operated the spruce industry in Oregon and Washington. The Air Service assigned more than 27,000 officers and enlisted men to the Spruce Division of the Aircraft Board. Working in the forests, mills, and railroads, they helped the industry increase production by 2500 per cent.

Civilians and military alike recognized from the beginning that the greatest problem would be production of combat planes fit for use in Europe. None had ever been produced in this country, and no one had the technical knowledge to do it quickly. There were not even any designs for such planes. The greatest deficiency was in engines. In 1917 the United States produced no engines that combined the light weight and high horsepower needed for use in combat planes.

The United States had to turn to its Allies for planes to equip its units on the front and for the technical knowledge that would enable it to produce combat planes for itself. The advice and guidance was sometimes more than a little tinged with self-interest and often showed a lack of real knowledge of the situation in America. But without the assistance of the Allies, the Air Service could not have made the gallant, albeit brief, combat record that it did.

To gather vital technical information, the Army sent a large mission to Europe in June 1917, headed by Major Raynal C. Bolling, a newly commissioned but long-time civilian leader in aeronautics. As a result of the mission's findings, the aircraft production authorities decided to build training planes initially and to buy pursuit planes chiefly from the French. Pursuit designs changed so rapidly that it was considered impracticable to manufacture them so far from the fighting front. The French agreed in August to produce for the United States almost 6000 planes—chiefly Spads, Nieuports, and Breguets—plus some 8500 engines, to be delivered by July 1, 1918. The United States would supply the raw materials.

Deciding the kinds of combat planes the United States should produce was a difficult problem. Efforts to standardize fighting planes during the war were unsuccessful because of rapid technical changes. During this relatively early stage of aeronautical development—1914–18—the British and French each developed more than fifty different types of fighting planes, the Italians more than thirty, and the Germans more than twenty-five. The United States used nine types of combat planes purchased from the Allies.

After much discussion and controversy, the Americans settled on the De Havilland 4 (DH-4), a two-place reconnaissance bomber of English design, for production in the United States. Eventually, American companies also placed the British Handley-Page bomber and the Italian Caproni bomber in production, but only the DH-4 was produced in quantity. The other programs were overtaken by the Armistice before any real progress was made. Production of other European models—including the Spad, Bristol, and Lepere—was considered or even undertaken in American factories, but none ever reached the production stage, usually because of technical problems. The chief American-designed combat plane developed during the war was the two-engine Martin bomber, built around the American Liberty engine. This plane did not get beyond the development stage before the end of the war, but, as the NBS-1, it became the standard bomber of the Air Service in the early 1920s. The Thomas-Morse Aircraft Corporation also developed a pursuit plane which came too late for use in the war, and Grover Loening developed the N-8 monoplane, adopted by the Navy after the war.

Certainly the outstanding contribution of the United States to aeronautical development during the war was the Liberty engine. Designed and produced in America, it was good enough to be sought after by the Allied countries. There is a story that two engineers designed the Liberty engine in two days at the end of May 1917 in a suite at the Willard Hotel in Washington. This is only partly true because engineers from a number of companies and from the U. S. Bureau of Standards also did a great deal of work on the engine. Produced in two versions—8-cylinder and 12-cylinder—the Liberty was destined to be the standby of the Air Service for more than a decade. In addition to the Liberty, American engine manufacturers during the war also produced in quantity two other domestic engines, the Curtiss and the Hall-Scott, and a number of foreign types, including the Hispano-Suiza, Gnome, and Le Rhone.

Beginning in the spring of 1917 the aircraft industry expanded feverishly, and sometimes haphazardly, in an effort to do its enormous job. Existing companies increased their capacities many times over, and a host of new companies came into the industry. But the narrow base of this expansion and the intricacies of the technical problems involved in putting new and foreign airplane and engine designs into production defeated the wholehearted efforts that most companies made to reach their goals.

In January 1918, production in the United States was at a monthly rate of only seven hundred engines and eight hundred planes, of which some seven hundred were primary trainers. Not one combat plane had been completed, and not one plane had been shipped to France. The country was aware in a vague way that the aircraft program was behind schedule, but even congressmen of the "watchdog" type were not especially disturbed. Ironically, the War Department itself touched off the uproar over aircraft production. It announced on February 21 that the first American-built planes were "en route to the front in France," implying carelessly that this was five months ahead of schedule. Actually, only one DH-4 had been shipped from Dayton, it did not leave Hoboken, New Jersey, until March 15, and the ship that carried it was torpedoed off the Azores. The first American DH-4 did not actually fly in France until May 17.

The revelation that the program was actually failing, instead of marching ahead as the War Department had implied, led to rumors that were followed by congressional and presidential investigations. Charges of graft and sabotage proved to be utterly false, but the presidential investigating committee, headed by Charles Evans Hughes, eventually strongly criticized the indecision, delay, defective organization, lack of knowledge and experience, and conflict of judgment that characterized the program.

Reorganization of the aircraft production machinery in the spring of 1918 brought renewed, if more sober, confidence in the ability of the aircraft industry to make a real contribution to the war effort. The basic problem was to shift quickly from production of trainers, of which there were plenty, to production of combat planes, especially the DH-4, which was adapted to the Liberty engine. The success of the shift is shown by the increase in DH-4 production from fifteen in April 1918 to 1097 in October. In all, the United States produced well over 3000 DH-4s before the Armistice on November 11. To these may be added about 7800 primary and advanced training planes, most of them the famous JNs or Jennies, plus a few hundred combat-type planes other than the DH-4, almost all of them experimental or test planes. The best estimates of production put the overall total for the war period at more than 11,000 planes, as against 27,000 originally ordered.

Engine production from July 1917 through November 29, 1918, totaled approximately 32,000, of which almost half were Liberty engines and a quarter OX-5s, a Curtiss-produced engine used in trainers. The remaining 8000 engines were foreign types, principally Hispano-Suizas and Le Rhones. One other type of aircraft—the balloon—played a prominent role in the air war in Europe and was produced in quantity. The country turned out more than a thousand balloons, including some 650 of the observation type.

Although training planes were indispensable to the building of an air force, the real measure of aircraft production had to be in terms of the number of planes it could put into the fighting in France. It was here that the greatest failure occurred. Of the almost 6300 planes delivered to the American Expeditionary Forces (AEF) in France, only some 1200 (all but three of them DH-4s) came from the United States. Almost 4800 came from the French, but most of these were training planes. Perhaps a truer index of the American contribution is the actual aircraft strength in U.S. units in the Zone of Advance on November 11, 1918. Of 1005 planes, 325 were American-built DH-4s, and all the rest were foreign-built planes, chiefly Spads and Salmsons; of 740 planes actually in squadrons at the front, only 196 were DH-4s. During their seven months of combat action in France, American pilots flew foreign planes most of the time. And since the French and British naturally kept their best planes for themselves, the Americans often found themselves flying outmoded types.

It is perhaps only fair to note that the tightness of shipping and the priority given shipment of ground forces in 1918 played a part in retarding the movement of American-built combat planes to France. The record would probably have been better had there been more shipping available when the planes began to roll off the lines.

And the United States was not alone in its failure to meet goals for aircraft production and expansion of air strength. In

August 1917 the Bolling Mission had contracted for the French to deliver to the AEF in France 5875 planes and 8500 engines by July 1, 1918, but only one-quarter of the planes could be delivered in time and the United States cancelled the contract before it expired. Nor did the French reach the combat strength they promised themselves. They never met their program of 4022 planes at the front by April 1, 1918, for at the end of the war they had only 3321 planes at the front.

Training

Fortunately, the human material from which to build an air force was not only available but willing. The air war in Europe had a strong romantic appeal for young men stirred by tales of the daring, individualistic feats of the great air aces—Georges Guynemer, René Fonck, and Charles Nungesser of France; Baron Manfred von Richthofen, Oswald Boelcke, and Max Immelmann of Germany; Albert Ball and Edward Mannock of Great Britain; and William A. Bishop of Canada. Between July 1917 and June 1918 more than 38,000 of the finest of America's youth volunteered for flying training in the Army. Transforming this raw manpower and many other thousands into trained fliers and ground crews was the most staggering task faced by the Air Service itself.

With its tiny handful of 1200 officers and men and its three flying fields as a nucleus, the Army's air arm began in April 1917 an expansion requiring it to multiply itself more than a hundred and fifty times over in little more than nineteen months. At the beginning there existed no real knowledge of what it would take to produce pilots who could fly in combat on the Western Front. No American military pilots had ever engaged in combat and few, if any, had ever flown in a combat plane. In fact, the Army had not one worthy of the name. Only from the Allies could there come the information and assistance that the United States needed to establish an effective training program.

The Aviation Section made certain basic decisions early, even before the full scope of the expansion became known. Training would have to be standardized; the personalized methods of prewar years would not serve to train thousands of pilots quickly. There would be three phases of flying training—ground, primary, and advanced. Most advanced training would be done overseas —in Great Britain, France, and Italy—where the right types of planes and experienced instructors were available. Large numbers of officers would be commissioned direct from civilian life in order to provide the planning and ground staffs needed for the expansion of the new training program.

After Foulois and others inspected the Canadian flying training system in April 1917, the Aviation Section took steps to launch the various phases of the training program. Hiram Bingham, a Yale professor commissioned in the Signal Corps, played a key role in the training program. Before the end of May, Bingham had started ground schools for cadets at six leading American universities—Massachusetts Institute of Technology, Cornell University, Ohio State University, and the Universities of Illinois, Texas, and California. Until the end of the program after the war, these six schools and two others—Princeton University and the Georgia School of Technology—received almost 23,000 cadets and graduated more than 17,500. The original eight-week curriculum was later increased to twelve and was of great value in giving the cadets a theoretical basis for flying training.

The expansion of primary flying training could not be done as quickly because most of the fields had to be built first. Meanwhile, the Canadians provided flying facilities in Canada during the summer months of 1917 in return for the use of American fields in the south during the winter. By the middle of December 1917, fifteen flying fields were in use, including some that were to become permanent landmarks of the air arm: Chanute, Selfridge, Kelly, and Scott. Wisely, the War Department built most of the fields in the southern states where flying conditions were good all year round. Ultimately, there were twenty-seven flying fields in the United States and another sixteen in Europe.

At the primary flying schools in the United States, cadets could earn their wings in six to eight weeks, after a total of

40 to 50 hours of flying, usually in the JN-4. Rated as Reserve Military Aviators (RMA), they received 25 per cent flying pay. In all, almost 15,000 cadets entered the primary flying schools in the United States, and 8688 received the RMA rating. Others received their training at oversea schools, making a total of more than 10,000 pilots trained during the war.

Training of Americans in Europe was handicapped by lack of facilities, late arrival of cadets, and the more urgent needs of the Allied air services, which naturally had first claim on planes and fliers. But cadets arrived in France as early as August 1917, and eventually some 2500 came from the United States or were recruited in France. Unfortunately, more than a thousand of these cadets who arrived during 1917 had to spend months waiting at Issoudun, Tours, and St. Maixent before they got a chance to begin training. Meanwhile, they were called on for construction work, cooking, guard duty, and any other jobs that needed to be done. Because they received the then handsome pay of $100 per month, they became known at Issoudun as the "Million Dollar Guard."

The Air Service, American Expeditionary Forces, began building its own schools in France in August 1917, since the French schools could not handle the expected arrivals. Eventually 16 fields—of which Issoudun was the largest and best known— were used to train American fliers. By November 1918 the American schools could give about 2000 pilots a month their final or "refresher" training. In all, more than 8000 pilots and observers received some form of flying training in France, the Air Service schools accounting for almost 1700 fully trained pilots and 850 observers. About 500 Americans received all or part of their flying training in Great Britain, and a few hundred more at two schools in Italy. The greatest contribution of these foreign schools was to give American pilots the feel of the planes they would fly in combat—planes that were not available in the United States.

But the French and British did not have enough training schools to handle the Americans, and the training establishment in the United States had to take over the greater part of the advanced pilot training. Specialized advanced schools were set up, beginning with the first observer school in September 1917. Aerial gunnery schools were also set up, and all flying personnel were supposed to have courses in gunnery, an absolute requirement for combat service.

Fliers alone did not make an air force. Engineers, supply and administrative officers, mechanics, and a host of other specialists and nonspecialists were needed on the ground if the air mission was to be fulfilled. The remarkable development of aerial photography and radio created a demand for large numbers of officers and enlisted men trained in these specialties. Schools for the various officer specialties were established at airfields or at educational institutions, and thousands completed the courses during 1917–18.

Any hope that enough mechanics could be obtained from civilian life was dispelled by the fall of 1917. Schools had to be opened to train enlisted men in a wide variety of specialties, including airplane engines, armament, armor, propellers, machine guns, ignition, welding, instruments, sail-making, vulcanizing, and copper work. At first, men were trained at factories and at northern flying fields that had to be closed down for the winter. Beginning in December 1917, heavy reliance was placed on large technical institutions to operate schools for the Air Service. By May 1918 more than 10,000 men had been trained at these various schools, more than half of them at the technical institutions. This met the most immediate needs. In June the Air Service concentrated all training of mechanics at its two large schools at St. Paul, Minnesota, and Kelly Field, Texas, and closed the others. More than 7600 men had been graduated from the various courses at these two schools by the end of the war.

The British also helped train American mechanics and other ground personnel at fields and factories in Great Britain. This was of mutual benefit as it helped relieve the British labor shortages also. Large numbers of mechanics were also trained at French factories and at American schools in France. Whole squadrons were trained in this manner.

Balloons played an important, if unspectacular, role in the war, and there was a constantly growing need for them. Balloon training remained completely separate from the rest of the Air Service training program. Special balloon schools trained pilots and observers and offered technical courses to the enlisted men of the balloon companies. Some balloon observers received their training in France. Up to the Armistice, balloon schools in the United States turned out 751 trained officers. The Air Service formed eighty-nine balloon companies of which thirty-three went overseas. Two companies were formed in France. By the end of the war the balloon force had a strength of more than 17,000 officers and men in the United States and abroad.

Air Service, AEF

On April 6, 1917 there were five U. S. Army aviation officers in Europe. Three were attending French flying schools; one was an assistant military attache in London; and the fifth was an air observer in Spain. But the observer in Spain was the energetic and aggressive Major William Mitchell, and he lost no time in getting permission to visit the front as an observer.

During the next few months Mitchell studied the air war intensively, visiting airfields, depots, and headquarters, spending ten days at the front and flying over the front lines. On his own initiative, and with French help, he drew up and sent to the War Department on April 20 a plan for the organization of an American air force in France. He followed this with a steady flow of reports on almost every aspect of the air war. It is likely that he had a hand in developing the aviation program for the United States laid down in the Ribot cable of May 26. By the time Pershing arrived in France with the staff of the American Expeditionary Forces in June, Mitchell was not only the best-informed but probably the best-qualified man to serve as Aviation Officer, AEF.

Mitchell presented Pershing with a proposal for an Air Service composed of two distinct forces. One consisted of squadrons attached to the ground armies, corps, and divisions and under the control of ground commanders. The other force consisted of "large aeronautical groups for strategical operations against enemy aircraft and enemy materiel, at a distance from the actual line." The bombardment and pursuit formations making up this force "would have an independent mission . . . and would be used to carry the war well into the enemy's country."

Here was clearly foreshadowed the classic controversy over the proper role of airpower that was to agitate the American military establishment for so many years. The heart of the controversy was destined to be the concept of strategic bombardment. Mitchell's ideas reflected the powerful influence of the foremost prophet of airpower of his time, the advocate of strategic bombardment and unified air command—Major General Hugh M. Trenchard, commander of the British Royal Flying Corps.

Pershing appointed a board of officers, including Mitchell, to recommend the composition and organization of the Air Service, AEF. The board began with the assumption that "a decision in the air must be sought and obtained before a decision on the ground can be reached." Therefore, it recommended a strategic force of thirty bombardment groups and thirty fighter groups and a second force of a size based on the strength of the ground forces to which it would be attached. Pershing did not accept the board's recommendations. The first program for the Air Service which he did approve provided only for units of the second type. Although later programs included bombardment and pursuit squadrons, at no time was permission granted to establish an American strategic bombardment force.

Actually, the composition of the Air Service in France was probably determined more by the nature of the aircraft obtainable than by programs or tactical doctrine. The programs adopted by Pershing's staff had some influence on aircraft production in the United States in 1918, but the hard fact remained that most of the American squadrons flew foreign aircraft in combat. The Americans had to take what the Allies could spare them over and above their own sometimes-desperate needs.

The Bolling Mission, which provided most of the technical

guidance for the American aircraft program in 1917, could not help but be impressed by the emphasis, in theory if not in practice, that the French, British, and Italians placed on strategic bombardment. But there had to be fliers before there could be an Air Service, and this meant that training planes would have to be given priority, at least intially. The American ground armies would need supporting air units if they were to do their part on the Western Front. For these reasons, the Bolling report to the War Department in July 1917 gave third priority to bombers and fighters for a strategic air force. By the time the United States was in a position to begin turning out bombers, the war had ended, and since the Allies did not have enough bombers for their own programs, the AEF was never able to build a bomber force of its own.

But in the summer of 1917 the aviation officers at AEF headquarters in Paris had no planes—only plans. Their first concern was to develop a staff and command organization that could handle the complex task of building an air force from scratch. On September 3, Pershing appointed Brigadier General William L. Kenly, a field artillery officer, as Chief of Air Service, AEF. Bolling served as assistant chief in charge of supply, while Mitchell became Air Commander, Zone of Advance. In November, Foulois, already a brigadier general, arrived in France with a ready-made headquarters staff of 112 officers and 300 enlisted men. After making a thorough inspection of aviation activities, Foulois succeeded Kenly as Chief of Air Service, AEF.

Building the Air Service in France proved to be a painful and halting process. Aside from the difficulties inherent in developing any military organization under the intense pressure of war, jealousy and friction within the Air Service further complicated matters. Air and ground officers were often at loggerheads. Earlier arrivals resented later ones (many of whom were newly commissioned civilians), and at the higher echelons such key officers as Bolling and Mitchell could not agree on their respective responsibilities.

By the spring of 1918 the lack of progress, aggravated to be sure by production failures at home and delays in French deliveries, could no longer be ignored. Pershing regarded the Air Service headquarters staff as a "lot of good men running around in circles." In May 1918 he brought in as Chief of Air Service a West Point classmate and senior Corps of Engineers officer, Brigadier General Mason M. Patrick. Pershing reasoned that Patrick would be able to stand above the strife of the ambitious young air officers, almost all of whom—including Mitchell and Foulois—were under 40.

Mitchell was subordinated to Foulois, who was placed in charge of aviation at the front in June with the title of Chief of Air Service, First Army, but it was difficult for the two to work together. The colorful, dashing Mitchell, determined to cut red tape and get things done no matter how, was bound to clash with the more studious and orthodox Foulois. Eventually, in an unusual act of self-denial, Foulois recommended that Mitchell be given the combat command and asked for himself the position of Assistant Chief of Air Service under Patrick. This change, in August, paved the way for Mitchell to become what he had wished to be all along—the outstanding American air combat commander of the war.

From this point on, the combat forces expanded rapidly, and new combat air commands were organized as new American armies came into the field. In October, Colonel Frank P. Lahm became Chief of Air Service, Second Army; and Mitchell, newly promoted to brigadier general, became chief of all Army aviation at the front on October 14. Pershing had told Patrick that he wanted Mitchell to command the combat forces at the front. Another pioneer Army flier, Colonel Thomas DeWitt Milling, succeeded Mitchell at First Army. The establishment of Air Service, Third Army, just before the Armistice, completed the air organization at the front as of November 11, 1918.

The Armistice saw the Air Service beginning to fulfill the promise expected of it. There were 58,000 officers and men in the Air Service in France, about 20,000 in training in England, and a small number in Italy. For every plane at the front, the Air Service estimated it needed thirty-five to forty men.

Air War in France

The U. S. Air Service made its combat record in World War I in a period of only seven months—from April to November 1918. It had required a full year for American aero squadrons to reach the point where they could support American ground forces at the front.

Aside from the logistical and training difficulties, there was a major difference of opinion between the AEF and the Allies, and this further delayed the appearance of American units. The French and British, already drained of their best men and hard-pressed by the Germans, looked on the American forces, both ground and air, as providing a fresh and growing manpower pool from which to draw replacements for their tired and depleted units. They wished to attach American battalions to French and British divisions and individual American pilots and observers to British and French air squadrons.

Pershing resisted strongly, and his insistence on a separate American army responsible for a separate sector of the front ultimately gave the Americans an opportunity to prove that they could fight as an independent force. But, meanwhile, the desperate manpower needs of the French and British in the face of powerful German attacks could not be ignored. Beginning in the fall of 1917, U.S. battalions and regiments served as parts of French and British divisions until they could be reunited into American divisions and eventually into the first U. S. Army on August 10, 1918.

The experience of the Air Service followed the overall pattern. Most of the American fliers and mechanics available for service at the front in late 1917 and early 1918 were trained in Europe. The Allies naturally wanted to use the young and fresh Americans to reinforce their own units, hoping to bolster Allied morale and discourage the Germans. Then, too, the Americans had as yet no combat planes of their own, and there was no other way in which they could get the combat experience they needed. The logic of this arrangement could not be disputed, and it was adopted as an interim measure, to be followed by the grouping of trained Americans into squadrons for use on French and British fronts. Later, when the American armies were formed, the American squadrons would be used with them.

There was little doubt that the Americans would fight well in the air. Since 1915, American volunteers had been flying with the French and British. Although the members of the Lafayette Escadrille were the most famous, many others had also won enviable reputations. After America entered the war, ninety-three trained pilots transferred to the Air Service and another twenty-six to the U. S. Navy, while a number remained with the French. In February 1918 the fliers of the Lafayette Escadrille became the nucleus of the 103d Pursuit Squadron, the first American squadron to fly as a unit in action. The 103d continued to serve with the French, since no other American squadrons were yet ready for action. In order to take advantage of the experience of the transferred pilots, the Air Service eventually distributed most of them through new American units as squadron commanders and flight leaders.

The 1st Aero Squadron, of Mexican border memory, arrived in France under the command of Major Ralph Royce on September 3, 1917—the first American flying unit to reach Europe. After training at French schools, it received French planes and further training as an observation squadron. Additional American squadrons arriving in France during the fall and winter followed a similar pattern of training. In preparation for the eventual transfer of a sector of the front to the American ground and air units, the Allied High Command decided that American units should be gradually concentrated in the Toul area, toward the eastern end of the vast front stretching from the Channel coast to Switzerland. The front in eastern France, comparatively quiet since the first year of the war, appeared to be a good place for blooding the new American forces.

The American buildup in the Toul sector began in February 1918 with the arrival in the Zone of Advance of the 95th Pursuit Squadron. The 94th Pursuit Squadron joined it on March

5, but neither unit had machine guns for the Nieuport fighters they were flying. In spite of this deficiency, which could have meant the difference between life and death, they began flying pursuit patrols over the lines on March 15. When the machine guns finally arrived, the 95th found that it still could not start regular operations because most of its pilots had never received instructions in gunnery. They had to be sent back to a French aerial gunnery school, leaving to the 94th the honor of being the first American-trained pursuit squadron to fight at the front. This famous "Hat in the Ring" squadron, later commanded by Captain Edward V. Rickenbacker, began its operations on April 3. On April 14, Lieutenant Alan F. Winslow and Douglas Campbell shot down the squadron's first two German planes. The 95th returned to the front on April 25, and the two squadrons were subsequently formed into the 1st Pursuit Group. The tendency toward larger units was almost inevitable as the number of squadrons increased; eventually, groups were organized into wings.

Meanwhile, the 1st Aero Squadron had arrived in the Toul sector on April 4, and on April 15 its pilots flew Spad two-seaters in the first reconnaissance missions over the lines. Two more squadrons arrived before the end of May, and the three were formed into the I Corps Observation Group, under French tactical control. Earlier, in March and April, balloon companies had begun operating with American divisions near Toul. The first day bombardment squadron to go into action was the 96th. Flying in French Breguets, the 96th began its operations in the Toul sector by raiding the railroad yards at Dommary Baroncourt on June 12. By the middle of June, therefore, representative units of all four elements of the Air Service had gone into action around Toul.

In a desperate effort to smash the Allies before American resources could permanently tip the scales against them, the Germans launched a series of mighty offensives in March 1918 that reached a furious climax in the Marne-Champagne battle of July. At the beginning of the offensive, the Germans used massed airpower for the first time. Some three hundred planes seized control of the air and attacked Allied troop movements. It required a still larger concentration of Allied planes to recapture control of the air. This lesson was taken to heart by the American air leaders.

At the end of June, American ground and air units moved to the vicinity of Château-Thierry, at the tip of the great salient the Germans had driven into the French lines. The American air units—1st Pursuit Group and I Corps Observation Group —together with some French units, were organized into the 1st Brigade under Mitchell and given responsibility for a portion of the battle area. Conditions were far different from those on the quiet Toul front. Great battles raged almost continually for weeks on end. The Germans had local superiority in the air because of greater numbers and the high quality of their *Jagdstaffeln*—pursuit squadrons. Outnumbered and facing superior planes—especially the latest version of the Fokker—the American pursuit pilots often found themselves outmatched. It was difficult to protect the observation planes in their missions behind the German lines, and formations of squadron size or larger became necessary.

The 1st Brigade found itself on the defensive throughout a five-week period during which the German attack was stopped and thrown back. The First carried out its primary mission of supplying information to the ground forces, but at a heavy cost in both observation and pursuit planes. In the most important offensive action of the air campaign, American pursuit planes joined British bombers and pursuits in attacking the large German supply base at Fère-en-Tardenois. Allied losses were heavy, but the attack forced the Germans to use fighters to protect their supply bases, weakening their strength over the front. The experience at Château-Thierry was a hard one, but it prepared the American fliers for future campaigns as the Toul sector never could have done.

In August, Patrick placed all American air units along the French front under the Air Service, First Army, with Mitchell as commander. These units had increased steadily during July and August, and Mitchell organized them, along with a number of

French groups, into three wings—pursuit, observation, and bombardment. Most of his bomber groups and some of his pursuit and observation groups were French. In all, the Air Service, First Army, had forty-nine squadrons, of which only about half were American. Mitchell also controlled a French aerial division with more than 40 additional squadrons, and he had the cooperation, but not the control, of nine British bombardment squadrons from Trenchard's Independent Air Force recently organized for strategic bombardment of Germany. Mitchell massed most of this strength behind an 80-mile front manned by the U. S. First Army and a French army corps under Pershing.

The Allied forces prepared to wipe out the St. Mihiel salient, which had been sticking into the French lines for four years. For several weeks before the attack began on September 12, the Air Service made ready for the assault. It succeeded in limiting enemy reconnaissance and collected the information needed by the ground commanders without arousing strong enemy suspicion of the American concentration. A significant measure of the degree of tactical surprise attained was the overwhelming superiority of the American and French forces at the beginning of the action—almost 1500 planes against an estimated 295 German planes. For this campaign Mitchell had what was up to that time "the largest aggregation of air forces that had ever been engaged in one operation on the Western Front at any time during the entire progress of the war."

For the first time the Americans had numerical superiority in the air. Mitchell used it to capture and maintain the offensive in spite of increasing opposition, including some of the best German pursuit units from other parts of the front. During the first two days of the battle, bad weather kept most of the planes on the ground, but their many attempts to carry out missions showed that the American fliers had gained greater experience and confidence. With better weather on September 14 and 15, Mitchell could put his plans in motion.

About a third of his force—some five hundred observation and pursuit planes—operated in support of the ground forces. The remainder struck behind the German lines, bombing communications and installations and strafing German columns. These attacks met strong German reaction in the air, and losses were heavy on both sides. The American day bombardment units met the strongest German opposition, and their losses were likewise heavy. But the overall results were good, since the Germans had been kept on the defensive and most of the action had taken place well behind their lines.

In September the Allies were advancing almost everywhere along the line. The success at St. Mihiel confirmed an earlier decision that the next American assault should be along the sector from the Meuse to the Argonne—in eastern France. After the Americans consolidated their lines on the St. Mihiel front, the ground and air units disengaged themselves and moved into the Meuse-Argonne area. Once more, as at St. Mihiel, the air units attempted to preserve secrecy. The Americans refrained from flying, other than as observers in French planes, until the attack was launched on September 26. They spent much of their time in training exercises with artillery and infantry units, a need revealed during the St. Mihiel campaign.

For this final campaign, Mitchell had a smaller force than at St. Mihiel, but it was augmented during October and November by new American units. His initial strength was more than eight hundred planes, of which almost six hundred were American. Here again, Mitchell sought every opportunity to concentrate his forces for large blows at the enemy, instead of parceling them out among the divisions and corps, where coordination of their activities was always most difficult. By incessant assaults on the German rear, he planned to keep the enemy on the defensive and prevent an attack on the American lines.

From the beginning of the offensive on September 26, the bombers played a key part in establishing air superiority over the battle area. The biggest air battles were usually provoked by these bomber raids, for the Germans regarded them as a serious threat. The largest and perhaps most successful of the missions took place on October 9, when a force of two hundred Allied bombers, accompanied by a hundred pursuit planes and fifty three-place planes flying in two echelons, struck a concentration point where the enemy was forming for a counterattack. The bombers dropped more than 30 tons of bombs in the face of strong attacks by German fighters. Other "huge" formations of up to 190 planes hit sensitive targets behind the lines on October 30 and November 4. To cope with these assaults the Germans reinforced their fighter units, and the American day bombers suffered grievous losses on a number of their missions.

Pursuit planes escorted bombers and observation planes and protected balloons. They also patrolled aggressively to force the Germans to fight. Some students of the air war believed that the lowflying patrols operating throughout the offensive in spite of bad weather proved "the outstanding success" of the campaign. From September 26 to October 1, American fighters claimed a hundred hostile planes and twenty-one balloons shot down. The 1st Pursuit Group, under Mitchell's direct control, operated over the battle lines against enemy planes and balloons, establishing a degree of air superiority that heartened the troops on the ground.

The observation squadrons were more successful in working with the infantry and artillery than they had been at St. Mihiel. They defended themselves better and adopted aggressive tactics, attacking enemy machine-gun emplacements and strongpoints. Their greatest success came in spotting enemy artillery and reporting visual reconnaissance. In this work, the balloon squadrons, of which there were twenty-three at the front by Armistice Day, also played an important part.

On November 11, 1918, Mitchell was in charge of all U. S. Army aviation at the front, directing the operations of the air services for the First and Second Armies and readying a third for action. He had 45 combat squadrons, with 767 pilots, 481 observers, and 23 aerial gunners. Two of these units—the British-trained 17th and 148th Pursuit Squadrons—had just rejoined the American forces after serving with the RFC on the British front since July 1918.

American officers continued to fly as individuals with Allied air forces even after American units appeared in strength at the front. In Italy, Captain Fiorello H. La Guardia led a detachment of eighteen bomber pilots into action against the Austrians in June 1918. In all, more than sixty-five American pilots saw action on the Italian front, flying Caproni bombers.

The combat record in France was not statistically impressive. The 740 American planes in squadrons at the front on November 11, 1918 constituted a little more than 10 per cent of the total aircraft strength of the Allies. The Air Service carried out 150 separate bombing attacks during which it dropped about 138 tons of bombs and penetrated as far as 160 miles behind the German lines. American losses in combat were 289 planes and 48 balloons, including 57 planes piloted by officers flying with the British, French, and Italians. A number of the 237 American officers and men killed in battle certainly could have been saved if the Air Service had required the use of the parachute. Although the German fliers used parachutes in the closing stages of the war, the Allied air forces refused to adopt them. The aviators themselves stubbornly rejected them—partly because of skepticism and partly because of a "freakish pilot fetish that it was a sign of cowardice and a lack of confidence in one's ability and equipment."

American pilots had confirmed claims of 781[*] enemy planes and 73[*] balloons shot down, but the true totals were less because of duplicate claims. The "Golden Age" of individual aerial combat, World War I saw the glorification of the fighter ace. Such American flying heroes as Captain Eddie Rickenbacker, Major Raoul Lufbery, and Lieutenant Frank Luke became better known to the American public than all except a handful of American generals. No fewer than 71 Americans qualified as aces—each shooting down five or more enemy aricraft. Altogether, they shot down some 450 planes and 50 balloons.

---

[*] An official USAF study published in June 1969, shows this to be 756 aircraft and 76 balloons.

CONSOLIDATED LIST OF AIRCRAFT CONTRACTS AND DELIVERIES IN U.S.

April 6, 1917–November 1, 1919

AERONAUTICAL & AUTOMOTIVE INDUSTRIES

1. *Curtiss Aeroplane & Motor Corporation*

JN-4   Primary Trainer; two-place biplane; 1850 lbs. gross weight; 43'7" span; 27'3" length; 1 Curtiss OX-5 engine; 90 h.p.; 75 m.p.h. top speed.

JN-4D   Primary Trainer; two-place biplane; 1920 lbs. gross weight; 43'7" span; 27'4" length; 1 Curtiss OX-5 engine; 90 h.p.; 80 m.p.h. top speed.

JN-4H   Advanced Trainer; two-place biplane; 2150 lbs. gross weight; 43'7" span; 27'1" length; 1 Hispano A engine; 150 h.p.; 93 m.p.h. top speed.

JN-6HG   Advanced Trainer; two-place biplane; 2700-50 gross weight; 43'7" span; 26'11" length; 1 Hispano A engine; 150 h.p.; 80 m.p.h. top speed.

Total Production, All Types   4,014

2. *Standard Aircraft Corporation*

Caproni   Bomber; biplane; 4-man crew; 12,350 lbs. gross weight; 76'9" span; 41'2" length; Three Liberty 12 engines; 350 h.p.; 103 m.p.h. top speed.

E-1   Light Pursuit Trainer; 1-place biplane; 1140 lbs. gross weight; 24'0" span; 18'11" length; 1 Gnome B-9 engine (100 h.p.) or 1 LeRhone C-9 engine (80 h.p.); 100 m.p.h. top speed.

Handley- Bomber; 4-man crew; 14,425 lbs. gross weight;
Page   100'0" span; 62'10" length; 2 Liberty 12-N en-
        gines; 350 h.p.; 94 m.p.h. top speed.

SJ-1   Primary Trainer; two-place biplane; 2070 lbs.
        gross weight; 43'10" span; 26'7" length; 1 Curtiss
        OX-5 engine; 90 h.p.; 70 m.p.h. top speed.

Total Production, All Types   1,033

3. *Wright-Martin Aircraft Corporation*

SJ-1   Primary Trainer; two-place biplane; 2100 lbs.
        gross weight; 43'10" span; 26'7" length; 1 Hall-
        Scott A-7a engine; 125 h.p.; 80 m.p.h. top speed.

Total Production, All Types   51

4. *L. W. F. Engineering Company*

V-1   Reconnaissance; 2-place biplane; 2670 lbs. gross
        weight; 42'0" span; 28'0" length; 1 Thomas
        Model 8 engine (135 h.p.) or 1 Sturtevant 5-A
        engine (150 h.p.); top speed approximately 90
        m.p.h.

Total Production, All Types   131

5. *Glenn L. Martin Company*

Glenn   3-man crew; 10,225 lbs. gross weight; 71'5" span;
Martin   46'10" length; 2 Liberty 12-A engines; 400 h.p.;
Bomber   113 m.p.h. top speed.

Total Production, All Types   10

6. *Thomas-Morse Aircraft Corporation*

S-4B   Pursuit Trainer; 1-place biplane; 1360 lbs. gross
        weight; 26'7" span; 19'10" length; 1 Gnome B-9
        engine; 100 h.p.; 95 m.p.h. top speed.

S-4C   Pursuit Trainer; 1-place biplane; 1354 lbs. gross
        weight; 26'6" span; 18'6" length; 1 LeRhone C-9
        engine; 80 h.p.; 90 m.p.h. top speed.

Total Production, All Types   599

7. *Lewis & Vought Corporation*
   VE-7 Two-place biplane; 1937 lbs. gross weight; 34'4" span; 24'6" length; I Hispano A engine; 150 h.p.; 106 m.p.h. top speed.
   Total Production, All Types 7

8. *Heinrich Corporation*
   Pursuit 1-place biplane; 1 Gnome 9 engine; 100 h.p.
   Total Production, All Types 2

9. *Gallaudet Aircraft Corporation*
   Twin Hy- 2-place biplane; 4200 lbs. gross weight; 48'0" droplane span; 34'6" length; 2 Hall-Scott A-5a engines; 125 h.p.; 82 m.p.h. top speed.
   Total Production, All Types 4

10. *Breese Aircraft Corporation*
   Penguin 1-place monoplane; 14' span; 1 Lawrence A-3 engine; 28 h.p.; Non-flying Ground Trainer.
   Total Production, All Types 300

11. *Burgess Company*
   Twin-Hy- Reconnaissance; 2-place biplane; 5380 lbs. gross droplane weight; 72'0" span; 32'5" length; 2 Sturtevant 5A engines, 150 h.p. each; 78 m.p.h. top speed.
   Total Production, All Types 1

12. *Fowler Corporation*
   JN-4D Primary Trainer; two-place biplane; 1920 lbs. gross weight; 43'7" span; 27'4" length; 1 Curtiss OX-5 engine; 90 h.p.; 80 m.p.h. top speed.
   Total Production, All Types 50

13. *Dayton-Wright Aeroplane Company*
   DH-4 Observation two-place biplane; 4297 lbs. gross weight; 42'6" span; 29'11" length; 1 Liberty 12 engine, 400 h.p.; 124 m.p.h. top speed.

SJ-1 — Primary Trainer; 2-place biplane; 2206 lbs. gross weight; 43'10" span; 26'7" length; engines used were Curtiss OX-5s, Hispano As, Hall Scott A-7as; top speed 70–80 m.p.h. depending on engine.

Total Production, All Types   3,506

14. *Packard Motor Car Company*

LUSAC-11 — LePere Fighter; 2-place biplane; 3746 lbs. gross weight; 41'7" span; 25'3" length; 1 Liberty 12 engine 425 h.p.; top speed 136 m.p.h.

Total Production, All Types   25

15. *Ordnance Engineering Company*

Orenco C — Scout-Pursuit Trainer; 1-place biplane; 1117 lbs. gross weight; 26'0" span; 18'10" length; 1 Le-Rhone C-9 engine; 80 h.p.; 102 m.p.h. top speed.

Total Production, All Types   8

16. *Fisher Body Company*

DH-4 — Same specifications as those under Dayton-Wright above.

SJ-1 — Same specifications as those under Dayton-Wright above.

Total Production, All Types   2,000

TOTAL Planes Aeronautical & Automotive Industries   11,742[a]

MISCELLANEOUS (EMERGENCY WAR ORGANIZATIONS, NEW CONCERNS, MISSIONS, ETC.)

1. *Pigeon-Fraser*

Pursuit — 1-place monoplane; 1250 lbs. gross weight; 37'11" span; 24'0" length; 1 Gnome 9 engine; 100 h.p.; top speed 103 m.p.h.

Total Production, All Types   3

2. *Liberty Iron Works*

JN-4D   Same specifications as under Curtiss Aeroplane & Motor Company, above.

Total Production, All Types   200

3. *Springfield Aircraft Company*

JN-4D   Same specifications as above.

VE-7   Same specifications as under Lewis & Vought above.

Total Production, All Types   588

4. *St. Louis Aircraft Corporation*

JN-4D   Same specifications as above.

Total Production, All Types   450

5. *U. S. Aircraft Company*

JN-4D   Same specifications as above.

Total Production, All Types   50

6. *Howell & Lesser*

JN-4D   Same specifications as above.

Total Production, All Types   75

7. *Schaefer & Sons*

R.S.   Light Pursuit Trainer; one-place biplane; 1 Gnome 9 engine, 100 h.p.

Total Production, All Types   1

8. *Canadian Aero Company*

JN-4D   Same specifications as above.

Total Production, All Types   680

9. *Pacific Aero Products Company (Later Boeing)*

EA   Primary Trainer; 2-place biplane; 2255 lbs. gross weight; 43'10" span; 27'0" length; 1 Curtiss OXX-3 engine; 90 h.p.; top speed 73 m.p.h.

Total Production, All Types   2

TOTAL Miscellaneous   2,152[b]

GRAND TOTAL   13,894[ab]

Note: In addition to the above the following companies were the principal producers of spare parts:

The Metz Co., Waltham, Massachusetts

Sturtevant Aeroplane Co., Jamaica Plains, Massachusetts

Wilson Body Co., Bay City, Michigan

West Virginia Aircraft Corporation, Wheeling, West Virginia

The Rubay Co., Cleveland, Ohio

Engel Aircraft Co., Niles, Ohio

Hayes-Ionia, Grand Rapids, Michigan

Sources: 1. Appendix I to U. S. Army Air Service Letter, dated April 6, 1921 as reported in 1922 Aircraft Year Book.
2. Fahey's "U. S. Army Aircraft," 1908–1946.
3. "America's Munitions 1917–1918," Report of Benedict Crowell, Assistant Secretary of War.

[a]Includes one airplane of unspecified type built by Sturtevant Airplane Co.

[b]Includes one airplane of unspecified type built by Italian War Mission, 2 planes of unspecified type built by Equipment Holding, and 100 built by various manufacturers of Handley Page Parts.